LEGAL WRITING STYLE

Third Edition

Antonio Gidi
Teaching Professor of Law
Syracuse University College of Law

Henry Weihofen
Late Professor of Law
University of New Mexico School of Law

HORNBOOK SERIES®

Hornbook Series is a trademark registered in the U.S. Patent and Trademark Office.

COPYRIGHT © 1961, 1980 by WEST PUBLISHING CO.
© 2018 LEG, Inc. d/b/a West Academic
      444 Cedar Street, Suite 700
      St. Paul, MN 55101
      1-877-888-1330

West, West Academic Publishing, and West Academic are trademarks of West Publishing Corporation, used under license.

Printed in the United States of America

ISBN: 978-1-63459-296-3

To Isabella and Sophia,
Who taught me to read and write.

And to Ana Claudia,
Who teaches us everything else in between.

Gidi

Preface

The first edition of this book was published in 1961, during the pre-history of modern legal writing. A pioneering work, well ahead of its time, it shaped the style of generations of lawyers and law students. A second edition, lightly updated, was published in 1980 at the dawn of the legal writing movement.

This sexagenarian classic, however, was left behind. It languished for decades, unfairly forgotten and badly out of shape. Although more than half was no longer useful, the core was timeless. It was destined to be discovered by someone with a passion for writing. I'm glad it was me. My research agenda was put on hold, and I dedicated myself to bringing Weihofen's vision back to life.

I originally thought the book would require only minor repairs to return it to a serviceable condition. Four years of research and more than 60 versions later, I'm honored to reintroduce Weihofen to the legal community, updated, developed, rewritten.

The book contains citations ranging from ancient Greek rhetoricians to 21st century writers; from English, German, and French stylists of previous centuries to contemporary American lawyers. Their insights show that many principles of good writing are independent of time, language, and culture. Let the masters inspire you to nurture your style.

This book addresses the key principles of writing, principles that have been debated for centuries. They are not immutable rules, but flexible, complementary, and conflicting guidelines that depend on context, objective, and, ultimately, your own taste and judgment. Take all these principles into consideration and you may write effectively; follow them blindly and your style will become formulaic.

The conscious writer will find here the tools to make strategic decisions about style. Instead of mechanical rules of thumb on writing well, you will find the intellectual framework needed to identify and produce superior prose. You will not only become a better writer, but will also grow to appreciate the reasons behind each principle.

As you cultivate an appreciation for style, you will learn to write deliberately instead of by accident. Only then can you exercise control over your message: you will say what you mean and mean what you say. Empowered by an understanding of the consequences of your stylistic choices, you will find your own voice.

Although short, this is not a leisure book for a carefree Sunday afternoon. But if you decide to take on the task of digesting it, you will become a more mature writer. It will change the way you think and write.

May this renewed edition of Weihofen's classic continue to guide generations of law students and professionals as they craft their own legal writing style.

GIDI

Acknowledgments

I couldn't have completed this project without the support of my Research Assistants over the past four years. They were an invaluable source of inspiration. Kathryn Wisner was the first who believed in the project; Daniel Viau helped shape it; David Katz helped refine it; and Erika Simonson helped it cross the finish line.

Several friends and colleagues also contributed and earned my appreciation: Aviva Abramovsky, Sally Ashkar, Emily Brown, Tessa Boury, Craig Boise, Edward Cooper, David Driesen, Shubha Ghosh, Mary Kay Kane, Arlene Kanter, Doug Moll, Lena Peters, Gail Provost, Kevin Schroeder, Mac Soto, Dixie Swanson, and Stephen Zamora.

I also acknowledge the many students, practitioners, and scholars who trusted me with their writings over the past two decades. Their reactions to my suggestions helped me forge my own theories on legal writing style.

At the library, Christine Demetros patiently coped with my excitement as she helped me discover obscure sources. At the office, always with a kind smile, Helen Neville and Kristin Stewart bound dozens of versions through interminable rounds of revisions.

Some colleagues exceeded expectations, reading the entire manuscript and making thoughtful recommendations: Ian Gallacher, Geoffrey C. Hazard, Jr., Robert Ragazzo, Richard Risman, and Mary B. Trevor.

When I sent an early version to Geoffrey C. Hazard, Jr., he was 87 years old, in the last year of his life. Within a few weeks, he mailed me a bound copy with hundreds of handwritten suggestions that made my writing sharper, more modern, and more vigorous. Age and disease might have taken a toll on his body, but not on his mind. He was a superb legal stylist, a friend, and a mentor; he refined my thinking and my writing. I miss him profoundly.

Finally, I thank my family, without whom I would have had more time to write a better book. But then I'd have no one to tickle.

Summary of Contents

Table of Contents

Note on Illustrations

Whenever examples are given side by side, the right-hand version or the one in parentheses is preferred.

LEGAL WRITING STYLE

Third Edition

Chapter 1

INTRODUCTION

> *There are two things wrong with almost all legal writing. One is its style. The other is its content. That, I think, about covers the ground.*
> Fred Rodell (1907–1980)[1]

For the lawyer, more than for other professionals, unless you can express your knowledge, you might as well have none.[2] The bricklayer, the surgeon, and the plumber do their work largely without words; they do not need to explain what they are doing to anyone or convince anyone that they are right.

Lawyers, however, are verbal creatures—words are their primary tools. Knowing the right answer is not enough; lawyers must explain their reasoning and persuade another lawyer, a judge, a jury, a client. Knowing and communicating are two different skills—a writer must bridge the gap between mind and paper through language.

Language, the greatest of humanity's inventions, is the only means we have for communicating ideas. Language is the only means for having ideas in the first place—"The limits of my language," said Ludwig Wittgenstein, "mean the limits of my world."[3] Herbert Spencer said something similar: "language must be regarded as a hindrance to thought, though the necessary instrument of it."[4] And Justice Robert Jackson intuitively reached the same conclusion, when facing a practical legal problem: "[p]eople do not have words to fit ideas that have never occurred to them."[5]

Writing is a skill acquired only with practice; one is not born with it. Aristotle taught that "for the things we have to learn before

---

[1]   Goodbye to Law Reviews, 23 Va. L. Rev. 38 (1936).

[2]   Thucydides (460 BC–400 BC). See also Aristotle, Rhetoric, Book III, Part 1 ("it is not enough to know what we ought to say; we must also say it as we ought").

[3]   Tractatus Logico-Philosophicus 5.6 (1921).

[4]   Philosophy of Style 11 (1915).

[5]   Nw. Bands of Shoshone Indians v. United States, 324 U.S. 335 (1945).

we can do them, we learn by doing them."[6] The pianist who plays Chopin flawlessly did not play Chopin the first time she sat down at the piano. The soccer team's star player did not shine the first day he handled a ball. You acquire skill, whether in playing the piano, playing soccer, or writing, by disciplined, self-critical practice. If you wish to be a good writer, said Epictetus two thousand years ago, write.[7] Bernard Shaw gave the same advice well over a century ago: you learn to write by making a fool of yourself until you learn how.[8] And Anne Lamott recently told us yet again, "Almost all good writing begins with terrible first efforts. You need to start somewhere."[9]

It is practice, then, that improves writing style. You learn by doing, not by reading advice on how to do it. A writing style manual can be helpful, just as a book on swimming can help you learn to swim. But the advice that you get from a writing style manual does not become meaningful until you put it into practice.

Style and substance are inseparable: style is the sculpture; substance, the clay.[10] A book on writing does not teach tricks or mannerisms to ornament your style. Style, said E. B. White, is not "a garnish for the meat of prose, a sauce by which a dull dish is made palatable. . . . The approach to style is by way of plainness, simplicity, orderliness, sincerity."[11]

The style should reflect the subject matter, the document's purpose, and the mood the writer wants to evoke in the reader. A lawyer might need to narrate facts, expound upon a legal principle, or argue a position. At one point, the mood the lawyer wants to convey will be one of calm impartiality, at another indignation or sympathy, stern justice or merciful pity. The writer does not begin by wondering what style to use. Instead, she asks, "What point am I trying to make? What do I want the reader to see, feel, or believe?"

If you know which effect you want to produce, a style will arise almost automatically. The words, the organization, and the rhythm of your prose will be those that most naturally express your attitude

---

[6]   Nicomachean Ethics, Book II, Ch. 1.

[7]   Epictetus (55 AD–135 AD), The Discourses of Epictetus 158 (1890).

[8]   Collected Letters (1874–1897) 465 (1965) ("You will never write a good book until you have written some bad ones . . . . write a thousand words a day for the next five years.").

[9]   Bird by Bird: Some Instructions on Writing and Life 25 (1994).

[10]   Gary Provost, Make Your Words Work 282 (2001).

[11]   William Strunk, Jr. & E. B. White, The Elements of Style 69 (1979).

and mood. They will convey excitement or calmness, deliberateness or impatience, judicious equanimity or passionate conviction:

> For ideally the style is the thought, freed from crudeness and incompleteness, and presented in its intrinsic power and beauty. And the writer's effort is not directed to achieving a style, but to satisfying the demands of his subject, in order to bring out in its fullness what is essentially there.[12]

The most powerful inspiration for true eloquence is a burning conviction. Light and heat, said Bernard Shaw, are the two vital qualities of literature.[13] Whoever writes with rational light and emotive heat can be eloquent without the aid of rhetorical devices. This is why even those without literary polish, let alone perfect English, have been able to write artful prose. Famous anarchists Nicola Sacco and Bartolomeo Vanzetti were convicted of murder based on controversial evidence and executed in 1927. After being sentenced, Vanzetti wrote:

> If it had not been for these thing, I might have live out my life talking at street corners to scorning men. I might have die, unmarked, unknown, a failure. Now we are not a failure. This is our career and our triumph. Never in our full life could we hope to do such work for tolerance, for joostice for man's onderstanding of man as now we do by accident. Our words—our lives—our pains—nothing! The taking of our lives—lives of a good shoemaker and a poor fish-peddler—all! That last moment belongs to us—that agony is our triumph.[14]

The most persuasive writing is sincere writing—writing that most naturally reflects the personality, the spirit, and the feelings of the writer. As Buffon famously put it, "the style is the man himself."[15] Arthur Schopenhauer said much the same: "Style is the physiognomy of the mind, and a safer index to character than the face."[16] And for Voltaire, "writing is the painting of the voice."[17] You are your style and your style is you.

But what is a natural writing style? All writing is artificial in the sense that it is something one must learn (and legal writing is

---

[12]   John Franklin Genung, The Working Principles of Rhetoric 19 (1900).

[13]   Man and Superman: A Comedy and a Philosophy xxxvi (1903).

[14]   Marion D. Frankfurter & Garner Jackson (eds.), The Letters of Sacco and Vanzetti v (1928) (as handwritten).

[15]   Discours sur le style [1753], in Lane Cooper (ed.), The Art of the Writer 153–54 (1952).

[16]   On style [1851], in Lane Cooper (ed.), The Art of the Writer 219 (1952).

[17]   5 Philosophical Dictionary 170 (1824).

more artificial than most). The student who reads good writing and tries to emulate good models is learning just as naturally as the one who follows poorer models, and the style she develops is as much her own.

How much is learned depends on the writer's conscious attention to the style of what she reads and how much effort she makes to emulate it. As P.D. James recommended, "Read widely and with discrimination. Bad writing is contagious."[18] When you read something that strikes you as effectively written, stop. Analyze the rhythm, the sentence structure, and the choice of words to find out how the writer obtained this effect. Look to the advice in this book; learn to identify bad habits and cultivate good practices. In time, you will develop your own natural way of writing.

The Fowlers' advice is timeless:

Anyone who wishes to become a good writer should endeavor, before he allows himself to be tempted by the more showy qualities, to be direct, simple, brief, vigorous, and lucid.

This general principle may be translated into practical rules in the domain of vocabulary as follows:

Prefer the familiar word to the far-fetched.

Prefer the concrete word to the abstract.

Prefer the single word to the circumlocution.

Prefer the short word to the long.

Prefer the Saxon word to the Romance.[19]

These principles summarize most of the advice in this book. We rearranged them into four objectives: be precise, concise, simple, and clear. The objectives overlap considerably, and sometimes contradict each other. Precision, for example, is in constant tension with concision, simplicity, and clarity; clarity and concision do not always go hand in hand either. Careful writers, however, are able to strike a balance among them.

The following four chapters include suggestions on how to achieve each of these qualities using elements of style including

---

[18] The Guardian, Feb 19, 2010.

[19] H.W. Fowler & F.G. Fowler, The King's English 1 (1908). See also Herbert Spencer, The Philosophy of Style (1884).

diction, phrasing, and sentence structure. We deal with them separately, not because they are independent, but because it is more orderly to focus upon each in turn, even though they often shade into one another.

Legal writing is intended to convince. Even "objective" and "predictive" writing carries an element of persuasion: you must convince the reader that your objective assessment is correct or that your prediction is sound. Persuasion results not only from the intrinsic merit of the argument, but also from how the message is conveyed. The chapter on forcefulness discusses how to make arguments more vivid and vigorous. The chapter on organization suggests improvements on the structure of sentences and paragraphs and on the orderly presentation of argument. The last chapter offers a touch of eloquence.

But before we get to any of these objectives, Aristotle's cardinal admonition must be emphasized: consider the audience.[20]

Effective writing is reader-centered. Good writers have "intellectual sympathy," a feeling for the reader's mental state, enabling them to adjust the phraseology and sequence of ideas to meet the reader's needs.[21] Put yourself in the reader's place and make a concerted effort to preempt doubts about meaning and to avoid verbosity, which slows and tires the reader. The central principle of writing, according to Herbert Spencer, is economy: you must present your ideas in a way that will spare the reader's attention, so the reader may apprehend them with the least possible mental effort.[22]

The ideal style is one that the reader will notice the least. "The greatest possible mint of style," said Nathaniel Hawthorne, "is to make the words absolutely disappear into the thought."[23] This aphorism is particularly apt for legal writing, which is read by busy people who cannot spend time admiring its artistry. Readers are best served by writing that allows them to grasp the substance without noticing its form. A noticeable style is not a good style. Even if it does not mislead or confuse the reader, it calls attention to itself and away from the message.

---

[20] The Art of Rhetoric.
[21] Herbert Spencer, 2 An Autobiography 512 (1904).
[22] Philosophy of Style: An Essay 11 (1915).
[23] See Mark van Doren, Nathaniel Hawthorne 267 (1949).

If the judge reading your brief is impressed solely with how well you write, you have defeated yourself—make the judge feel that your client has a good case, not a good writer. When friends told Cicero that he was the greatest orator, he replied: "Not so, for when I give an oration in the Forum people say, 'How well he speaks!' but when Demosthenes addressed the people they rose and shouted, 'Come, let us up and fight the Macedonians!' "[24]

You never merely write. You always write to someone; you write with a purpose. Part of knowing how and what to write is determining to whom you write. Once you know your audience, write to that person as you would want that person to write to you.[25] Improve the golden rule by writing to that person as that person would wanted to be written to. Even a novelist or a journalist does not write for everyone. An article for *The New Yorker* is written in a distinctly different style from one for *Sports Illustrated*, not only because the topics are different but also because the readers are different.

The lawyer, of all writers, has the easiest task when it comes to identifying her readers. Usually, she is writing for an audience of one—one client, one lawyer, one judge. In fact, the lawyer knows her readers much better than most other writers and has some idea of what appeals to them. The lawyer may know something of their tastes and interests; their political, social, and economic points of view; their hobbies; and the public figures they respect. A lawyer must keep a mental picture of the person being addressed and measure every statement against the effect it will have on that person. Even when a lawyer does not know her reader, the audience of a legal text is significantly more uniform than that of most other forms of writing.

Sometimes the lawyer's audience is not a legal professional. A letter to a doctor has a different audience than the one addressed to a person with limited education and should be written accordingly. Language appropriate for a corporate mortgage is not appropriate for addressing a jury. A contract, although usually written for only two lay people, must be drafted with a further audience in mind—lawyers and ultimately judges who may have to interpret it. Because it is difficult to develop a variety of styles, a lawyer may mistakenly write a letter to a client as though drafting

---

[24]   See Merving James Curl, Expository Writing 12 (1919).

[25]   Joseph M. Williams & Joseph Bizup, Style: Lessons in Clarity and Grace 177 (2017); Robert Gunning, The Technique of Clear Writing 4 (1973).

a legal instrument or compose a brief as though arguing orally in court. The lawyer who uses one kind of writing style when another is more appropriate is likely to write poorly.

Rigorous writing is excellent training in rigorous thinking. "Thought and speech are inseparable from each other," said John Henry Newman. "Matter and expression are parts of one: style is a thinking out into language."[26] To write properly, one must think properly. Writing, said Justice Roger J. Traynor, is "thinking at its hardest."[27]

Consistent concern for form naturally leads to improved substance. The lawyer who strives to be precise and clear may discover the need to think through a point more thoroughly before he can express a thought unambiguously. A text written with fuzzy words was probably the result of fuzzy thought. Trying to write with clarity helps the writer perceive that he lacks a clear understanding of the subject, and so spurs him to master the content more thoroughly.

Language and thought—style and substance—are so closely interconnected that it is impossible to dissociate one from the other, as it is impossible to dissociate an author from his or her style.

---

[26] The Idea of a University 276 (1852).

[27] Some Open Questions on the Work of State Appellate Courts, 24 U. Chi. L. Rev. 211, 218 (1957). See also William Zinsser, On Writing Well 147 (2006) ("Writing is thinking on paper. Anyone who thinks clearly can write clearly"); Robert Gunning, The Technique of Clear Writing 11 (1973).

Chapter 2

PRECISION

> *Words are the source of misunderstandings.*
>
> Antoine de Saint-Exupéry (1900–1944)[28]
>
> *You can always write and erase and do it over.*
>
> Toni Morrison[29]

§ 2.1 Introduction

On your own, you do not have to write with precision. It is your prerogative to write any way you want and blame the reader who fails to understand your meaning. But you do not have that freedom when you represent a client's interest.

The lawyer must write more precisely than almost anyone else. Most writers can expect their work to be read in good faith, with an honest desire to understand what was intended. But the lawyer must write constantly aware of a hostile reader: the party who wants the contract to have contradictions or loopholes; the disappointed heir who wants the will read to defeat the testator's intention; the criminal defendant who wants the statute interpreted so as not to cover a certain act; and all the others who want to twist the meaning of words for their own ends.

Not every legal document will be attacked. If all goes well, no question will ever arise. But lawyers never know which of their efforts will someday be the subject of disagreement. Therefore, they must take pains to say precisely what they mean—no more and no less—not only so that a person reading in good faith can understand, but also so that a person reading in bad faith cannot misunderstand.[30]

---

[28] Le Petit Prince 80 (1943).

[29] Toni Morrison: Write, Erase, Do it over, https://alanrinzler.com/2015/03/toni-morrison-write-erase-do-it-over.

[30] See Quintillian (35 AD–100 AD), Institutes of Oratory § 8.2.24 (95); *In re* Castioni, 1 QB 149, 167–68 (1891).

An ambiguous text is vulnerable to various interpretations: reasonable misunderstandings, good faith misinterpretations, even intentional manipulations. You cannot avoid interpretation of your text because this task belongs to the reader: all writing must be interpreted to be understood. But you must make an effort to maintain control over your message. When you write an ambiguous text, you delegate the construction of a substantial part of your message to the reader.[31] This is particularly risky in contracts because courts may interpret ambiguous clauses against the interest of the drafter.

The risk of misinterpretation, however, is only the beginning of your troubles. Finding language that will stand the corrosive effect of time is more difficult to address:

> If the lawyer had only to write language that fools could not misunderstand and knaves could not twist, the problem of precision would be vastly simpler than it is. A greater difficulty, an insuperable one, is to write language that time will not change. It is more often changed circumstance and changed minds rather than foolishness or knavery that strains the language of the law.[32]

The lawyer who fails to draft clearly and precisely fails to reflect the client's objectives. But saying precisely what we mean is not easy; success depends on diction, phrasing, and sentence structure. "[M]ost of the disputes in the world arise from words," said Lord Mansfield.[33] Sometimes small words are the center of large-scale disputes. Every word can be ambiguous in context; control each one, or they will betray you. Even experienced lawyers make mistakes and find themselves litigating the meaning of their writing.

Ambiguities arise in any legal setting. A lawyer must be especially careful in wording a will. It is a mournful characteristic of probate cases that the testator is never available to explain what she meant. The drafter should therefore express the client's wishes without ambiguity.

A will provided that the testator's property should be "divided equally between all of our nephews and nieces on my wife's side and my niece." Did this mean that half of the property was to be divided

---

[31]   But see § 5.15, Use Ambiguity Strategically.

[32]   David Mellinkoff, The Language of the Law 397–98 (1963).

[33]   Morgan v. Jones, 98 Eng. Rep. 587, 596 (1773).

among the twenty-two nephews and nieces "on my wife's side," and the other half to go to "my niece," or that each person was to receive a twenty-third interest? The Arkansas Supreme Court held that the testator's niece was entitled to a full half share because the will used the word *between*, which applies only to two objects. If the intended reference had been to more than two, the preposition would have been *among*.[34] We can only trust that the drafter understood the distinction so that the court's interpretation left the testator resting easy in his grave.[35] But, even so, the lawyer's wording cost the estate a lawsuit, which could have been avoided by expressing the testator's intent clearly.

A charter of incorporation required that directors "shall be elected on a vote of the stockholders representing not less than two-thirds of the outstanding capital stock of the Corporation." Does this mean that a candidate needs the votes of the owners of two-thirds of the outstanding stocks to be elected? Or merely that the owners of two-thirds of the outstanding stocks must be present at the meeting at which the election is held? Control of the corporation depended on the interpretation. The court said the answer was in the word *on*. If a two-thirds vote for election had been intended, the charter should and presumably would have said "by a vote." "On a vote" meant that the charter meant a two-thirds quorum requirement.[36] Careful drafting—which would have separated quorum and voting requirements or defined the terms—would have avoided this lawsuit and perhaps prevented the client's losing control of the corporation.

An old Iowa statute prohibited lascivious acts with a child "of the age of sixteen years, or under." If a person commits such an act with a child who is sixteen years and six months old, is that person guilty? The State Supreme Court said no. Taking the words "of the age of sixteen years" in their ordinary meaning, said the court, a child is sixteen only on the sixteenth birthday. Before that day, a child is "under sixteen"; after that day, "over sixteen."[37] A careful

---

[34] Lefeavre v. Pennington, 230 S.W.2d 46 (Ark. 1950).

[35] See *In re* Welsh's Estate, 200 P.2d 139 (Ca. 1949) ("where the will is drawn by a lawyer whose experience and competence is beyond question, the presumption that legal terms embodied in the will are used in their legal sense is all but conclusive.").

[36] State v. Briede, 52 So.2d 568 (La. App. 1951).

[37] Knott v. Rawlings, 96 N.W.2d 900 (Iowa 1959). See also *In re* Smith, 351 P.2d 1076 (Okla. Cr. 1960) (interpreting a statutory definition of rape by a person "over eighteen years of age" and holding that when one reaches the age of 18 years he or she is "over the age of 18").

drafter might have detected the ambiguity and avoided the controversy. If the drafter intended to include the entire sixteenth year, then it could be said clearly and simply, "under the age of seventeen years." More precise language could have avoided unnecessary grief and litigation. Indeed, the current Iowa statute lowered the age of consent and avoided the ambiguity: "unless another age is specified, a 'child' is any person under the age of fourteen years."[38]

Writing clearly and precisely, however, is much more than resolving a single question, such as the right preposition to use in a particular situation. Because the elements of style overlap considerably, achieving clarity requires multiple assessments. This chapter addresses using the right word to express precise meaning. But imprecision and ambiguity may also be caused by various defects of sentence structure, such as improper word order, misplaced modifiers, and wrong punctuation, discussed elsewhere.

The elements of style also contradict each other. Brevity is a vice if it conceals ambiguity; simplicity is a vice if it conceals complexity. Sometimes, using more words is more helpful than using fewer: there is nothing wrong with adding a word or two (or a sentence or two) to make an idea more precise and clear. Sometimes, using more words creates confusion and ambiguity.[39]

§ 2.2   Choose the Right Word

Alexander Hamilton, a master of effective expression, said that the selection of the right word (diction) calls for the exercise of the greatest faculty of the human mind—judgment. Mastering words demands an appreciation of differences in shades of meaning. "Let the meaning choose the word," said George Orwell, "and not the other way about."[40]

In a quest for impressive words, inexperienced writers sometimes ignore the meaning of the words they use:

> Not all comedic performance should be *shrouded* in legal protection.

The writer obviously does not know what a *shroud* is.

> The employer *accedes* to proprietorship of any copyrightable material an employee generates in the course of employment.

---

[38]   Iowa Code § 702.5 (2017).

[39]   See Julie A. Oseid, The Power of Brevity: Adopt Abraham Lincoln's Habits, 6 J. ALWD 28, 29 (2009) ("The goal of brevity should be clarity").

[40]   Politics and the English Language (1946).

Here again, the writer uses a word without fully grasping its meaning, perhaps confusing *accede* with *succeed*.

> The UCC allows these commercial transactions to be carried on in an *aura* of certainty.

Aura, which denotes a subtle or vaporous emanation, is an inappropriate word to depict certainty.

A Seattle law firm approached a physician to serve as an expert witness:

> Your testimony is most important. Without it our position becomes extremely *tenable*.

Tenuous is the right word here.

These malapropisms are often the result of "the hankering of ignorant writers after the unfamiliar or imposing."[41] Many people use words they do not understand. They have a vague, general feeling about a word's connotation, which may be a shade or two off its true definition, or even the opposite of the intended meaning. The con artist spouting rich polysyllables may impress an uninformed audience, but a lawyer cannot afford to toss words around with abandon.

A good writer is a student of words. It is not enough to know the approximate meaning of a word; one must also discern the subtle difference between synonyms. The difference between the right word and the almost right word, said Mark Twain, is the difference between lightning and the lightning bug.[42] It's an endless search for precision. "You'll never make your mark as a writer," William Zinsser warned, "unless you develop a respect for words and a curiosity about their shades of meaning that is almost obsessive."[43]

Writers sometimes give a misleading coloration to their statements because they do not appreciate the transformative power of different shades of meaning. To say that a man's acts were heroic is one thing; to refer to them as heroics is altogether different.

No two words are exactly synonymous. Each has its own emotional wavelength. *Informant* and *informer* denote the same thing, but *informer* has a negative connotation. Inept writers, with

---

[41]   H.W. Fowler & F.G. Fowler, The King's English 13 (1908).

[42]   In George Bainton (ed.), The Art of Authorship 87–88 (1890).

[43]   On Writing Well 32 (2006).

no feeling for the emotional tone of words, sometimes describe actions or arguments in ways that are damaging to their client's interest. Of two words denoting the same thing, one may inspire sympathy or other favorable feeling, while the other evokes only ridicule or contempt. Compare:

childlike, childish   institute, instigate
depreciate, deprecate   manager, boss
difference, discrepancy   masterly, masterful
endless, interminable   obedient, submissive
enormousness, enormity   question, interrogate
fervent, fervid   strategy, plot
humble, meek   unusual, weird

Bertrand Russell demonstrated the fallacy of what he called conjugating "irregular comparatives."

I am firm; you are stubborn; he is pigheaded.

We all play this game. Our purpose is to liberate the oppressed; theirs is to stir up disorder and foment revolution. They use spies; we enlist counterintelligence officers. I negotiated a settlement; you worked a deal; they made out like bandits. Mine is a plan; yours is a scheme; theirs is a plot. I am a freedom fighter; you are a guerrilla; they are terrorists. We have reasons for what we do; you have excuses; they have rationalizations.

Consider the nuances:

affirm, assert, allege
apt, likely, liable
avert, avoid, evade
avowed, professed, ostensible, specious
difference, distinction, discrepancy, disparity
difficulty, hindrance, obstacle, obstruction
just, fair, equitable, upright
justifiable, defensible, excusable
legal, lawful, licit, legitimate
look, watch, stare, glare
murder, killing, homicide, assassination, execution
meticulous, scrupulous, punctilious
retire, retreat, withdraw, quit
work, job, labor, toil, employment, grind

In the measured and precise world of legal analysis, some familiar words may seem out of place.

In this case, the promise ran directly to the beneficiary, but the intent was the *overpowering* factor.

Using a wrong word, like *overpowering* in this sentence, is as jarring as a sour note in a symphony. It diverts the reader's attention from what is being said to how it is being expressed.

Hear the sour note in each of the following:

By *instigating* the student loan program, the government hoped to provide an incentive for the study of science.

It is with *unbridled* pride that I present . . . .

Judge Blank deserves the most *fulsome* praise.

This is to acknowledge your *lengthy* letter . . . .

Even writers who know better are sometimes betrayed by carelessness.

Contrary to disclosure, the parties need to request production of discovery.

The writer did not mean *contrary to*, but *in contrast to* or *unlike*.

A book on brief writing tells us:

The acquisition of an extensive vocabulary is, probably, for the average person a skill seldom attained or mastered.

Acquisition may require certain skills, but it is not itself a skill.

The word *literally* is sometimes used to mean the opposite: figuratively. And the word *precise* is sometimes used imprecisely—even by eminent writers:

The action of New York tends to restore some of the *precise* irritants which had long affected the relations between these two great nations.[44]

What was meant was not *precise* irritants, but *very* or *precisely the same* irritants.

The legal writer must always seek precision. Consider Mark Twain's criticism of James Fenimore Cooper:

Cooper's word-sense was singularly dull. When a person has a poor ear for music he will flat and sharp right along without knowing it. He keeps near the tune, but it is not the tune. When a person has a poor ear for words, the result is a literary flatting and sharping; you perceive what he is intending to say, but you also perceive that he

---

[44]   United States v. Pink, 315 U.S. 203, 232 (1942) (Douglas, J.).

doesn't say it. This is Cooper. He was not a word-musician. His ear was satisfied with the approximate word.[45]

To illustrate his criticism, Mark Twain listed three dozen examples, collected from half a dozen pages of the tale *Deerslayer*, where Cooper made poor word choices: verbal for oral; unsophisticated for primitive; precaution for caution; mortified for disappointed; different for differing; insensible for unsentient; distrusted for suspicious.

"Some words approach the desired meaning; others capture it, embody it, nail it to the wall in a way that leaves both the writer and the reader satisfied."[46] Word choices that miss the mark, even minor mistakes, have consequences, for "[w]ords that draw attention to themselves distract from the concept they're representing."[47]

The task of finding the right word is particularly challenging because meaning and connotation are contingent on time, place, and context. As Learned Hand noticed, "words are chameleons, which reflect the color of their environment."[48]

You develop an ear to distinguish the right word from the almost-right word by building a vast vocabulary through extensive reading; you put it into practice through attentive writing. It helps if you make it a habit to use reference materials.

§ 2.3　Use a Thesaurus and a Dictionary

You will continually encounter situations where you cannot think of the exact word you need. The words that come to mind don't quite hit the mark. You are sure there is a better one, but you don't know or can't recall it. Take time to find it. Make it a practice to consult a dictionary and a thesaurus to help you liberate "the word

---

[45]　Mark Twain, Fenimore Cooper's Literary Offenses, North American Review (1895).

[46]　Anne Enquist, Laurel Oates & Jeremy Francis, Just Writing: Grammar, Punctuation, and Style for the Legal Writer 91 (2017).

[47]　Ian Gallacher, Legal Communication and Research: Lawyering Skills for the Twenty-First Century 130 (2015).

[48]　Commissioner v. Nat'l Carbide Corp., 167 F.2d 304, 306 (2d Cir. 1948). See also Town v. Eisner, 245 U.S. 418, 425 (1918) (Holmes, J.) ("But it is not necessarily true that income means the same thing in the Constitution and the Act. A word is not a crystal, transparent and unchanged, it is the skin of a living thought, and may vary greatly in color and content according to the circumstances and the time in which it is used.").

that's right on the tip of your tongue, where it doesn't do you any good."[49]

A thesaurus serves a different function than a dictionary. It gives no definitions, only synonyms and antonyms. It is useful when you know the meaning of the word but are looking for another to convey the right shade of meaning, give a different nuance, or say something in a fresher way.

Insecure writers use a thesaurus to unearth fancy words they have never heard before merely to decorate their prose. That is not its proper use: "the thesaurus is a place for meeting friends, not for picking up strangers."[50] Just as you don't ask a question in open court unless you know the answer, you don't use a word unless you know its meaning.

When typing a document, you can access a basic thesaurus in your word processor with a right click of the mouse; you can find others on the internet. They are not as comprehensive as published materials, but they're easy to use. Use them often.

When you do not know the exact meaning of a word, or the exact difference in shades of meaning between two words—between *continuous* and *continual*, or between *compel* and *impel*, for example—you need a dictionary. And sometimes you will only find a satisfactory answer in usage dictionaries. Don't be lazy—consult dictionaries often to learn a word's precise meaning and usage while expanding your vocabulary.

The purpose of usage dictionaries is debated. Descriptive usage dictionaries merely record language as it is actually used by native speakers; they do not favor one form of language over another. Prescriptive ones, by contrast, focus on correct and effective usage to promote language that "sound[s] grammatical and relaxed, refined but natural, correct but unpedantic."[51] Because legal writers must write in a formal style, they have little use for descriptive usage dictionaries.[52]

Sometimes you recognize that the word you have written is not precisely what you want, but you cannot find another that will do. Consider recasting the whole sentence to put the thought in another

---

[49] William Zinsser, On Writing Well 35 (2006).

[50] Gary Provost, Make Your Words Work 291 (2001).

[51] Bryan A. Garner, Garner's Modern English Usage xiv–xv (2016).

[52] See Appendix, Further Readings (discussing descriptive and prescriptive usage dictionaries).

way. Suppose you are writing a letter to opposing counsel, rejecting an offer of settlement. You write:

> My client is unwilling to accept anything less than the amount of her claim. She has instructed me to file suit next Monday unless you will agree to the amount she asks.

On rereading, the last word, *asks*, strikes you as weak, but you cannot think of a better one. You resort to the thesaurus for synonyms, but only *request*, *claim*, and *demand* come close to what you need. *Request* and *claim* seem to be no better than *ask*, while *demand* is too strong. Well, don't stick to that line of inquiry; when the well runs dry, quit and drill another. Try rewording the last clause: She has instructed me to file suit next Monday . . .

> unless the full amount is paid.
>
> unless we receive a satisfactory reply.
>
> unless we receive a satisfactory proposal for settling this matter.

Which wording you use depends on what thought you are trying to convey. If you are determined to take nothing less than the full amount and want to close the door to any further offers of settlement (or want to give that impression), the first formulation will do. The second is not quite so unbending. It hints that the door you have just closed is not locked: although your client wants the full amount, it is just possible that you might persuade him to accept a little less. The third invites another offer.

Unless the writer questions a word's correct usage, she is helplessly unaware. There is no hope for the person who does not know what she does not know. One who knows enough to doubt will look it up.

§ 2.4   Trust Spell Check, but Proofread

Part of precision is respect for the rules of grammar and spelling. Spelling has always been a major challenge for any writer. Automated spell checks minimize the problem. If you misspell a word, the bells will go off: either the computer will autocorrect the error, or the offending word will be highlighted by a red squiggly underline so you can fix it, if need be, with a click of the mouse. Our lives are easier now, and we are certainly safer from a major blunder, but the problem has not yet gone away.

When an associate wrote that a contract clause was "duplicitous," the partner retorted that he should have said "duplicative." The associate argued that "duplicitous" was a word according to his computer's spell-check. Of course it *is* a word, the partner said, but not the right word in this situation.[53]

Today's writers battle errors that spell check cannot catch, words that are misspelled in one context but that in another would be correct: words such as principal and principle; affect and effect; who and whom; through and thorough; you're and your; they're, their, and there. Usage mistakes and inartful constructions are more difficult to catch than grammatical or spelling errors. Software is getting more sophisticated, but do not think it unnecessary to proofread your document just because you have spell check. Trust spell check, but proofread.

Autocorrect creates yet another problem. Lawyers employ a rich, sophisticated, technical vocabulary that is currently beyond the capabilities of an automated device, which may autocorrect incorrectly. The advantages are too small in relation to the risks. To keep the advantages and avoid the risks, leave spell check on but disable autocorrect. When you see a squiggly line under a word, determine whether it is, in fact, a mistake—you will avoid the blunder of an unwanted autocorrection, recognize your weak spots, and learn from your mistakes.

§ 2.5   Don't Be Afraid to Repeat a Word

Precision often demands repeating the same term to express the same idea. Never be afraid of repeating a word when necessary. Inexperienced writers mistakenly think there is an ironclad rule against using the same word twice in a sentence, in a paragraph, or within a certain number of lines. Although the rule is useful, it is not absolute. Many more sentences are spoiled by trying to avoid repetition than by repetition itself.[54]

> This common law doctrine was recognized both by the executive before the *enactment* of federal *laws* and by the courts after the *passage* of the *statutes*.

In a misguided attempt to be elegant, the writer shifts from *enactment* to *passage* and from *laws* to *statutes*. The last five words of the sentence should be replaced by "their enactment."

---

[53]   Janet S. Cole, A Brief Guide to Brief Writing 5 (2013).

[54]   See §§ 3.9, Not All Repetition is Pointless, 6.11, Use Reiteration Deliberately, and 8.5, Reiteration.

Fowler, who was not known for his patience, was merciless with writers who practiced what he sarcastically called "elegant variation":

It is the second-rate writers, those intent rather on expressing themselves prettily than on conveying their meaning clearly, and still more those whose notions of style are based on a few misleading rules of thumb, that are chiefly open to the allurements of elegant variation.[55]

If repetition is to be avoided, techniques other than elegant variation can work. One way of avoiding the monotonous effect of repeating a word without sacrificing exactness: using pronouns. For some reason, lawyers seem to think they must avoid this simple solution. After referring to a statute, instead of saying, "in its first section," they feel an obligation to say, "in the first section of said statute," or "in the first section thereof."

There is no reason for this practice. The pronoun *it* can do a lot to help take the stuffiness out of legal writing style, especially to avoid legalisms like *such, said, therein, thereof*, and *thereto.* "Thank you for your letter and for the information it contained" is better than "thank you for your letter and the information contained therein."

Even when not aiming for elegance, some writers vary words simply, it seems, out of fear of repetition.

Most *employers* would agree, but some *owners* have taken a contrary view.

Instead of hunting for a different word for *employers*, the writer could simply have used another approach to avoid repetition: omitting the noun the second time: "but some have taken a contrary view" or, better yet, "but some would not."

Not all commonly-used means of limiting repetition work well. Avoid using terms such as "the former . . . the latter," "the first . . . the second," and "party of the first part . . . party of the second part." They require the reader to pause, even if only momentarily, to go back and recall who was former and latter, first and second. Don't cause your reader unnecessary effort. If a short word or phrase, used consistently, can identify the reference, the reader can move on without having to figure out what is meant. *Buyer* and *Seller*, *the company* and *the union* are examples of identifying labels.

---

[55]   H.W. Fowler, A Dictionary of Modern English Usage 148 (2d ed. 1965).

Divorce settlement agreements and other contracts sometimes refer to the parties simply by their first names.

At times, though, repetition is the best choice. Repeating words and phrases may impair the literary quality of your work, but sometimes legal writers must sacrifice grace for precision. If you substitute a variation to avoid repeating a word, your reader may think you are making a distinction that you are not.

> Two of the seven Democratic delegates are *women*, whereas all of the Republican delegates are *ladies*.

The hapless writer merely wanted to avoid repeating the word *women*, but by using *ladies* he suggests that the Democratic women were somehow something less.

In statutory drafting especially, the same term must be used every time the same concept is referred to. This is so important that it is sometimes called "the drafter's golden rule." Variation for the sake of variety is not permissible. Thus, what is called a *motor vehicle* in one section or sentence must not be called an *automobile* in another.

Conversely, one term must not be used to refer to several ideas. *Unlawful* must not be used to mean criminal in one sentence and tortious in another.

Variation can also be dangerous in drafting wills and contracts. If you use a different term the second time, the reader will assume that you did it for a reason. If you had meant the same thing, you would have used the same term.

> I give the *farm* to my sister Amy. If she predeceases me, the *property* is to go to my brother George.

This invites litigation over what George will inherit—the farm, or something else?

Referring to the same person in different ways is confusing:

> Where *the manager* of a radio station conceived the title and principal characters of a program and employed *another person* to prepare the scripts and act in the production, but said nothing about the ownership of the program, *the broadcaster* owned the program and its title, even though *the script writer* copyrighted the first ten scripts in her own name without consulting *her employer*.

This story seems to have five actors: the manager, another person, the broadcaster, the scriptwriter, and her employer.

Actually there are only two, but the reader has to sort out five labels and assign them to the proper people.

You will make it easier for your reader to follow the story if you always use the same designation for the same party. Do not call a party Appellant in one sentence and Smith or Defendant in another. Consistency enables the court more easily to identify the parties with the issues. It may be helpful sometimes to refer to "Plaintiff Ames" and "the Defendant railroad," or to "Defendant-Appellant" and "Plaintiff-Appellee."

Rule 28(d) of the Federal Rule of Appellate Procedure discourages lawyers from using the terms *appellant* and *appellee*, preferring the parties' actual names, a descriptive term ("employer"), or the same designation used in the court below. It is always preferable to assign a person or entity a name rather than labeling them by their status in litigation. This applies to civil or criminal cases, regardless of the party you represent.

Some lawyers refer to their clients by name to make their story personal and compelling, but call the opposing party "the Appellant" or "the Defendant" to dehumanize the opponent. This may be a bad idea: the asymmetry of having a defendant without a plaintiff or an appellant without an appellee is confusing. Moreover, as Bryan Garner has noted, it is better to associate your opponents' bad deeds with their names instead of allowing them to hide behind a procedural label.[56]

Deliberate repetition is appropriate, but when you notice unintentional repetition, listen closely for a disruptive effect. Avoid repeating the same word so often in a sentence that the repetition becomes noticeable. Words often repeated include *in*, *of*, *the*, and *that*.

> The essence *of* many *of the* opinions *of the* Court *of* Appeals on *the* subject *of*
>
> She said *that* it was not true *that that* was the incident *that* led to *that* result.

§ 2.6   Use Gender-Neutral Language

(1) The Problem with Gendered Writing

Employing male terminology as a generic term for both genders invidiously implies male superiority and excludes women.

---

[56] Legal Writing in Plain English 57 (2013).

Language does not only reflect reality; it also influences our perceptions of reality. Language, therefore, may be a guiding force to effect changes in reality—in fact, language shapes reality.

Studies have shown that generic statements about *man* evoke, to a statistically significant degree, images of males only, whereas corresponding statements that avoid using the word *man* evoke images of both males and females.[57] That's "the subtle power of linguistic exclusion."[58] Moreover, statements that affirmatively include both words—*man* and *woman*—have an inclusive effect: they fairly and precisely reflect reality and avoid gender stereotypes.

For many centuries society operated under a convention that "the masculine included the feminine."[59] There had always been occasional objections to this practice, which perpetuated the cultural assumption that male is the norm and female is a deviation. But the feminist movement only began to challenge the convention more steadfastly in the 1970s. By the late 1980s, change was widely accepted, and by the late 1990s, most of the English language had been fully degendered.

Contemporary legal writing style, therefore, avoids male-centric language.

We have come a long way in recent years, and any reader would now cringe to read a text that consistently uses words like *man* or *he* to refer generally to men and women. Chief Judge Judith S. Kaye predicted this evolution in 1991: "I believe that gendered writing . . . will one day be immediately recognized as archaic and ludicrous."[60] She was a visionary—it has been for a long time now.

Gender imbalance will make your message imprecise, old-fashioned, unfair, and offensive; it will distract the reader and affect your credibility.

Many states and countries have already adopted gender-neutral language in official publications, including bills and

---

[57] See Casey Miller & Kate Swift, Words and Women 24 (2000).

[58] Id. at 41.

[59] See, e.g., 1 U.S.C. § 1 (2012) ("In determining the meaning of any Act of Congress, unless the context indicates otherwise . . . words importing the masculine gender include the feminine as well."); Cal. Civ. Code § 14 ("Words used in this code . . . in the masculine gender include the feminine and neuter.").

[60] A Brief for Gender-Neutral Brief-Writing, N.Y.L.J., 21 Mar. 1991, at 2.

regulations. Private companies have adopted similar policies. Women are invisible no longer.

The main categories of gendered language to watch for are: (a) the general designation of humans; (b) occupational labels; and (c) pronouns. But we also have to be careful with (d) subliminal hints within the message.

(2) Designation of Humans

When speaking about people, good writers say people or humans instead of men; human rights instead of the rights of man; and humankind, humanity, or human beings instead of mankind. Instead of manpower, they say workforce and instead of man-made, artificial or synthetic.

In search of a gender-free standard, the law has erased all references to its traditional mythic reasonable man, and adopted the more inclusive but equally elusive reasonable person.[61] Law students today do not read the offending expression in their Torts casebooks, so they are unaware it was once the standard.

(3) Occupational Labels

Occupational sex-biased titles are also disfavored. The careful writer uses epicene nouns, which have only one form for either gender. Instead of juryman, juror; instead of fireman, firefighter; instead of workman, worker.

Avoid job titles that are formed with a feminine suffix (-*woman*, -*trix*, -*ess*, -*enne*, -*ette*, -*mistress*), such as executrix, testatrix, administratrix, prosecutrix, heroine, actress, headmistress, stewardess, heiress, waitress, headmistress, businesswoman. These terms may lead to the perception that the male category is the norm, and that women filling these positions are somehow a deviation and thus lesser.

Avoid gendered nouns even when the gender of the subject is known. Gendered nouns can create gender bias and stereotyping, contributing to gender inequality and sexism. Instead of chairman, chairwoman or chairperson, say chair; instead of draftsman, draftswoman or draftsperson, say drafter; instead of policeman,

---

[61] See Ronald K.L. Collins, Language, History and the Legal Process: A Profile of the "Reasonable Man," 8 Rutgers Camden L.J. 311 (1977); Naomi R. Cahn, Looseness of Legal Language: The Reasonable Woman Standard in Theory and in Practice, 77 Cornell L. Rev. 1398 (1992).

policewoman or policeperson, say police officer; instead of anchorman, anchorwoman or anchorperson, say anchor; instead of salesman, saleswoman or salesperson, say sales representative; instead of congressman, congresswoman or congressperson, say representative.

Stay away from gratuitous gender references such as "male nurse," "cleaning lady," "lady lawyer," and "female doctor." They betray a perception that some professions are typically or properly performed by people of a specific gender.

Drawing up a full list of gendered job titles is unnecessary because some of them are archaic, and most have been obsolete for at least a generation. Although the substitution process was the artificial result of conscious effort, rather than the natural evolution of the language, it has been a success: if originally the gender-free words felt forced and were objects of ridicule, they are now quite ordinary.

(4) Personal Pronouns

Getting rid of gendered personal pronouns, however, has proved to be a more difficult matter, and the search for gender-free pronouns has been unsatisfactory. Plural pronouns, *they* and *them*, are common for both genders, but the English language does not have a gender-neutral third-person singular pronoun yet. We have *he, she, it*, and that's it.

Careful writers have developed several techniques to address this deficiency of the English language.

(a) The most common method is to double the pronoun, one for each gender (*he or she*), making sure not only that no one is excluded, but also that everyone is included. So, instead of saying,

> A taxpayer can expect to be audited at least once during *his* life,

prefer,

> A taxpayer can expect to be audited at least once during *his or her* life.

The use of *he or she*, although inartful and inefficient, may serve to affirmatively validate the presence of women and their active role in society.[62] But the clumsy effort to fill this void by writing *he or she, him or her, his or hers, himself or herself* every time you need to use a pronoun soon becomes a drag and saps the

---

[62] Francine Wattman Frank & Paula A. Treichler, Language, Gender and Professional Writing 160 (1989).

strength of your sentences. It is particularly objectionable when used repeatedly, and unbearable when it appears twice in the same sentence. Use this approach sparingly.

> [A] litigant may raise a claim on behalf of a third party if the litigant can demonstrate that *he or she* has suffered a concrete, redressable injury, that *he or she* has a close relation with the third party, and that there exists some hindrance to the third party's ability to protect *his or her* own interests.[63]
>
> The plaintiff must submit *his or her* complaint to preserve *his or her* claim. The claim should be filed in *his or her* home district unless there is evidence that *his or her* claim may be better processed in another court.

Pronouns are useful: they make sentences flow smoothly without repeating the noun. Indeed, pronouns are essential to good writing style—the preceding sentence, for example, just used the pronoun *they* in place of the word *pronouns*. But using a pronoun that is more awkward than the noun defeats the very purpose of pronouns. Despite its wide use, therefore, *he or she* is not conducive to good writing style: it's wordy, it's long, it's weak, it's slow. It shows that the writer gave up on style. Moreover, putting the male pronoun first does not really resolve the broader issue of gender neutrality. That's why careful writers use it sparingly or avoid it.

Instead, you can recast the sentence, and

(b) Use the plural.

> Taxpayers can expect to be audited at least once in *their* lives.

(c) Use *you*, *I*, *we*, or *one*.

> You (we, I, one) can expect to be audited at least once in *your* (our, my, one's) life.

(d) Omit the pronoun.

> A taxpayer can expect to be audited at least once *in* life.

(e) Repeat the noun.

> A taxpayer can expect to be audited at least once during *the taxpayer's* life.

(f) Use another noun, like *person* or *party*.

> A taxpayer can expect to be audited at least once in that person's lifetime.

(g) Use an article, like *a* or *the*, instead of the pronoun.

> A taxpayer can expect to be audited at least once in *a* lifetime.

---

[63] Edmonson v. Leesville Concrete Co., 500 U.S. 614, 629 (1991).

More controversially,

(h)   Use the singular *they*.

> A taxpayer can expect to be audited at least once during *their* life.

(i)   Use the generic *it*.

> A taxpayer can expect to be audited at least once during *its* life.

There are several other alternatives to the gendered pronoun. For example, you can

(j)   Use the passive voice.

> A writer should always define the meaning of a word he is using.
>
> A writer should always define the meaning of a word *being used*.

(k)   Use a relative clause or indefinite pronoun, like *who*.

> If a lawyer cannot write well he should not pass the bar.
>
> A lawyer *who* cannot write well should not pass the bar.

(l)   Convert a noun into a verb.

> The client must give his consent before a lawyer can settle.
>
> The client must *consent* before a lawyer can settle.

A resourceful writer uses various methods to avoid the gendered pronoun. Sometimes, however, none of the alternatives is appropriate and the only solution is to

(m) Rewrite the sentence.

You can generally choose from several alternatives, but not every method is appropriate in every situation: some might be inartful or slightly change the meaning. For example, you can repeat the noun only a few times and only if the repeated words are not too close to each other; the use of passive voice usually weakens your prose; the singular *they* and the generic *it* are still considered ungrammatical; *one* is stilted; and *you* may be seen as too informal.

In addition, the plural may disguise the point the writer wants to make and is weaker than a statement in the singular—"a judge must be careful" does not convey quite the same meaning as "judges must be careful." The sense of individual responsibility implicit in the original text is lost in its translation to gender-sensitive language.[64]

---

[64]   See William Strunk, Jr. & E. B. White, The Elements of Style 60 (2000) (the use of plural nouns and pronouns will make your prose sound "general and diffuse"); William Zinsser, On Writing Well 82 (2006) ("[P]lurals . . . weaken writing because they

So choose the method that best captures your message and is the most idiomatic and unobtrusive in the context. But avoid using the same method repeatedly or your style will soon become stale.

Another successful way of avoiding gendered pronouns, without falling in the trap of using the awkward *he or she* and still maintaining the sentence in the singular, is to

(n) Judiciously apportion the traditional singular pronouns *he* and *she* throughout the text.

This last approach is used in this book. It should be used in combination with all other available methods, and reserved to secondary statements, particularly those that have little chance of being quoted by another writer. If well done, the reader will not notice. This method, however, is not available for professional legal writing style; it is only useful in long, book-length documents, where you will face the issue dozens of times.

One recent treatise uses *she* for all plaintiffs and *he* for all defendants, openly acknowledging the risk (if not the certainty) that this choice gives the appearance that women are always victims and men are always tortfeasors, which is offensive to both.[65] A more neutral solution would have been to alternate the usage in the several chapters of the book or to randomly and equitably assign singular pronouns.

Remember, however, that you are not merely throwing in a pronoun as a generic singular—you are referring the reader to the image of a hypothetical person. It is essential, therefore, to be consistent: if the lawyer is male and the client is female in an example, maintain that gender choice until the next example, when the prosecutor can be male and the judge, female. If you change the gender of your characters in the middle of an example you will confuse your readers.

This method presents its own risks because it may inadvertently suggest stereotypes. Consider the following sentence: "An autobiography coming into a library would be classified as non-fiction if the librarian believed the author, and as fiction if she

---

are less specific than the singular, less easy to visualize."); Garner's Modern English Usage 460 (2016) ("The disadvantage [of pluralizing] is that it often too strongly suggests a singleness of mind in the group, as opposed to the uniqueness of an individual mind.").

[65] Dan B. Dobbs, Paul T. Hayden, & Ellen M. Bublick, Hornbook on Torts vi (2016) ("If it creates a sense that women are always plaintiffs and men always tortfeasor defendants, it is unfortunate, inaccurate and not our aim.").

thought he was lying." Whoever wrote that sentence seems to have assumed the librarian to be female and the book author to be male, which is gender-stereotypical. But if the writer had inverted the pronouns some might object that the message remains sexist: women lie and men make judgment.[66]

Or you might risk the opposite outcome: in a "spasm of overcompensation," you might use exclusively male pronouns for burglars, embezzlers, and liars while exclusively using female pronouns for doctors, lawyers, and judges.[67] If you do so, you may call the reader's attention to your choices, diverting attention from the message: "alternating pronouns in either a fixed or random pattern may . . . attract the attention of the feminist, who will probably pause to consider instances that either perpetuate or overturn strong stereotypes [or of the] sociologist, who will find the writer's behavior much more interesting than the writer's argument."[68] But if the personal pronouns are randomly distributed throughout the text, any accusation of biased language limited to isolated issues would be unfair.

The language is still gendered because it uses the generic *he* and the generic *she*, but it is not sexist because their use is balanced. Although objected to by some scholars, the advantages of a streamlined text exceed the disadvantages.

(5) The Search for a Gender-Neutral Singular Pronoun (*They* and *It*)

The English language has yearned for a third person gender-neutral singular pronoun for far too long, at least as far back as Middle English.[69] It is surprising that a language may experience an unfulfilled void for centuries without devising a solution. Yet the language cannot thrive without it. As long as nobody questioned the generic *he*, no one missed a gender-neutral singular pronoun. But now that its use is impermissible, the void must be addressed.

Because English has no central authority to impose language and grammar rules, it was easier to destroy offending practices

---

[66] Francine Wattman Frank & Paula A. Treichler, Language, Gender and Professional Writing 163 (1989).

[67] See Beverly Ray Burlingame, Reaction and Distraction: The Pronoun Problem in Legal Persuasion, 1 Scribes J. Leg. Writing 87, 106 (1990).

[68] Id.

[69] Webster's Dictionary of English Usage 499 (1989).

than to build good solutions. But good solutions do exist: the singular *they* and *it*.

The *Oxford English Dictionary* cites several examples of singular *they* in every century, going back to 1375 (*they*), 1382 (*their*), 1450 (*themself*), and 1548 (*them*). Amongst its most prestigious users are Austen, Bagehot, Byron, Carroll, Chaucer, Chesterfield, Defoe, Dickens, Fielding, Fitzgerald, Kipling, More, Orwell, Shakespeare, Shaw, Spencer, Swift, Thackeray, Whitman, Wilde, Woolf, and the King James Bible.[70]

So several American presidents were in good company when they used the singular *they*:

> And if anyone doubts that democracy is alive and well, let them come to New Hampshire.—Ronald Reagan[71]
>
> If anyone tells you that America's best days are behind her, they're looking the wrong way.—George Bush[72]
>
> No American should ever live under a cloud of suspicion just because of what they look like.—Barack Obama[73]
>
> The Cambridge police acted stupidly in arresting somebody when there was already proof that they were in their own home.—Barack Obama[74]

The singular *they* is most common after a noun phrase with one of the indefinite determiners or pronouns that are grammatically singular but notionally plural: either, neither, who, any, no, each, some, every, one, no one, anyone, everyone, someone, anybody, nobody, somebody, everybody.

> Every taxpayer can expect to be audited at least once during *their* life.

But it could be used in any situation:

> A taxpayer can expect to be audited at least once during *their* life.

Despite its centuries-old prestigious pedigree going back to Middle English, the singular *they* has been considered ungrammatical since the eighteenth century, and opposition is still

---

[70] See Oxford English Dictionary (2013). See also Webster's Dictionary of English Usage (1989); Random House Webster's Unabridged Dictionary (2001); and Webster's Third New International Dictionary (Unabridged) (1993).

[71] Remarks to Citizens in Concord, New Hampshire, September 18, 1985.

[72] Address Before a Joint Session of the Congress on the State of the Union, January 29, 1991.

[73] Statement by the President on the Supreme Court's Ruling on Arizona v. the United States, June 25, 2012.

[74] Helene Cooper, Obama Criticizes Arrest of Harvard Professor, NY Times, July 22, 2009 (commenting on the arrest of Professor Henry Louis Gates, Jr.).

strong. As a result, lawyers cannot use it in formal prose, at least not until it becomes accepted as Standard English.

But it seems to be the inevitable choice—it is only as ambiguous as the singular *you*, and is more melodious than the unpronounceable *s/he* or the unspeakable *s/he/it*. Purists are too detail-oriented to accept the nonstandard number agreement and too uncreative to recognize the historical precedent of the singular *you*. But it is better to upset a few grumpy old grammarians than to stall the development of the English language.

South Africa, Australia, Canada, and other English-speaking countries have embraced *they* as a singular gender-neutral pronoun.

> Everyone has inherent dignity and the right to have *their* dignity respected and protected.[75]

> "[C]onsumer" means any person who . . . purchases . . . a tobacco product . . . for *their* own use . . . or on behalf of . . . a principal who desires to acquire it for use . . . by *themself* . . . .[76]

The singular *they* has become unremarkable, particularly in speech by young people, and is gathering widespread popularity—it will eventually be acceptable in formal writing. The trend, considered irreversible at the end of the twentieth century[77], is now stronger than ever.[78] Indeed, experimental research on cognitive psychology has shown that readers use minimal processing effort to understand the singular *they*, giving scientific credence to our intuition.[79] *They* is coming, and there's nothing you can do to stop it.

---

[75]   Constitution of the Republic of South Africa, Section 10 (1996).

[76]   Ontario's Tobacco Tax Act, Section 1 (1990).

[77]   The New Fowler's Modern English Language 779 (R.W. Burchfield, ed., 3d ed. (1996).

[78]   See, e.g., Associated Press Stylebook (2017) (accepting singular *they* in limited circumstances); The Chicago Manual of Style § 5.48 (2017) (same). In 2015, the American Dialect Society selected the singular *they* as the word of the year.

[79]   See Julie Foertsch & Morton Ann Gernsbacher, In Search of Gender Neutrality: Is Singular "They" a Cognitively Efficient Substitute for Generic "He"? 8 Psychological Science 106, 110 (1997) ("the increased use of singular *they* is not problematic for the majority of readers"); Anthony J. Sanford & Ruth Filik, "They" as a Gender-unspecified Singular Pronoun: Eye tracking Reveals a Processing Cost, 60 Q. J. Experimental Psychology 177 (2007) (the brain recognizes *they* as a plural pronoun, not singular; while eye-tracking reveals a mismatch effect, it is rapidly accommodated by the brain as an accepted deviation). See also Steven Pinker, The Sense of Style 255–62 (2014).

Using *it* would not be a bad choice either and has the advantage of being singular and short. The feeling that *it* dehumanizes the subject will fade with widespread use—it is already used for babies.

> A taxpayer can expect to be audited at least once during *its* life.

International institutions like UNIDROIT and UNCITRAL use *it* in their enactments:

> A party cannot act inconsistently with an understanding *it* has caused the other party to have and upon which that other party reasonably has acted in reliance to *its* detriment.[80]

So does the United States:

> A party asserting a claim, counterclaim, crossclaim, or third-party claim may join, as independent or alternative claims, as many claims as *it* has against an opposing party.[81]

The original 1938 version of this Rule was, "the plaintiff . . . may join . . . as many claims . . . as *he* may have against an opposing party." In 1987, the text was changed to "as many claims as *the party* has." The current version (above) is from the 2007 restyling of the Rules. True, *party* is a genderless word, and may refer to a corporation, but it may also refer to a person. Instead of writing "he, she, or it," the rulemakers decided to adopt the generic *it*.[82]

These sentences seem unremarkable for a modern English speaker. Worse choices of epicene pronouns have been devised over the years—dozens of them—and none has taken hold. As with any pronoun choice, however, *they* and *it* should never be used when imprecision or ambiguity would result. The historical evidence and increasing social acceptance of their use in various contexts, however, suggest that such concerns are less warranted than they once were.

Whatever the solution, it will probably be awkward and artificial for a generation, so we'd better start using it soon. Once the users of the language settle on the gender-neutral pronoun, this section will be deleted (it's mostly obsolete already). Then another battle, already started, will be waged to include other groups excluded from the traditional singular pronouns, such as

---

[80]   Unidroit Principles of International Commercial Contracts, art. 1.8 (2004). See also Unidroit Convention on International Interests in Mobile Equipment, arts. 4(1), 4(2), 11(2), 13 (2001); UNCITRAL Model Law of Secured Transaction, art. 2(*o*) (2016).

[81]   FRCP 18(a).

[82]   See, among dozens of examples, FRCP 38(c) and 81(c)(3)(B)(i), which correspond to a generic *he* in the original 1938 version.

transgender, transsexual, queer, intersex, and other gender-nonconforming people. Binary conceptions of gender (he or she and male or female) may have become too rigid to express reality. That's how language evolves—incrementally. Meanwhile, writers will have to make do with evasive tactics instead of a solution.

(6) Biased Message

The problem of gender-biased language is acute in the use of exclusionary language: the generic *man*, the generic *he*, and the professions. But it may also be hidden in the message itself.

Avoid expressions implying that virtue is found only in men: facing danger "with manly courage," or "like a man." Things would certainly be no easier for a woman were she to endure childbirth like a man. Also, avoid the opposite temptation to find virtue only in women. As Madeleine Albright said, "I'm not a person who thinks the world would be entirely different if it was run by women. If you think that, you've forgotten what high school was like."[83]

If you say, "judges are so overworked that they often neglect their wives and children," you will make some husbands feel doubly neglected. The same will happen if you say, "all judges and their wives are invited to the ceremony." Say *families*, *partners*, or *spouses* instead.

A careful writer is wary of unconscious sexual bias.

(7) Conclusion

The use of gender-neutral language is a matter of precision, fairness, and credibility. If you use sexist language, your statement will be imprecise and unfair because it will exclude a significant portion of the population. It may also be ambiguous. Gendered usage is now borderline ungrammatical. You will also lose credibility with readers, men and women, who will find your style objectionable. Most important, whatever your readers' opinions on the matter, they will notice your misstep. You will then have shifted their attention from your message, one of the most egregious flaws in writing style, particularly when you have the ethical duty to represent someone else's interest.

For the same reasons, avoid the temptation to make a political statement by using *she* as the gender-neutral pronoun. It is neither

---

[83] Madeleine Albright on Barriers Broken and Barriers that Remain, Wall St. J., May 7, 2012.

gender neutral nor precise—you cannot combat the generic *he* with the generic *she*. Moreover, it, too, distracts from your message.[84]

Don't be overzealous. When you know the gender of the person or when discussing issues that affect only one gender, such as cervical or prostate cancer, use the appropriate gender-specific pronoun. It would be ludicrous to say, "A person should not drink alcoholic beverages if he or she is pregnant."

When you need to transcribe old texts with gendered usage, do so unapologetically. We should not abandon our forefathers' (a word used consciously here) wisdom only because of their dated writing style. If it is irrelevant for the point you are making, there is no need to call attention to the issue by labeling the text sexist—it is unfair and cowardly to mistreat writers of another era. We can only hope the next generation will show a similar courtesy towards our mistakes. If you cannot paraphrase, either transcribe the text with the offending usage and let readers sort it out, or update it with brackets.

Write so that the gender issue will be invisible, and will not even occur to your reader, who will focus on your message, instead of seeing your writing either as sexist or awkwardly or ostentatiously nonsexist.[85]

§ 2.7 Abstract Words Are Inexact

Lawyers must constantly deal with abstract legal concepts, like negligence, malice, consideration, intent, fraud, reasonableness, and the even wider concepts of right, wrong, property, duty, justice, and freedom. In fact, the law mainly consists of abstract general principles.[86]

While we cannot avoid using such words, we can recognize the ambiguity inherent in them. Because they are big words, they do not have one exact meaning. *Justice* or *democracy* does not connote for one person quite what it does for another. A writer using such a

---

[84] Francine Wattman Frank & Paula A. Treichler, Language, Gender and Professional Writing 164–65 (1989); Beverly Ray Burlingame, Reaction and Distraction: The Pronoun Problem in Legal Persuasion, 1 Scribes J. Leg. Writing 87, 107 (1990).

[85] Bryan A. Garner, The Winning Brief 356–59 (2014). See also Beverly Ray Burlingame, Reaction and Distraction: The Pronoun Problem in Legal Persuasion, 1 Scribes J. Leg. Writing 87 (1990).

[86] See §§ 4.6, Prefer Concrete to Fuzzy Nouns; Avoid Vogue Words (concrete words are simpler) and 6.7, Use Specific and Concrete Rather than General and Abstract Words (specific and concrete words are stronger than general and abstract ones).

word should pause to define the sense in which it is being used, first for himself and then for the reader; and then use it consistently in that sense.

> Your allegation that the function of our courts is protective and corrective solely would lead to the conclusion that our courts should not be termed courts of justice but rather courts of expediency.

It would be futile to debate this proposition without first defining in what sense the words *justice* and *expediency* are being used.

> The court reached an equitable conclusion which in its essence stated that a broad principle of public policy is essential to public welfare.

What does this say, if anything?

Some writers become so addicted to the use of abstract words that they use them even for concrete things:

There are a variety of forms that the courts have approved.	The courts have approved various forms.

Abstract terms appeal to writers who have not clearly thought through what they want to say and those afraid that a more specific statement may be incorrect. Because these words are vague, they can be used without any precise meaning, offering an easy way out for the lazy and the fuzzy-minded. A Birmingham, Alabama ordinance once provided that "no nude be displayed unless it is art."

The process feeds on itself: because our thoughts are fuzzy, we use woolly phrases, and the availability of these woolly phrases allows us to be content with fuzzy thoughts. A. Parker Nevin once constructed an all-purpose political speech, made up of reverberating sentences such as this:

> The crucial test for the solution of all these intricate problems which confront and challenge our ingenuity is the sheer and forceful application of those immutable laws which down the corridor of time have always guided the hand of man, groping as it were for some faint beacon of light for his hopes and aspirations.[87]

We confirm this caricature by listening to almost any political speech, whether made by the head of government or by a candidate for county commissioner. Here is a sentence from a speech by President Franklin D. Roosevelt:

---

[87]   An Address to End All Addresses, Princeton Alumni Weekly (1948).

> In our inner individual lives we can never be indifferent, and we assert for ourselves complete freedom to embrace, to profess, and to observe the principles for which our flag has so long been the lofty symbol.[88]

The example is taken from President Roosevelt intentionally, not because he was one of the worst offenders but because he was one of the least. He could be vividly specific, as in the following passage:

> I have seen war. I have seen war on land and sea. I have seen blood running from the wounded. I have seen men coughing out their gassed lungs. I have seen the dead in the mud. I have seen cities destroyed. I have seen two hundred limping, exhausted men come out of line—the survivors of a regiment of one thousand that went forward forty-eight hours before. I have seen children starving. I have seen the agony of mothers and wives. I hate war.

A writer's job is to create a mental picture through words. Abstract words are difficult to understand because they offer the reader no image to visualize. Fred Rodell was particularly critical of legal language: "legal words and concepts and principles float in a purgatory of their own, halfway between the heaven of abstract ideals and the hell of plain facts and completely out of touch with both of them."[89]

Concrete words, on the other hand, evoke facts—real experiences and real people—and the reader can identify with them. One such concrete picture—soldiers coughing out their gassed lungs—activates our imagination more than a thousand words declaiming against war's irrationality, horrors, and other abstractions. If you must use abstract words, "make them as concrete as possible by tying them to the specific facts of [the] case."[90]

§ 2.8   Words to Watch

There are dozens of controversial words to watch. Some of them are traps for general use, others are unfit for formal writing or for legal writing; some are wrong, others inappropriate, still others merely offer the risk of ambiguity. If you are to attain precision, you must consider every word; if you are to attain concision, you must remove those that are taking up bandwidth without any useful

---

[88] This and the next quotation are taken from Stuart Chase, The Tyranny of Words 381–82 (1938).

[89] Woe unto you, Lawyers! 136 (1957).

[90] Theresa J. Reid Rambo & Leanne J. Pflaum, Legal Writing by Design 472 (2013).

function (the topic of the next chapter). As an artist, a careful writer chooses each word with discrimination.

A good writer must develop an ear for words, just as the musician must develop an ear for notes. The best way to do so is to read good prose, but this process can be aided by creating the habit of consulting good dictionaries, dictionaries of usage, and thesauruses.[91]

It is not the purpose of this book to teach vocabulary, usage, or grammar. You have presumably learned the essentials of correct English before starting law school; if not, you have some important catching-up to do. But experience has shown that certain words give legal professionals special trouble. Below are some of them.

affect, effect

Because these words sound almost the same and there is correlation in meaning, even experienced legal writers confuse them.

Effect is usually a noun, meaning "consequence" or "result" ("actions have effects"). It is also used idiomatically in "personal effects," "visual effects," "to take effect," "with immediate effect."

Effect is also less commonly used as a verb, meaning "to bring about," "to accomplish," "to execute" ("the new policy will effect changes in society").

Affect is usually a verb, meaning "to have an effect on" or "to influence" ("her death affected me"). The difficulty exists because of the correlation between the verb *affect* and the noun *effect*: when you affect something, you have an effect on it.

Affect can occasionally be used as a noun in the field of psychology.

aforementioned, aforesaid

"Afore" is an archaic prefix meaning "before." The words *aforementioned* and *aforesaid* (previously mentioned, previously said) are often useless or ambiguous. They are useless when the reference is clear, serving merely as fancy decoration; they are ambiguous when it is unclear which earlier item they refer to.

They are archaic legalese to be avoided in all kinds of legal writing, particularly in less formal documents such as letters.

---

[91]   See § 2.3, Use a Thesaurus and a Dictionary and Appendix.

Sometimes, however, the qualification that a word was previously mentioned in the text is useful and unambiguous. In these cases, prefer simple constructions like "named above," "mentioned earlier," "previously mentioned," or "abovementioned." When necessary to avoid ambiguity, say precisely where the word was previously mentioned, referring to the exact section or clause of the document.

See *said*, *such*, and *same*. See also *herein*.

alibi

Alibi means "elsewhere" in Latin. It is a term of art for the criminal defense in which the suspect alleges innocence for having been somewhere other than the crime scene at the relevant time.

For over a century, however, the word has been colloquially used in the United States to mean any excuse, pretext, or explanation, real or fabricated. When an American athlete who was favored to win an event in the 1960 Olympics was beaten by two Russians, he said, "I don't have any alibis; I was beaten fair and square." This was commendable sportsmanship but hardly commendable phrasing, unless he meant merely to admit that he had been present at the games. The word is also loosely used to designate the person who will provide the defense: "Mary is my alibi."

A layperson may get away with using the word in the loose sense, but a lawyer needs to use precise legal terminology.

alleged, allegedly

Because the law presumes a person to be innocent until proved guilty, we should not call someone not yet convicted a criminal, not even an alleged (or accused or suspected) criminal. The word is more appropriately applied to actions, events, situations, conditions, and things, not to persons. A crime was allegedly committed, and a person allegedly committed criminal acts, because that's what the police allege; but the person is not an "alleged criminal."

The word is also improperly used as an unnecessarily cautious hedge to report an established unpleasant fact: if a person is a suspect, it is wrong to call that person an "alleged suspect."

and, or

These seemingly precise words may lead to ambiguity, as thousands of litigated cases can attest.[92] Sometimes it is difficult to determine whether *or* is being used in a disjunctive sense, marking an alternative (A or B, but not both), or in an inclusive sense (A or B, or both).

The same kind of ambiguity afflicts the interpretation of *and*. Does the writer mean the several *and* (A and B, together or separately) or the joint *and* (A and B together only, not separately)? Sometimes that distinction is important.

To make matters worse, sometimes writers use *and* when they mean *or* and use *or* when they mean *and*. Use conjunctions with care.[93]

Despite what your middle school teacher told you, and despite the grammar checker in your word processor, it is acceptable to begin a sentence or a paragraph with *and* or *or*. Actually, these two words are an excellent way to begin a sentence or paragraph. The same is true for *but, so,* and *because.* Go ahead. Try it.

and/or

Fierce controversy has raged for almost two centuries over the use of *and/or*.[94] In a heated debate in the 1930s and 1940s, judges called it a linguistic abomination devoid of meaning and incapable of classification by the rules of grammar and syntax.[95] It was held to violate a constitutional requirement that judicial proceedings be conducted in English.[96] A judge called it,

> that befuddling, nameless thing, that Janus-faced verbal monstrosity, neither word nor phrase, the child of a brain of someone too lazy or too dull to express his precise meaning, or too dull to know what he did mean, now commonly used by lawyers in drafting legal documents,

---

[92] See 3A Words and Phrases 166–210 (2007 & Supp. 2016) (summarizing hundreds of cases litigating the meaning of *and*) and 30 Words and Phrases 47–111 (2008 & Supp. 2016) (same for the meaning of *or*). See also Reed Dickerson, The Fundamentals of Legal Drafting 104–114 (1986).

[93] See § 5.9, Distinguish Between the Conjunctive and the Disjunctive.

[94] See Cuthbert v. Cumming, 10 Exch. 809 (1855).

[95] See Comm. Standard Ins. Co. v. Davis, 68 F.2d 108 (1933); State v. Smith, 184 P.2d 301 (1947); Am. Gen. Ins. Co. v. Webster, 118 S.W.2d 1082 (1938).

[96] Tarjan v. Nat'l Surety Co., 268 Ill. App. 232 (1932).

through carelessness or ignorance or as a cunning device to conceal rather than express meaning. . . .[97]

The *American Bar Association Journal* called it "a device for the encouragement of mental laziness."[98] Many lawyers endorsed this attack ("anti-andorians"). But others ("andorians") defended it as a useful abbreviation to avoid ungainly circumlocution, with precise meaning in most situations, "generally neither awkward nor ambiguous," "a perfectly legitimate offspring of the necessity for brief and precise expression," under "the authority of logic as well as long and honorable precedent."[99]

Whether *and/or* is an aberration or a useful addition to the English language, it might not be as precise as one might think, as more than a century of litigation has proved. Courts have had to construe its meaning in hundreds of cases, including those in which affidavits, ballots, indictments, ordinances, statutes, judgments, findings, decrees, jury instructions, convictions, and verdicts were held void or ineffectual; pleadings were stricken; and options, leases, pensions, insurance policies, bonds, deeds, mortgages, and other contracts were subjected to the hazard of judicial interpretation.[100]

The phrase is clear and precise when used by careful writers to connect two items in a simple situation. The sentence "A and/or B" clearly means A alone, B alone, or both A and B together. The *Oxford English Dictionary* defines it as "a formula denoting that the items joined by it can be taken either together or as alternatives." It means "both or either." Indeed, the phrase has operated in innumerable situations without incident, including in thousands of cases.[101] The U.S. Supreme Court alone has used the phrase in more than 1,600 opinions.[102]

---

[97] Employers' Mutual Liability Ins. Co. v. Tollefsen, 263 N.W. 376 (1935).

[98] Editorial, 18 A.B.A.J. 456 (1932).

[99] See An and/or Symposium 18 A.B.A.J. 574 (1932); Note, In Defense of and/or, 45 Yale L.J. 918 (1936). See also Roger Sherman Hoar, Words and Phrases—Meaning of Words "and/or", 20 Marq. L. Rev. 101 (1936).

[100] See 3A Words and Phrases 220–25 (2006 & Supp. 2016); 118 A.L.R. 1367; 154 A.L.R. 886; 3 C.J.S. 1069. See also David Mellinkoff, The Language of the Law 147–52, 306–10 (1963) (discussing the historical background and giving examples of litigation and conflicting interpretation).

[101] See, e.g., Daughters of Sarah Nursing Home Co., Inc. v. Lipkin, 145 A.D.2d 808 (1988); Horseshoe Bay Resort, Ltd. v. CRVI CDP Portfolio, LLC, 415 S.W.3d 370 (2013).

[102] See, e.g., Bell Atl. Corp. v. Twombly, 550 U.S. 544 (2007) (a class of all "subscribers of local telephone and/or high speed internet services"); Ashcroft v. Iqbal,

But *and/or* may become ambiguous and invite controversy in a complex setting, especially when careless writers use the phrase irresponsibly without considering what they mean.[103] It may be particularly confusing when used to connect three or more items (A, B, and/or C) or when used several times.[104] The ambiguity therefore lies not in the phrase itself but in the complexity of the situation or in its inappropriate use.[105]

The use of *and/or* may increase concision at the expense of precision. Its use in a contract, said David Mellinkoff, is a signal that the drafter has abandoned the duty to speak on behalf of the client and has delegated this task to the courts.[106] If the drafter will only stop and think about what she is trying to convey, she will find more precise alternatives. Sometimes it is best to say "A or B, or both"; sometimes, "A or B" is enough; sometimes, what you mean is "A and B"; sometimes, you mean something else.

Use it sparingly, if at all.

as (for "because," "since," or "for")

As serves many useful functions in conversational English, but it invites trouble in legal writing when used to show cause.

> The Senate bill passed as the Vice President cast the tie breaking vote.

---

556 U.S. 662 (2009) (allegation that the defendant discriminated "on account of religion, race, and/or national origin").

[103] See *In re* Estate of Massey, 317 N.J. Super. 302 (1998) (finding ambiguity in a will directing that property should pass to "my niece and/or grandniece"). The court chastised the attorney for using the phrase: "considering the universal scorn for 'and/or,' and the harrowing prospect of deciphering sense out of any English sentence in which it is contained, it is startling to find 'and/or' in a will drafted by an attorney at law. . . . [T]he use of 'and/or' in a will bespeaks negligence on the part of the drafter."

[104] See State v. Gonzalez, 130 A.3d 1250 (2016) ("we find the judge's repeated use of the phrase 'and/or'—in defining what the jury was obligated to determine—so confusing and misleading as to engender great doubt about whether the jury was unanimous. . . .").

[105] See Note, In Defense of and/or, 45 Yale L.J. 918 (1936) (one may "criticize the term because of difficulties inherent in the ideas expressed rather than in the manner of expression"); David Mellinkoff, The Language of the Law 308 (1963) ("it is only the simplicity of the facts—not the formula—that prevents confusion").

[106] The Language of the Law 309–10 (1963) ("And/or is sometimes shorter, but never more precise, than ordinary English. It is usually uncertain. It is completely unnecessary."). *See also* Mellinkoff's Dictionary of American Legal Usage 28 (1992) ("The allure of brevity and the phony appearance of mathematical precision convince the lazy, the ignorant, and the harried that at one stroke and/or covers all the possibilities of both conjunctions").

Did the Senate pass the bill while the Vice President cast a vote or because the Vice President cast a vote? *As* in this sentence should either be replaced by *because* or *for*, or it should be deleted and the comma replaced by a semicolon:

> The Senate bill passed because the Vice President cast the tie breaking vote.
> The Senate bill passed, for the Vice President cast the tie breaking vote.
> The Senate bill passed: the Vice President cast the tie breaking vote.

The causal *as* may create unintentional ambiguity. In some situations, it may not be clear whether it means a cause (in which case you should use *because*) or a description of a time frame (in which case you should use *while*).

> *As* the plaintiff remained silent, the defendant entered the house.

The reader is unsure whether the defendant entered the house *because* the plaintiff remained silent or *while* the plaintiff remained silent.

Good writers avoid causal *as* clauses, except in two situations: if it is placed before the main sentence ("as she only laughed at my arguments, I gave it up") or if the reader necessarily knows the fact introduced by the clause ("I need not translate, as you know German").[107]

Some usage experts defend the causal *as* because the context would disambiguate the sentence. They claim that examples of ambiguity in published writing are rare.[108] Not only is this a dubious proposition, the argument is also inapplicable to legal writing: published writings go through a professional editorial process that legal writing rarely does. Moreover, writing an inadvertently ambiguous sentence hoping it will be understood in context is not the hallmark of good writing style. A sentence must be clear independent of context.[109]

In legal writing, use *as* cautiously. It's safe for comparisons and if used as a preposition, but avoid it for timing and causation.

See *since* and *while*.

---

[107] See H.W. Fowler & F.G. Fowler, The King's English 300 (1908); H.W. Fowler, A Dictionary of Modern English Usage 36 (2d ed. 1965).

[108] See Webster's Dictionary of English Usage 122 (1989).

[109] See § 5.16, Do Not Rely on Context to Cure Ambiguity.

aspect

What you see when you look out from a *viewpoint* (*standpoint, perspective, point of view*) is an *aspect*. A person who takes a position on a foggy viewpoint is likely to have a foggy view or aspect. Who knows what a writer means when speaking of "the main aspects of the case," "the most difficult aspects of the problem," or "a vital aspect of the rule"?

See *factor*.

case

Few words are used more loosely than *case*. The word has many correct uses: "a federal case," "a case of libel" (or "of measles"), "stating a case," "the plaintiff has no case," "in case of need."

But it is often a flabby way to express what could be said more precisely and concisely:

as was formerly the case	formerly
in cases in which	if, when
in the case of	in
in many cases	often, frequently
in every case	always
it is often the case that	often
it is not the case that	[rewrite]
in the case of both men and women	of (by, for) (both) men and women
in many cases they refused	many refused
in any case	[rewrite]

Sometimes, as in the last example, *case* may be replaced by a longer phrase. "The minority rule is impractical in any case" is not objectionable because it is wordy, but because it is unclear. It may mean literally that the rule would be impractical to apply in any situation or in any litigated case; it may mean that it is impractical from any point of view; or, coming after enumeration of other objections, it may mean "finally," "in any event," or "whatever the merits of these other arguments."

Sometimes a phrase like "in this case" is ambiguous: it could mean "in this situation" or "in this lawsuit." Other times, the phrase is unnecessary: instead of "in some cases taxpayers went bankrupt" prefer "some taxpayers went bankrupt."

Inexperienced legal writers sometimes refer to a precedent by saying "in the case of *Roe v. Wade*" or "in the *Miranda* case." Instead, say simply "(in) *Roe v. Wade*" or "(in) *Miranda*." They also sometimes refer to a just-cited precedent as "this case," creating ambiguity as to whether the phrase refers to the precedent or the current situation. The solution, again, is to refer to the precedent by name.

Because *case* has many different meanings, it should be carefully used.

compare to, compare with

When one thing is likened to another or when making an analogy, the proper term is *compared to*. When two things are examined to find their differences and similarities, it is *compared with*.

> She compared his efforts *to* those of his predecessor.
> The bill needs to be compared *with* the Senate version.

If your friend compares you *to* Gandhi, it is probably a compliment; but you might not like it if she starts comparing you *with* Gandhi.

Usage experts argue that it is also acceptable to use *compare to* when one examines to find differences and similarities.[110] Even if this is true in regular usage, stick to the traditional rule in legal writing, which requires more precise and predictable prose.

comprise, constitute, compose

Do not confuse *comprise*, *constitute*, and *compose*. *Comprise* means "embrace." The Bill of Rights comprises substantive and procedural rights, i.e., it embraces, contains, or includes, both. The House and Senate constitute (compose, form, make up) the Congress.

"The parts *compose* the whole; the whole *comprises* the parts. The whole is *composed* of the parts; the parts are *comprised* in the whole . . . The phrase *is comprised of* is always wrong and should be replaced by either *is composed of* or *comprises*."[111]

---

[110] Webster's Dictionary of English Usage 317–18 (1989); The New Fowler's Modern English Usage 164–65 (R.W. Burchfield, ed., 3d ed. 2000); The New Fowler's Modern English Usage 168–69 (Jeremy Butterfield, ed., 4th ed. 2015).

[111] Garner's Dictionary of Legal Usage 188–89 (2011). See also H.W. Fowler, A Dictionary of Modern English Usage 102 (2d ed. 1965); Theodore Bernstein, The Careful Writer: A Modern Guide to English Usage 113 (1985).

data, datum

Datum is an English word taken from Latin; its English plural also uses the Latin form, *data*. Thus, "the data are," not "the data is." Prefer plural modifiers like "these," "many," "a few of," instead of "this," "much," and "little." And never use *data* with a cardinal number: "five data."

Some usage experts accept the use of *data* as an abstract mass noun (like "information"), taking a singular verb and a singular modifier. But the plural is more common and preferred by editors.[112] If you use the plural, therefore, you don't run the risk of distracting your reader. A recognized exception is computer data, which is singular, and will eventually swallow the rule.

Other Latin or Greek plurals to watch:

addendum, addenda	memorandum, memoranda
alumna, alumnae	minutia, minutiae
alumnus, alumni	momentum, momenta
bacterium, bacteria	phenomenon, phenomena
criterion, criteria	stimulus, stimuli
curriculum, curricula	stratum, strata
dictum, dicta	symposium, symposia
medium, media	

Some Latin words are properly used only in the plural, like *trivia* and *paraphernalia*. Other words, originally plural, are now singular, like *agenda* and *insignia*. Still others have lost their original plural form: we say *campuses* not *campi* and *focuses* not *foci*. *Memoranda* and *memorandums* are equally acceptable, but prefer *memoranda*, although *memos* is a common informal variant.

deem

As a way to say "think," "consider," or "believe," *deem* is a false elegancy. Here is the United States Supreme Court being tacky:

> We do not deem it necessary, however, to consider either of these questions, because, in our opinion, the court below was without jurisdiction of the cause.[113]

Deem is correctly used in a technical sense to imply the inferential as opposed to the actual: a legal fiction. Thus, we say that a person who acts knowing that it is likely to result in death is

---

[112] Webster's Dictionary of English Usage 317–18 (1989).
[113] Louisville & Nashville RR. v. Mottley, 211 U.S. 149, 152 (1908).

deemed to have intended to kill. It is also correctly used when a defaulting defendant is deemed to have admitted the truth of fact allegations in the complaint. The correct use is illustrated in another Supreme Court opinion holding that although a corporation is not a citizen, it

> seems to us to be a person, though an artificial one, inhabiting and belonging to that State, and therefore entitled, for the purpose of suing and being sued, to be deemed a citizen of that State.[114]

disinterested, uninterested

Disinterested means impartial, unbiased, without a personal bias or interest in the outcome of a dispute; *uninterested* means indifferent, uncaring, lacking attention or interest. A judge should be disinterested, but not uninterested, in the case before her.

fact

A fact is something that has been done or has happened. Careless writers sometimes use it loosely when they mean idea, opinion, theory, or alleged fact. Use it only when you are talking about an actual occurrence. If you bear this in mind, you will not be guilty of the following misuses:

> Rule 13(g) makes clear the fact that a party may file a crossclaim only if it arises out of the same transaction or occurrence.
>
> The fact that the decision is likely to be reversed never crossed his mind.
>
> The fact to be determined is whether a reasonable person would interpret the seller's words as a guarantee.
>
> The facts are inaccurate.

"True fact" is tautology; "false facts," contradiction; "alternative facts," aberration.[115]

factor

Factor is one of those terms that we reach for when we are too lazy to hunt down the right word to say exactly what we mean: "one factor in the court's opinion." You can usually find a word that is clearer and more exact, such as circumstance, component, element, fact, event.

Other similarly loose words: *consideration, notion.*

See *aspect.*

---

[114] Louisville, C. & C. R. Co. v. Letson, 43 U.S. 497, 555 (1844).

[115] See § 3.2, Eliminate Unnecessary Words (discussing *the fact that*).

find, finding

A finding is the determination of an issue of fact. It should not be used to refer to a court's holding on a matter of law. The trier of fact (court or jury) makes findings of fact ("finds that . . .") and the court makes holdings or conclusions of law ("holds that . . .").

> In an action tried on the facts without a jury . . ., the court must find the facts specially and state its conclusions of law separately.
>
> A party may later question the sufficiency of the evidence supporting the findings.[116]

See *rule, ruling.*

forthwith

If ordered to do something forthwith, how promptly must you comply? Within an hour? A day? A month? The word has no fixed meaning. It means promptly, within a reasonable time, without unreasonable delay under the circumstances. But it must be interpreted in context—and interpretation means litigation.

"*Forthwith* has been given every shade of meaning in the spectrum of time."[117] Some cases held that two or three hours was too long; others held that three months was not. Some cases held that *forthwith* means immediately; others held it did not.[118]

Instead of inviting a lawsuit by using this seemingly imperious but actually ambiguous term, be specific if possible: say "within 24 hours," "within 30 days."

herein

Herein means "in this." But this what? This sentence? This paragraph? This section? This chapter? This document? This statute? This contract? "The exact point of reference remains obscure, and depends completely on context, which is another way of saying that your writing is going to be interpreted,"[119] for "*herein* is the start of a treasure hunt rather than a helpful reference."[120]

A statutory phrase, "except as herein expressly provided," was held by a trial court to refer to the entire statute. The appellate

---

[116] See Fed. R. Civ. P. 52.

[117] David Mellinkoff, The Language of the Law 311 (1963).

[118] See citations to cases, running to several pages, in 37 C.J.S. 128–31; 17A Words and Phrases 112–34 (2004). See also David Mellinkoff, The Language of the Law 310–12 (1963).

[119] David Mellinkoff, The Language of the Law 315 (1963).

[120] David Mellinkoff's Dictionary of American Legal Usage 283 (1992).

court reversed, holding, three-to-two, that *herein* meant "in this section." This holding was in turn reversed by the state supreme court, which held that it clearly referred to the entire statute.[121]

To avoid litigation, be specific. Say, "except as provided in this section," or "except as provided in paragraphs 10 and 11."

Avoid *therein, hereafter,* and other similar terms.[122]

See *aforementioned, aforesaid.*

however

However usually serves its purpose best when placed after the first significant phrase or unit, not first in the sentence.

> We are told, however, that the rule is obsolete.

If you want to emphasize the contradiction with the previous sentence, start with *but.*

> But we are told that the rule is obsolete.

However is properly placed first when it means "in whatever way" or "to whatever extent."

> However we look at it, the rule is obsolete.

individual

This word is not a synonym for "person." It more properly denotes a separate or private person as opposed to a group of persons, the family, or the community as a whole. It is correctly used in the following sentences:

> This assembly is a constituent body, not a mere aggregation of individuals.
> We must protect both society and the individual.

In the following sentences, *individual* is incorrectly used and should be replaced with *person*:

> Any individual may be admitted to a hospital upon written application by the head of any institution in which such individual may be.
> We must protect society against such individuals.

involve

"The foggy mind's best friend,"[123] the word *involve* is "overworked as a general-purpose verb that saves the trouble of

---

[121] Owen v. Off, 218 P.2d 563 (Cal. App.1950), *vacated* 227 P.2d 457 (Cal. 1951).

[122] See § 4.7, Avoid Outmoded Wording.

[123] I. A. Richards, How to Read a Page 141 (1942).

precise thought."[124] Strictly, it means to roll up in itself to gather in or embrace; to wrap up in something. Figuratively, it is used to mean entangle in difficulties or embarrassment ("involved in a crime"). But instead of being used only to connote such an entanglement or complication, it is often loosely used to mean nothing more than include, influence, or contain. Here are some examples of how not to use it:

(1) A full hearing may involve excessive cost.
(2) More than ten agencies are involved in caring for the patients.
(3) The reorganization plan involves the issuance of securities to the public.
(4) The proposal would involve an increase in personnel.
(5) Such a decision would involve the overruling of a long line of cases.
(6) The facts of the case involving Olivia Smith are omitted.
(7) The risks involved are serious.

In these sentences, *involve* means: (1) entail; (2) concerned, dedicated to; (3) contemplates; (4) call for; (5) require, mean; (6) against, related to. In (7), omit the word.

Use *involve* only when you want to connote entanglement or complication.

irregardless

A misguided blend of *irrespective* and *regardless*, this word is the result of sloppy thinking. It is useless because it means the same as "regardless." It is also a double negative: it contains the negative prefix *ir-* and the negative suffix *-less*, which cancel each other.

One cannot say that *irregardless* is a nonword because it is used as a word and recorded in most dictionaries. But it is unacceptable, especially in formal writing.

jury

This is a group name, used as a singular collective noun to refer to the jury as a unit ("the jury returned its verdict"). When referred to as a number of people, a plural verb is proper ("the jury were all working people"). Avoid ambiguity by using "jurors" or "members of the jury" in the second situation.

---

[124] H.W. Fowler, A Dictionary of Modern English Usage 302 (2d ed. 1965).

like, as

Like should not be confused with *as*. *Like* is a preposition that governs nouns and pronouns; *as* is a conjunction that governs verbs, phrases, and clauses.

He argued this case *like* he argued the previous one.	He argued this case *as* he argued the previous one.
His argument in this case was *as* his argument in the previous one.	His argument in this case was *like* his argument in the previous one.[125]

So, after *like* you will find a noun or noun phrase; after *as* you will find a verb or verb phrase.

literally

The adverb *literally* means "not figuratively" and is properly used to make sure the reader will believe a statement even if it seems exaggerated.

> When my client lost her business, she was literally left with one dollar in the bank.

But the word is more frequently misused for "figuratively"—that is, for "not literally":

> I literally sank through the floor.
> My head was literally exploding.

The abuse is so pervasive that even small children use the word—it has become part of regular speech.

One way to avoid misusing this word is not to use it. This is not hard to do; a lawyer will not often have legitimate use for it. You may have occasion to talk of a "literal interpretation" of a contract or a statute, that is, one adhering closely to the words. But you do not need to say you mean exactly what you say. This use is redundant and therefore unnecessary—counsel should no more need to protest her literalness (as by interjecting, "it really happened that way") than her truthfulness (as by interjecting, "to tell the truth").

The practice of using the adverb hyperbolically (usually prefacing a metaphor) has been denounced for more than a century, and it is common across several different languages and cultures.

---

[125] Garner's Dictionary of Legal Usage 545 (2011).

Like the adverb *actually,* *literally* is superfluous: it inartfully adds emphasis to a statement that often does not need it.[126]

Misuse has become so frequent that most major dictionaries have recently recognized the colloquial definition. But this does not justify its use in a profession that demands precision and credibility.

majority

Do not use *majority* as a grandiose synonym for "most." Use *most.*

The majority of the cases turned on questions of fact.	Most cases turned on questions of fact.

personal, personally

These words are overused. "My personal opinion" and "my personal friend" usually means nothing more than "my opinion" and "my friend." If emphasis is desired, it is simpler to say "my own opinion." *Personal* is proper, however, when used to distinguish private from official:

> As trustee, I am bound to refuse, but my personal opinion is that . . .

Personally may be correctly used in at least two other senses: (1) in person, not through others; and (2) as a person.

(1)   The President conferred the medals personally.

(2)   She is personally likable, and a brilliant trial lawyer.

But often the word overemphasizes the self and gives off an air of self-importance: "I personally prefer tea."

practically

This word is misused and abused. It does not always mean what the writer intended, and sometimes it does not have any meaning at all. "The court practically overruled *Doe v. Eton*" means that for practical purposes, or, so far as future practice is concerned, the case is no longer a precedent.

It is less precise (although not incorrect) to say, "the court awarded practically the full amount of the damages sued for."

The word means "in practice" or "for practical purposes" and is contrasted to "hypothetically" or "theoretically": "theoretically your

---

[126] Claire Kehrwald Cook, Line by Line: How to Edit Your Own Writing 185 (1985).

theory is sound, but practically it doesn't work."[127] Delete the word if unnecessary or use adverbs with the intended meaning, such as *almost*, *nearly*, or *substantially*.

presume, assume

Although much alike in meaning, these words are not always interchangeable. When you mean to "take for granted," "believe without proof," or "suppose," in the ordinary lay sense, use *assume*. *Presume*, because of its relation to "presumption," carries a legal connotation and has a stronger inferential value.

Prefer adverbs derived from *presume*, such as *presumably* (it is to be presumed) or *presumptively* (there is a legal presumption).[128]

principal, principle

Because these words sound alike, even experienced legal writers confuse them, but discriminating readers don't, and won't forgive you. And spell check is unlikely to save you from a blunder.

As an adjective, *principal* is fancy for "most important," "leading," "main" ("she is one of the principal lawyers in the law firm," "this is one of his principal achievements").

As a noun, *principal* refers to a person occupying a superior position (a school principal, a principal at a firm, a principal represented by an agent) and the original sum of money invested, as distinguished from the interest later accrued.

Principle is never used as adjective; it's a noun meaning a law or moral rule ("I am a person of principles") or a general proposition that is the foundation of a system of belief or reasoning ("the principles of tort law").

This book discusses the principal principles of writing.

proven, proved

As a past participle of "prove," *proven* is archaic; modern usage favors *proved*. But *proven* is still used as an adjective: "this is a proven fact" or "innocent until proven guilty"; but "we have proved our case."

---

[127] Theodore Bernstein, The Careful Writer. A Modern Guide to English Usage 338 (1985).

[128] Garner's Dictionary of Legal Usage 87 (2011).

rule, ruling

Like *find* and *finding*, lawyers sometimes use *rule* and *ruling* when they mean "hold," "holding," or "opinion."

> The Supreme Court ruled [read *held*] that the state court's failure to allow reasonable time to secure counsel violated the 14th Amendment.

> The Supreme Court issued a ruling [read an *opinion*] that surprised most observers.

A rule or ruling is an order or direction of a court or tribunal on a point of law. The judge *rules* on motions and on objections to evidence; ultimately the judge *holds* for the plaintiff or for the defendant.

See *find, finding.*

said

Used as an adjective, *said* means "aforementioned" or "aforesaid"; it refers the reader back to something mentioned before (the antecedent). Lawyers use it in the misguided hope that it will confine the meaning of the word and consequently add precision to the text: it is not any farm; it is *said* farm (or *the said* farm).

In a pleading, a prayer for relief against "said defendants hereinafter named" was construed not to include a defendant who had not been previously named.[129] In that case, the word *said* was probably thrown in without any purpose. The following excerpt from a complaint shows how seriously addicted some lawyers become:

> [O]n *said* railroad track . . . opposite *said* curve in *said* highway, large quantities of highly volatile coal were unnecessarily thrown into the firebox of *said* locomotive . . . preventing proper combustion of *said* coal. . . . [Defendant] knew *said* smoke would fall upon and cover *said* curve in *said* highway when *said* engine reached a point on *said* railroad tracks opposite *said* curve, unless *said* smoke was checked in the meantime.

Exposure to this language apparently infected the court. After quoting this passage, the opinion continued with a sentence starting, "said paragraph of the complaint" and containing seven more *saids*.[130]

Modern readers do not realize, however, that the use of *said* in narratives was a necessary feature of common law and code

---

[129] Wheeler & Wilson Mfg. Co. v. Filer, 28 A. 13, 14 (N.J. Ch. 1893).

[130] Button v. Pa Ry. Co., 57 N.E.2d 444 (Ind. App.1944), quoted by Evans, "Words, Words, Words," 2 Ky. State Bar J. No. 1, p. 19 (Dec. 1946). See also Hughes v. Moore, 11 U.S. 176 (1812) (a four-page Supreme Court opinion containing 57 *saids*).

pleading. The pleading rules mandating its use disappeared many decades ago, but we keep using the word because we think that real lawyers write that way.[131]

Not only it is an archaism to be avoided, it is unnecessary and ambiguous: "if the antecedent is certain, *said* is unnecessary . . . . When there is any possibility of *said* referring to two things . . . litigation is invited."[132] Writers other than lawyers get along without using *said* at all. Legal writers should avoid this tasteless legalese.

See *same* and *such*. See also *aforementioned, aforesaid*.

same

Used as a pronoun, *same* is another example of the heavy-footed jargon used by some lawyers. Like *said*, it refers to something previously mentioned. It is an archaism to be avoided. Discriminating readers will think it offensive.

> The plaintiff took the check and endorsed the *same* [read *it*] over to the bank.
>
> Please sign the enclosed releases and return *same* [read *them*] to this office.
>
> The partner logged the information and sent the *same* [read *it*] to her associate.

See *said* and *such*. See also *aforementioned, aforesaid*.

shall, may, will, must

Shall imposes an obligation to act: it's a must. But *shall* has been used loosely to mean *may* or *should*, and this abuse has led to ambiguity and litigation.[133] Avoid it. Prefer *must* or *will*.

When conferring a privilege or a discretionary right, use the indicative or *may*, not *shall*: "the owner has the right to" or "the owner may," not "the owner shall have the right" or "the owner shall." Using *shall* states the right as if it were a duty.

Shall, however, is not completely useless; its value rests precisely in its ambiguity: "it has imperative overtones, but often

---

[131] See § 3.10, Repeating and Realleging Facts is Pointless (the use of *said*, *aforesaid*, and *same* was legally required in some situations).

[132] David Mellinkoff, The Language of the Law 318–19 (1963).

[133] See 39 Words and Phrases 173–259 (2006 & Supp. 2016) (summarizing more than a thousand cases over the past century litigating the meaning of *shall*).

preserves some measure of discretion."[134] If you need ambiguity, *shall* is perfect.[135]

When denying or abridging a right or privilege, use "may not" or "must not," not "shall not." With a negative subject, use *may*, not *shall*: "no person may," not "no person shall."

Avoid the passive voice. Do not say "is directed to"; say "must." Not "is authorized to" or "is entitled to," but "may."

Be consistent. It may not avoid all ambiguities, but it helps.

since

This word refers to time; it means "after," "subsequent to the time that." But it is also used as a causal conjunction, meaning "because." Avoid using it in a way that leaves the reader in suspense as to how it is being used.

> Since the statute, following protracted litigation in both the state and federal courts, was finally upheld and enforcement vigorously initiated . . .

At this point, the reader does not know whether *since* here means "after" or "because." When you want to stress the causal connection, use "because," even if the sentence is clear in context.[136]

See *as (for "because," "since," or "for")* and *while*.

state, say

Most lawyers seem to think it beneath a court's dignity for it to say anything. It must always state or claim. Even Jesus Christ was content merely to "say unto you." It's not contempt of court to have judges do the same.

Strictly, *state* means to express fully or clearly. The word is correctly used in the following sentences:

> The precise terms of every new appointment must be *stated* in writing.
> I proceeded to *state* my reasons.

The same happens with the word *write*: lawyers are too important and their fees too high to just write something—they

---

[134] Edward Cooper, Restyling the Civil Rules: Clarity Without Change, 79 Notre Dame L. Rev. 1761, 1777 (2003-2004).

[135] See § 5.15, Use Ambiguity Strategically.

[136] See § 5.16, Do Not Rely on Context to Cure Ambiguity.

draft it.[137] Lawyers don't *tell* nor *say* anything either—they *advise* or *indicate*.[138]

such

The adjective *such* sometimes serves a useful purpose, as when it saves having to repeat a concept (the antecedent) that cannot be easily referred to in a word or two. In statutes and regulations, for example, it may be necessary to make clear that the second reference is to exactly the same concept mentioned previously. The word *such* is the simplest way to do so.

But some lawyers get into the habit of tagging *such* on to almost any noun they have already used in the same passage.

> Whenever application is made to a judge stating under oath that a person needs hospital care, *such* judge may order *such* person . . .

Here, it would be simpler to say "the judge."

> A contract of insurance is void if *such* a contract . . .

In this sentence there is no reason for not saying "the contract," or better yet, "it."

> The Act is an attempt to remedy the situation in the construction industry already described, but *such* attempt can succeed only if *such* situation . . .

This would read more naturally if "such attempt" read "the attempt" or "this attempt," and if "such situation" read "that situation" or "the situation."

See *said* and *same*.

that, which

Many people use *which* in writing, when in talking they would use *that*—perhaps feeling that *which* is more literary and *that* is too colloquial.[139] This is a myth: more often than not, *that* is the word they want. Or they shift from the one word to the other without any reason other than a desire for variation.

> The agreement compels the parties to engage in practices *that* they would rather avoid, and to refrain from activities *which* they would like to undertake.

---

[137] David Mellinkoff, Legal Writing: Sense and Nonsense xi (1982).

[138] See Peter M. Tiersma, Legal Language 103 (1999).

[139] H.W. Fowler, A Dictionary of Modern English Usage 625 (2d ed. 1965).

The two clauses in this sentence are parallel, and the shift from *that* to *which* is without reason.

Generally, we should use *that* as the defining or restrictive relative pronoun, and *which* as the non-defining or non-restrictive. Thus, if the clause being introduced could be omitted without changing the meaning of the noun it modifies, we should use *which*. If omitting the clause would change the meaning, we should use *that*.

> The Eighth Amendment, *which* defendant relies upon, forbids cruel and unusual punishments.

The subject is "the Eighth Amendment," and omitting the clause would not change the message: "the Eighth Amendment forbids cruel and unusual punishments." We therefore use *which*.

> The constitutional provision *that* forbids cruel and unusual punishments is the Eighth Amendment.

Here, the subject is not merely "the constitutional provision," but rather "the constitutional provision that forbids cruel and unusual punishments." The clause is thus a restrictive one, introduced by *that*.

The choice between *that* and *which* is not a grammatical mandate, but a direction to improve clarity and precision: "[i]f writers would agree to regard *that* as the defining relative pronoun, and *which* as the non-defining, there would be much gain both in lucidity and in ease."[140] This distinction is not always observed, however, and we cannot assume that others will read it into our own writing. If a clause is intended to be purely descriptive and not defining, it is better not only to use *which*, but also to set the clause off with commas.

though, although

The conjunctions *though* and *although* are synonymous. But *although* is preferable at the beginning of a sentence and *though* for introducing short supplementary clauses or phrases.

> *Although* the court accepted the principle, it refused to apply it in this case.
>
> The plaintiff was careless, *though* not willfully so.

---

[140] Id. at 626.

Otherwise, choose one word or the other depending on the rhythm and on the formality of what you are writing. *Although* is more formal.

various

Various means "differing from one another," or "of several kinds." It should not be used to mean "several" or "many." It is correct to say, "[n]ow the power to regulate commerce embraces a vast field, containing not only many, but exceedingly *various* subjects, quite unlike in their nature."[141] It is incorrect to say, "these laws gave birth to a problem that has plagued *various* courts [read *several*]."

where, when

Where denotes place only. One can speak of "states where the rule is followed," but "cases where the rule is followed" should be changed to "cases in which the rule is followed" or "cases that follow the rule."

Crops and animals are not the only property *where* an after-acquired property clause may be used.	Crops and animals are not the only kinds of property *for which* an after-acquired property clause may be used.

When *where* means "if," use *if* or *when*.

Contracts are only valid *where* all the formal requirements have been observed.	Contracts are only valid *if* (*when*) all the formal requirements have been observed.

whereas

This vague word has spawned litigation for more than two centuries. Sometimes it means nothing; sometimes it has any of several meanings. If a contract of sale reads, "whereas there are 4,000 square feet of floor space in Seller's house," does it mean that Seller warrants? Does it mean that the parties have examined the house and agreed that whether it has more or less than 4,000 square feet of floor space will not affect the contract? Or does it mean that if it has more or less than 4,000 square feet the price will be adjusted?[142]

---

[141] Cooley v. B. of Port Wardens, 53 U.S. 299 (1851).

[142] David Mellinkoff, The Language of the Law 324 (1963).

When you find yourself about to indulge in a *"whereas,"* consider whether it means anything. If not, delete it. If you intend to say something meaningful, say it in clearer language.

while

Originally, this word was related to the notion of time, and meant "during the time that," "as long as," "at the same time as." But it has come to be used also as an adversative conjunction, meaning "although," "but," or "whereas." It is better to avoid this use, especially when it leaves the meaning unclear.

> *While* such combinations were expressly prohibited by statute, this venture flourished.

The reader is not sure whether the venture flourished during the time it was prohibited, or although it was prohibited.

See *as (for "because," "since," or "for")* and *since.*

Chapter 3

CONCISENESS

Brevity is the soul of wit.
Shakespeare (1564–1616)[1]

Less is more.
Robert Browning (1812–1889)[2]

§ 3.1   Introduction

If the first aim in writing is to communicate with accuracy, the second is to do it with dispatch. Conciseness is particularly important for lawyers, who, more than most writers, must say exactly what they mean, no more and no less. Every additional word is one more potential source of ambiguity, error, or conflict.

"Lawyers are wordy," wrote David Mellinkoff, "it takes them a long time to get to the point."[3] Indeed, "[t]he one thing about legal writing that everyone agrees on is that there is too much of it. Everyone complains of everyone else's verbosity."[4]

Lawyers write for busy professionals. Picturing the judge reading your brief late at night may inspire you to make your point in the fewest words possible. And you will not only spare the reader's time and energy, but also increase your material's vitality. Consider Chief Justice Roberts's reaction: "I have yet to put down a brief and say, 'I wish that had been longer'. . . . Almost every brief I've read could be shorter."[5]

Almost every scholar who has addressed writing style has had strong opinions on concision—ironically, it's the most discussed topic. "[T]he aim," said Herbert Spencer, "must be to convey the greatest quantity of thoughts with the smallest quantity of words."[6] "Every word that can be spared," said Arthur Schopenhauer, "is

---

[1]   Hamlet (1602).

[2]   Andrea Del Sarto (1855).

[3]   The Language of the Law 24 (1963).

[4]   Legal Writing: Sense and nonsense 126 (1982).

[5]   Interview with Bryan A. Garner, 13 Scribes J. Leg. Writing 5, 35 (2010).

[6]   The Philosophy of Style [1852], in Lane Cooper (ed.), The Art of the Writer 260 (1952).

hurtful if it remains."[7] In persuasive writing, this lesson means that "[e]very fact, every observation, every argument that does not positively strengthen your case positively weakens it by distracting attention."[8] Being concise, says Kristen Konrad Tiscione, "helps you make intentional choices," and leads to more powerful writing.[9]

> A writer must make a sparing use of the reader's time, patience, and attention; so as to lead him to believe that his author writes what is worth careful study, and will reward the time spent upon it. . . . Therefore, the quintessence only! To use many words to communicate few thoughts is everywhere the unmistakable sign of mediocrity. To gather much thought into few words stamps the man of genius.[10]

Verbosity is contagious: "[w]ordy complaints invite wordy answers. Extra words by lawyers stimulate extra words from the bench. A long . . . majority produces a longer dissent."[11] It's a vicious circle: "[l]ong opinions also provide fodder for professors to chew over in long law review articles. Long law review articles provide grist for the brief and opinion writers."[12] When law review editors enter the profession, the circle is closed. The whole legal community suffers as a result.

A leisurely style, adorned with rhetorical ornaments, is more likely to arouse impatience than admiration. Patricia Wald gives the judge's perspective:

> The more paper you throw at us, the meaner we get, the more irritated and hostile we feel about verbosity, peripheral arguments and long footnotes. . . . Many judges look first to see how long a document is before reading a word. If it is long, they automatically read fast; if short, they read slower. Figure out yourself which is better for your case. . . . With the docket the way it is—and growing

---

[7]   On style [1851], in Lane Cooper (ed.), The Art of the Writer 229 (1952).

[8]   Antonin Scalia & Bryan A. Garner, Making Your Case. The Art of Persuading Judges 182 (2008). See also Sidney F. Parham, Jr., The Fundamentals of Legal Writing 5, 53-54 (1967).

[9]   Rhetoric for Legal Writers 229 (2016).

[10]   Arthur Schopenhauer, On style [1851], in Lane Cooper (ed.), The Art of the Writer 228–29 (1952).

[11]   David Mellinkoff, The Language of the Law 411 (1963).

[12]   Tom Goldstein & Jethro Lieberman, The Lawyer's Guide to Writing Well 114 (2016).

.... we judges can only read briefs once. We cannot go back and re-read them, linger over phrases, chew on meanings. Your main points have to stick with us on first contact—the shorter and punchier the brief the better.[13]

We like writers who can communicate in a straightforward way, without circumlocutions or redundancies. So, tighten up your style: make every word work hard for the privilege of being a part of your message. "If it is possible to cut a word out," said George Orwell, "always cut it out."[14] This is not an easy task. Even Orwell was unable to follow his own lesson—he could have expressed the same thought cutting three unnecessary words: "If it is possible to cut a word, cut it." "Fighting clutter is like fighting weeds," warned William Zinsser, "the writer is always slightly behind."[15]

In an apocryphal case, a taxpayer testified, "as God is my judge, I do not owe this tax." Judge J. Edgar Murdock answered, "He's not, I am; you do."[16] We need not strip our writing down to the irreducible minimum, but we can try to be less wordy.

"It is possible to make the same point verbosely or briefly," said David Mellinkoff.[17] A master of style, Winston Churchill, said, "give us the tools and we will finish the job."[18] Anthony Eden expressed the same thought: "we shall not let go until we have done the job, and we welcome all those who will give us a hand to finish it."[19] Eden's sentence is certainly not verbose. But Churchill's is clearly better—it is the one that sticks in our memory. This illustrates what is generally true: the briefer form is livelier and more forceful.

Insecure writers sometimes employ a flowery style as a smokescreen. "[M]any people," noticed Arthur Schopenhauer, "try to conceal their poverty of thought under a flood of verbiage."[20] Other writers ramble because of an undisciplined enthusiasm for their own words. Abraham Lincoln skewered one practitioner: "He

---

[13] 19 Tips from 19 Years on the Appellate Bench, 1 J. App. Prac. & Process 7, 9–10 (1999).
[14] Politics and the English Language (1946).
[15] On Writing Well 12 (2006).
[16] Memorial Proceedings, 68 TC XII (1977).
[17] The Language of the Law 412 (1963).
[18] Radio Broadcast, February 9, 1941.
[19] Quoted in San Bernardino Sun, July 6, 1941.
[20] On style [1851], in Lane Cooper (ed.), The Art of the Writer 228 (1952).

can compress the most words into the smallest ideas [better than] any man I ever met."[21]

Good style conveys meaning directly, with minimum interference or digression. Taking the long way around to make your point slows you and the reader down. "Prefer the single word to the circumlocution," say the Fowlers.[22] "Use no more words than are necessary to express your meaning," says Ernest Gowers, "for if you use more you are likely to obscure it and to tire your reader."[23] And you will obscure your thoughts even from yourself: like the cuttlefish, you'll hide yourself in your own ink.[24]

Learn to say more with less: get to the point directly and quickly, then get out.

§ 3.2 Eliminate Unnecessary Words

One simple way to reach your point more quickly is to cut out unnecessary words that clutter the path, "the deadwood that does nothing but detract from both substance and style."[25]

> Vigorous writing is concise. A sentence should contain no unnecessary words, a paragraph no unnecessary sentences, for the same reason that a drawing should have no unnecessary lines and a machine no unnecessary parts. This requires not that the writer make all his sentences short, or that he avoid all detail and treat his subjects only in outline, but that every word tell.[26]

Good writing never has extra words—if you pull any word out of a well-crafted sentence, it collapses.

We all tend to use unnecessary words. When you read your writing looking for flab, you will probably be astonished to find how many words would never be missed. "Good writing," said Ernest Hemingway, "is writing wherein you can't remove one word without changing the meaning."[27] Trimming away the fat gives you a

---

[21] I The Works of Abraham Lincoln 378 (1908).

[22] H.W. Fowler & F.G. Fowler, The King's English 1 (1908).

[23] Plain Words 34 (1948).

[24] John Ray, The Wisdom of God Manifested in the Works of the Creation 339 (1743).

[25] Claire Kehrwald Cook, Line by Line: How to Edit Your Own Writing 2 (1985).

[26] William Strunk, Jr. & E. B. White, The Elements of Style 23 (1979).

[27] Lilless McPherson Shilling & Linda K. Fuller. Dictionary of Quotations in Communications 277 (1997).

leaner, more muscular style. "Perfection is finally attained not when there is no longer anything to add, but when there is no longer anything to take away."[28]

Monitor your writing for unnecessary words and phrases:

all of

What does the word *of* contribute in the following passages?

> A pardon restores all of their civil rights.
> All of the world is sad and dreary.
> In all of these cases.
> All of Hell broke loose.

Some pronouns require *of*: all of us, all of them. Elsewhere, it's fluff.

as to

The words *as to* in phases such as "as to whether," "as to what," "as to who," and "as to how" are almost always superfluous. The Fowlers called them "a hideous combination."[29] Yet these constructions pervade legal writing. Consider it a failure to let sludge like "there is no question as to" fleck your briefs.

Below are six passages taken from one United States Supreme Court opinion:

> If, however, the above-quoted provision of § 380a *as to* docketing is a prerequisite . . . .
> *As to* dismissals the first sentence of Rule 47 requires . . . .
> The assumed controversy between affiant and the Civil Service Commission *as to* affiant's right to act . . . .
> We can only speculate *as to* the kinds of political activity appellant desires to engage in . . . .
> There is no question *as to* the exhausting of administrative remedies.
> There is no problem of judicial discretion *as to* whether to take cognizance of this case.[30]

In some of these passages, *as to* means "concerning" or "about"; in others, it means "of," and in the last it is merely superfluous.

---

[28]   Antoine de Saint-Exupéry, Wind, Sand, and Stars 66 (1939).

[29]   H.W. Fowler & F.G. Fowler, The King's English 333 (1908).

[30]   United Public Workers v. Mitchell, 330 U.S. 75 (1947). This decision contains about three dozen uses of *as to*.

the fact that

The fact that "should be revised out of every sentence in which it occurs."[31] Simpler and better wording can be found.[32]

owing (due) to the fact that	because
notwithstanding the fact that	although
the fact that defendant was negligent	defendant's negligence
the fact that this contention ignores is that	this contention ignores
despite the fact that	although, even though, despite
except for the fact that	except for
in light (view) of the fact that	because, given that
the fact (of the matter) is that	[omit]
as a matter of fact	[omit]

that

In a long sentence, it is easy to forget that you have already used *that* as a conjunction and to repeat it, as in the following sentence:

> The court held *that* if the statute is interpreted in accordance with the intent of Congress as reflected in the committee reports and the debates in both houses, *that* the Board's decision must be upheld.

Even where the repetition is not erroneous, *that* can sometimes be omitted, especially when it appears more than once in a sentence. Train your ear to sense when a statement sounds better without it. Delete one *that* from each of the following sentences:

> It was only reasonable to suppose, as the evidence shows that she did suppose, that a felony was being committed.
>
> Whether this is a provision that should be retained is a question that the committee ignored.

Not every instance of *that* should be summarily eliminated. In many situations, suppressing *that* can create ambiguity or disrupt the balance of the sentence. If it is doing work, leave it.

there are, there is, it is

Starting a sentence with *there are, there is* or *it is* is a word-wasting habit that leads to weak introductions.[33] It is good practice, whenever you find yourself writing such a sentence, to consider whether you should revise it. Did you notice the weak introduction

---

[31]   William Strunk, Jr. & E. B. White, The Elements of Style 24 (1979).

[32]   See § 2.8, Words to Watch (discussing *fact*).

[33]   See § 6.12, Put Words to be Stressed at the Beginning and the End of Sentences.

in the previous sentence? It reads better if revised to, "whenever you find yourself writing such a sentence, consider revising it."

The following examples show that eliminating these useless introductory words often makes the sentence shorter and stronger. Incidentally, the previous sentence would have been weaker if it had started like this: "there are several examples that show that . . . ."

It is the contention of the petitioner	Petitioner contends
It is not necessary for you to	You need not
There are a few states that have rejected the rule.	A few states have rejected the rule.
There are no precedents that support this claim.	No precedent supports this claim.
It has been held by most courts	Most courts have held
It was the judge who ordered	The judge ordered
There was uncontradicted evidence to support this finding.	Uncontradicted evidence supported this finding.
There are several legal issues that would arise.	Several legal issues would arise.
There have been many courts that have decided	Many courts have decided

Avoid these expressions when they are mere throat clearers, adding nothing to the meaning of the text and sapping its vitality.[34] You may use them, however, if you are stating the existence of something, or if a weak statement serves your purposes.

> It's now or never.
> It's too late now.
> There are several paintings in the living room.
> There were several prominent lawyers at her birthday party.
> There is a woman in the lobby, and she looks suspicious.

It is difficult to give examples that cannot be improved in context. Although the construction is weak, you may use it occasionally—many writers have done so successfully.

> There are more things in Heaven and Earth, Horatio, than are dreamt of in your philosophy.—William Shakespeare, *Hamlet*.
> There is nothing more atrociously cruel than an adored child.—Vladimir Nabokov, *Lolita*.

---

[34]   See § 3.5, Eliminate Throat Clearers.

There are only two ways to live your life. One is as though nothing is a miracle. The other is as though everything is a miracle.—Albert Einstein.

There is no such thing as a free lunch.—Anonymous.

There is no place like home.—L. Frank Baum, *The Wonderful Wizard of Oz*.

It was the best of times, it was the worst of times . . . —Charles Dickens, *A Tale of Two Cities*.

who, which, who is, that is, which was

These words can often be deleted as unnecessary.

This case, which was the first one decided in this state,	This case, the first decided in this state,
John Doe, who was the first witness to testify,	John Doe, the first witness to testify,
Nutraceuticals is a company that is engaged in processing	Nutraceuticals is engaged in processing (or, processes)

§ 3.3   Eliminate Wordy and Useless Expressions

Many wordy phrases consist of compound prepositions and conjunctions. Often these three- or four-word combinations can be replaced by a single word. Prepositions encumbered by nouns can be unshackled and allowed to stand alone. The word inside the parentheses in the list below replaces the wordy phrase to its left:

adequate number of (enough)

adequate amount of (enough)

adjacent to (next to, close to)

a large amount of (much)

a large number of (many)

a limited number of (few)

along the lines of (like)

anterior to (before)

a number of (many, several, some)

as a consequence of (because)

as a means to (to)

as a result of (because)

as of yet (yet)

a small amount of (a little)

a small number of (a few)

as regards (about)

at all times (always)

at an earlier date (before)

at such time as (when)

at that point in time (then)

at that time (then)

at the place that (where)

at the present time (now)

at the time at which (when)

at the time of (when)

at the time when (when)

at this point in time (now)

at this time (now)

be able to (can)

by means of (by)

by reason of (because)

by virtue of [the fact that] (by)

cause injury (injure)

check to see (check)

concerning the matter of (about)

distance of ten feet (ten feet)

do an analysis of (analyze)

during such time as (while, during)

during the course of (during)
during the period when (when)
during the time that (while)
equally as . . . as . . . (as . . . as . . .)
excessive amount of (too much)
excessive number of (too many)
for the duration of (during, while)
for the period of (for)
for the purpose of (for, to)
for the reason that (because)
for this reason (so)
in accordance with (by, under)
in addition to (additionally)
in all probability (probably)
in an effort to (to)
in a position to (can)
in a situation in which (when, if)
in a situation where (when, if)
in a timely manner (soon, timely)
in case of (if)
in cases in which (where)
in circumstances in which (when)
including but not limited to (including)
in conjunction with (with)
in connection with (with, about)
in excess of (more than)
in favor of (for)
in order to (to)
in reference to (about)
in regard(s) to (about)
in relation to (about)
in respect to (about)
in spite of (although)
in spite of the fact that (although)
in terms of [omit]
in the absence of (absent, without)
in the case at bar (here)
in the course of (during, in)
in the event of (if)
in the event that (if)
in the instant case (here)
in the interest of (for)

in the matter of (about)
in the nature of (like)
in the near future (soon)
in the neighborhood of (about)
in the same way as (like)
in the vicinity of (near)
in the year of 2018 (in 2018)
in this case (here)
in view of (because)
it is certain that (certainly)
it is directed that (must)
it is imperative that (must)
it is necessary that (need)
it is not necessary for you to (you need not)
it is often the case that (often)
it is possible that (possibly, may)
it is probable that (probably)
it is the duty of (must)
it shall be lawful (may)
it shall be the duty of (must)
it shall not be lawful (may not, must not)
it would appear that (apparently)
located in (in)
neither of them (neither)
no later than (by, before)
notwithstanding (although)
notwithstanding the fact that (although)
on account of (because)
on a daily basis (daily)
on a number of occasions (often,
    sometimes)
on behalf of (for)
one and the same (the same)
one of the reasons (one reason)
on many occasions (often)
on or about (on, about)
on or before (by)
on the basis of (from)
on the ground(s) that (because)
on the occasion of (when)
on the part of (by)
or, in the alternative (or)

period of time (period, time)

period of two months (two months)

pertaining to (about, of)

piece of legislation (act, statute)

previous to (before)

prior to (before)

provided that (if)

similar to (like)

so as to (to)

State of Ohio (Ohio)

subject to (if)

subsequent to (after)

sufficient amount of (enough)

sufficient number of (enough)

the question as to whether (whether)

the majority of (most)

the manner in which (how)

the moment when (when)

the time when (when)

the reason being that (because)

the reason for (because)

the reason is because (because)

the reason is that (because)

to a large extent (largely)

to the effect that (that)

under circumstances in which (when)

until such time as (until)

under the provisions of (under)

whether or not (whether)

with a view to (to)

with reference to (about)

with regard to (on, about, regarding)

with respect to (on, about, regarding)

with the exception of (except)

with the result that (so that)

These wheezy expressions are time-and-paper-devouring verbosities. They are rarely used in conversation—that alone should make them suspect. Law students may feel impelled to use them because they are impressed with the formality of legal writing. "I am writing a legal opinion," they think, "so I must sound like a lawyer." But a lawyer is not required to use a stuffy tone, and legal writing need not be padded with windy words. The student should learn to distinguish a style that is dignified and formal from one that is overstuffed and flabby.

Some writers may have no conscious purpose in using these compound phrases. Having no precise meaning, they can be used without much thought. Like abstract words,[35] they have a strong attraction for the hazy and the lazy writer.

---

[35] See §§ 2.8, Abstract Words are Inexact and 6.7, Use Specific and Concrete Rather than General and Abstract Words.

Prepositions can often be omitted:

climb up [down] (climb)	stand up (stand)
cut out (cut)	start in (start)
end up (end)	start off (start)
explain about (explain)	start out (start)
head up [down] (head)	try out (try)
rise up (rise)	up until (until)
sit down (sit)	win out (win)

Prepositions and conjunctions are "glue words" that hold together the "working words," mainly nouns and verbs, which carry the meaning of the sentence. Glue words are essential to obtain cohesion, but they are unemphatic. Make sure you are not using more than you need. Concise, forceful writing has a higher proportion of working words.[36]

Clauses can sometimes be cut down to phrases:

While the trial was going on	During (the) trial
The court decree which was handed down in July ordered that payments be made each month on the mortgage.	The July court decree ordered monthly mortgage payments.
She is a person who	She
This is an issue that needs	This issue needs

A phrase or clause can sometimes be replaced by a single adjective or adverb:

The fact that the defendant was present at the meeting of June 10 cannot be denied.	Undeniably, the defendant was present at the June 10 meeting.
Plaintiff testified in a frank and unhesitating manner.	Plaintiff testified frankly and unhesitatingly.
Plaintiff accepted the offer that the defendant had made to settle the case for $75,000.	Plaintiff accepted the defendant's $75,000 settlement offer.
There can be no doubt but that	Doubtless, no doubt

---

[36] See Richard Wydick, Plain English for Lawyers 7 (2005). See also Richard A. Lanham, Revising Prose (2007) (avoid sentences with long strings of prepositional phrases).

Participles (verbs used as adjectives) are useful for making *which* clauses more concise.

Courts which follow the majority rule	Courts following the majority rule
The measures which were enacted in 2017	The measures enacted in 2017

Sometimes a whole phrase may be replaced by a colon or a dash.[37]

Management now faced its most serious crisis, in the form of a threatened walk-out by the union representatives.	Management now faced its most serious crisis: a threatened walk-out by the union representatives.

Some sentences are so marbled with verbal fat that it is better to start over and recast the sentence than to try to delete superfluous words.

The particular weakness of the defendant's argument arises in connection with its basic premise relative to the primary purpose of the legislature.	Defendant's argument is weak because it assumes that the legislature's primary purpose was . . . .

Combining sentences can sometimes achieve conciseness, as by reducing a sentence to a subordinate clause.

The first case to pass on the issue was *Dow v. Dow*. In that case, the court held	In *Dow v. Dow*, the first case to pass on the issue, the court held . . . .

Adjectives and adverbs may often be deleted—they are ineffective, especially for most lawyers' purposes.[38] Changing a noun or an adjective to a strong action verb often makes the wording more concise and forceful.[39]

The writer who violates the advice to avoid wordy expressions lacks what Thomas Jefferson called "the most valuable of all talents, that of never using two words where one will do."[40] Do not take this advice to the extreme, however: do not sacrifice every phrase that has a single-word equivalent—they may provide the rhythm, variety, or emphasis you need.[41]

---

[37] See § 7.13, Continuity Through Punctuation.
[38] See § 6.3, Intensifying Adverbs and Adjectives Weaken Your Prose.
[39] See §§ 4.5, Don't Overuse Nouns and 6.4, Use Action Verbs.
[40] Letter to Bernard Moore [1765], 27 American J. of Ed. 546 (1877).
[41] Claire Kehrwald Cook, Line by Line. How to Edit Your Own Writing 12 (1985).

Conciseness, in its finest sense, is obtained by hitting upon just the right word or phrase. When Thoreau said, "the mass of men lead lives of quiet desperation," he expressed a thought that might have sounded commonplace if put in other words; "quiet desperation" made it memorable.[42]

§ 3.4   Eliminate Unnecessary Determiners and Modifiers

Careless writers commonly use words and expressions that contribute no meaning to the sentence. Although they may have meaning or add balance in some situations, they are often verbal tics that can be easily omitted. Here are some useless adjectives and adverbs:[43]

absolute, absolutely	near, nearly
actual, actually	necessary, necessarily
basic, basically	obvious, obviously
certain, certainly	particular, particularly
clear, clearly	perfect, perfectly
complete, completely	practical, practically
considerable, considerably	pure, purely
current, currently	real, really
definite, definitely	reasonable, reasonably
due, duly	relative, relatively
entire, entirely	respective, respectively
exact, exactly	serious, seriously
extreme, extremely	simple, simply
fair, fairly	specific, specifically
final, finally	substantial, substantially
full, fully	sure, surely
general, generally	total, totally
high, highly	true, truly
individual, individually	undue, unduly
literal, literally	utter, utterly
mere, merely	virtual, virtually

---

[42]   Walden 10 (1854).

[43]   See also See § 6.3, Intensifying Adverbs and Adjectives Weaken Your Prose (discussing elimination of adjectives and adverbs).

Although valuable when used properly, the following words are frequently useless filler and should be handled with care:

any	little	sort of
both	much	such
even	now	that
given	pretty	the
here	quite	then
in reality	rather	type of
indeed	so	various
just	some	very
kind of	somehow	well
largely	somewhat	

Strunk and White showed no patience for useless qualifiers:

> Rather, very, little, pretty—these are the leeches that infest the pond of prose, sucking the blood of words. The constant use of the adjective little (except to indicate size) is particularly debilitating; we should all try to do a little better, we should all be very watchful of this rule, for it is a rather important one and we are pretty sure to violate it now and then.[44]

§ 3.5   Eliminate Throat Clearers

Insecure writers have a verbal tic of using throat clearers—meaningless phrases at the beginning of a sentence preparing the reader for the main message. They are an exhalation, a padding that can usually be replaced by a word or omitted. They are amateuristic attempts to transition or to emphasize.[45]

Nothing bogs down your writing more than the habit of introducing each new point with a long-winded introductory phrase. Because of this practice, "some sentences seem to take forever to get started."[46]

> As far as . . . is concerned
>
> The next question that must be discussed is
>
> The first issue that must be considered is
>
> Another significant point that we wish to call to the court's attention is
>
> Consideration should be given to the possibility of

---

[44]   The Elements of Style 73 (1979).

[45]   See § 6.2, Avoid Ineffective Techniques to Emphasize.

[46]   Joseph M. Williams & Joseph Bizup, Style. Lessons in Clarity and Grace 145 (2014).

It should be noted in connection to . . . that

A key aspect of this case, which must not be overlooked, is that

It is unnecessary to point out how important it is

Another important issue that has loomed large during the trial of this case is the question of whether

Few, if any, of the issues in this case were the subject of more conflicting testimony than that of whether

Even short throat-clearers must be avoided. As they accumulate, your style becomes slow and bloated.

All things considered

As a matter of fact

I think that

In a manner of speaking

In my opinion

In the final analysis

In this regard

It has come to my attention that

It is my (considered) opinion (contention) that

It seems (to me) that

It would appear to be the case that

Needless to say

Notice (note) (observe) (remember) that

One must not ignore (forget) that

The fact (of the matter) is that

The truth is that

Undoubtedly

It should (must) be noted (stressed) (remembered) (emphasized) that

It is important (interesting) (essential) (crucial) to remember (bear in mind) (point out) (note) (say) (stress) (recall) that

It is clear (obvious) (noteworthy) (apparent) (significant) (expected) (evident) (widely known) that

Because the beginning is the second most emphatic place in a sentence,[47] throat clearers waste valuable real estate. But they should also be avoided in the middle of a sentence: *that is to say, in fact, indeed, in effect.*

These expressions are not throat clearers, however, when they have a purpose. You must start a sentence with *I think that* when it is not clear from the context that what follows is your own

---

[47] See § 6.12, Put Words to be Stressed at the Beginning and the End of Sentences.

opinion. To start a sentence with *in the final analysis* reminds the reader of what you said before and prepares him for the conclusion.

Sometimes entire sentences and even paragraphs are useless padding. Here is a sentence that seems to consist almost wholly of empty words:

> It may be stated without fear of successful contradiction that although our opponents have filed a replication relative to the proposals made in connection with the several issues in dispute, the clearly apparent conflict as to basic philosophy and approach in regard to the concept of management prerogative remains wholly unresolved.

Wordy introductions are often nothing but warming-up motions, verbal crutches for hesitant writers. You may need these warm-up phrases to start the words flowing. But when you edit, remember that they're functional to the writer, not the reader. Delete them—the best introduction moves swiftly into the argument.

§ 3.6   Avoid Doublets and Triplets

(1) Introduction

Avoid phrases that needlessly repeat an idea. The legal language is addicted to a simple form of repetition (called pleonasm by grammarians, word pairs by etymologists, binomial expressions by linguists, and doublets and triplets by legal writers): using two or more conjoined synonyms or near synonyms, when any one of them would serve the purpose.[48]

acknowledge and agree	annul and set aside
acknowledge and confess	apparent and obvious
act and deed	approve and accept
adaptations and modifications	assume and agree
advise and assist	authorize and direct
agree and covenant	authorize and empower
agree and declare	authorize and require
agreed upon and understood	bind and obligate
aid and abet	breaking and entering
aid and comfort	buy or purchase
all intents and purposes	by and on behalf of
alter, change, or modify	by and under
alter or change	by and with

---

[48] See Garner's Dictionary of Legal Usage 294–97 (2011) and Mellinkoff's Dictionary of American Legal Usage 129–32, 325–66 (1992).

cancel and terminate
cancel, annul, and set aside
cease and come to an end
cease and desist
cease and terminate
chargeable and accountable
confess and acknowledge
consent and agree
convey, transfer, and set over
covenant and agree
cover, embrace, and include
deem and consider
devise and bequeath
dispute, controversy, or claim
due and owing
due and payable
due care and attention
execute and perform
facts and circumstances
fair, reasonable, and adequate
false and untrue
final and conclusive
finish and complete
fit and proper
for and during
fraud and deceit
free and clear
free and unfettered
full and complete
full faith and credit
full force and effect
furnish and supply
general, vague, and indefinite
give and grant
give, devise, and bequeath
goods and chattels
grant and convey
grant, bargain, and sell
if and when
indemnify and hold harmless
in lieu, in place, instead, and in
    substitution of

in my stead and place
just and reasonable
keep and maintain
lands and tenements
last will and testament
kind and nature
law and order
legal and valid
let or hindrance
lewd and lascivious conduct
liens and encumbrances
lot, tract, or parcel of land
made and entered into
made, ordained, constituted, and
    appointed
maintenance and upkeep
mind and memory
make and provide
modified and changed
mutually understood and agreed
name, constitute, and appoint
new and novel
nominate and appoint
null and void
null and void and of no force or effect
of and concerning
of any sort or kind
ordain and establish
order, adjudge, and decree
order and direct
other and further
own or possess
pain and suffering
pardon and forgive
perform and discharge
possession, custody, and control
power and authority
practice and procedure
produce and disclose
quiet and peaceable possession
ratify and consent
release, remise, and discharge

relieve and discharge	terms and provisions
remise, release, and forever discharge	to have and to hold
remise, release, and forever quitclaim	totally and completely
repeat and reallege	true and accurate
repeat, reallege, and reiterate	true and correct
represents and warrants	truth and veracity
request and demand	understand and agree
rest, residue, and remainder	undertake and agree
right, title, and interest	unless and until
save and except	vague, nonspecific, and indefinite
seized and possessed	void and of no effect
shall and will	void and of no force
sole and exclusive	ways and means
supersede and displace	willing and able
terms and conditions	

Some of these phrases, like *cease and desist, aid and abet, pain and suffering*, became terms of art and must be used as a pair when appropriate. Lawyers will eventually realize that they are tautological and unnecessary.

Other phrases may not be objectionable in some situations. For example, you may argue that *if and when* is not pleonastic because the words express different meanings. Take this sentence: "if and when a complaint is filed, I will order a detailed investigation." *If* alone would not suffice because you want to say that if the event happens you will act and that you will act promptly; *when* alone will not do, because it assumes that the event will happen, whereas you want to imply that it may not. Very well then, use both—no one would urge you to cut out words that serve a purpose.

But when you find yourself writing *if and when*, ask whether both words serve a purpose or whether you have fallen into the habit of treating them as a team that must always be hitched together. "Many writers seem to have persuaded themselves" said the Fowlers, "that neither *if* nor *when* is any longer capable of facing its responsibilities without the other word to keep it in countenance."[49] Fowler compared the writer who abuses this formula to "a timid swordsman who thinks he will be safer with a second sword in his left hand."[50]

---

[49]   H.W. Fowler & F.G. Fowler, The King's English 335 (1908).
[50]   H.W. Fowler, A Dictionary of Modern English Usage 264 (2d ed. 1965).

The same argument is applicable to several entries in this list that are formed by near, but not complete, synonyms. *Unless and until* is not pleonastic either, but it is difficult to find a situation in which one of the two would not suffice.[51] *If and when* and *unless and until* are useless clichés. Avoid them.

Pointless repetition flourishes in deeds and wills. In old deeds, the granting clause sometimes *witnesseth* that the grantor "has granted, bargained, sold, remised, released, conveyed, aliened, and confirmed, and by these presents does grant, bargain, sell, remise, release, convey, alien, and confirm."

In wills, many drafters (perhaps their clients) like the rolling repetitiveness of traditional phrases, such as "sound and disposing mind and memory," "not acting under duress, menace, fraud, or undue influence of any person whomsoever," "to make, publish, and declare," "hereby expressly revoke and cancel any and all other wills, codicils, legacies, bequests, and testamentary dispositions heretofore at any time made by me." Fifty years ago, the president of the Illinois State Bar Association estimated that from 25% to 40% of the words used in a simple will were meaningless or redundant.

In contracts, introductory words such as "whereas" and "now therefore" add nothing. "It is agreed" is usually needed only once, if not at all, and certainly not in every paragraph. There is no need to say, "it is agreed upon and understood." The consideration clause can often be less wordy than the formulations frequently used. If the parties' undertakings are well stated, no recitation of consideration may be needed. Whatever recitals of agreement and consideration you write into the contract should be expressed only once; do not repeatedly say that in consideration of so and so, a party agrees to do this and that. "Buyer will" is just as effective as "it is further understood and agreed that buyer will" or, "In consideration of the aforesaid . . . buyer hereby undertakes and agrees that she will." If you want a formal heading in your contract, just write, "in consideration of the mutual benefits provided by this agreement, the parties agree as follows." Or, "the parties agree as follows." Or don't write anything; it makes no difference.

Statutes are now edited by legislative drafting counsel. Yet many still on the books are grievously verbose. Despite recent amendments and the 2007 restyling of the Federal Rules of Civil Procedure, Rule 23(e) still provides that a class action may be

---

[51]   Id. at 665–66; Ernest Gowers, Plain Words: Their ABC 102 (1957).

"settled, voluntarily dismissed, or compromised" if the settlement offer is "fair, reasonable, and adequate." How these superfluities have survived is open to question, debate, and speculation.

(2) Historical and Linguistic Explanations

Scholars have acknowledged the historical origin of some paired legal phrases. For several centuries after the Norman Conquest in the eleventh century, English courts conducted business in Law French, a mix of Medieval Latin and Medieval French. From the twelfth to the seventeenth centuries in England, the language of the courts was French; the language of government, religion, and learning was Latin; and the language of the people was English. Few English people outside the legal profession understood French, so English words were also needed to convey legal meaning to the populace. Slowly, lawyers started to speak in pairs of words, one French and one English, a legacy still seen today.[52]

The theory of bilingualism seems to be preferred by most legal scholars who have addressed the pairings issue. It does explain many doublets formed by French and English words. But it does not explain strings of synonyms that do not have the expected etymological origins. Nor does it explain their use in England before the Norman Conquest or outside the law.

Bilingualism also does not explain why countries with no history of dual language also have doublets or triplets. Medieval German law, for example, was often expressed through alliteration ("homestead and house," "right and righteous"); in triplets ("true, loyal, and obedient"); in negative synonymy ("free and not servile"); and in rhyme ("without keep or staff").[53] The same practice existed in several languages and countries. Spanish law is another example: "*daños y perjuicios*", "*nulo y sin efecto*," etc.

Doublets, therefore, have several other explanations. They may have been used because they give a sense of elegance, balance, and rhythm, a ritual that lends legitimacy to any statement. The rhetorical function of doublets should not be underestimated.

---

[52] Ernest Weekley, Cruelty to Words 43 (1931). This phenomenon was not limited to word pairs in legal English; it arose in the English language in general. See John Earle, Philology of the English Tongue §§ 77, 78 (1879); Otto Jespersen, Growth and Structure of the English Language 135–36 (1905). See also § 4.9, Prefer Saxon Over Latin Words.

[53] Rudolf Huebner, A History of Germanic Private Law 10 (1918) (the rhyme exists only in German: *ungehabt und ungestabt*).

Tellingly, when something makes no sense, we say that it was done "without rhyme or reason." Old folk verses, magic formulas, and sayings were often in rhymed or alliterative forms to aid memory in a time when knowledge was passed down orally. These were the expressions that survived the test of time; the others were forgotten.

As George Philip Krapp concluded, "the real explanation of the use of words in pairs is rhetorical and oratorical rather than etymological. By the use of two words a writer often gets a richer cadence, an oratorical amplification of the expression that may seem . . . more effective than the use of a single word would be."[54]

(3) False Precision

Whatever the origin of this practice, it made a lasting impression on the legal profession: careful lawyers must use several synonyms to cover all possibilities.[55] This impression is difficult to overcome.

Lawyers read and hear these doublets and triplets frequently. These phrases enter the legal unconscious and give a false impression of legal precision. People think that's the way lawyers talk, that's the traditional technical legal terminology. "[T]he repetition of these phrases," said David Mellinkoff, "accustoms the profession to the unprecise pattern of two-words-for-one . . . . If the mature lawyer uses these phrases sufficiently long, pride rationalizes habit into conviction . . . we write what we read."[56]

Good lawyers are cautious and busy: they can't afford to write "null" and run the risk that the absence of "and void" might lead to litigation. Nor can they spend hours of research to debunk expressions that have survived decades or centuries and are still widely used. Instead, a lawyer who wants to protect the client's interest will be under pressure to write "null and void, and of no

---

[54] Modern English: Its Growth and Present Use 250–53 (1909) (without overlooking the bilingual explanation). See also David Mellinkoff, The Language of the Law 38–39, 121–22, 144, 325–66 (1963). *Compare* Peter M. Tiersma, Legal Language 13–16 (1999) (discussing alliterative binomial expressions in Old English, long before the Norman Conquest and the rise of Law French) *with* Tiersma at 31–34 (discussing binomial expressions attributed to bilingualism). But see Garner's Dictionary of Legal Usage 294 (2011).

[55] Chester Lloyd Jones, Statute Law Making in the United States 123 (1923).

[56] The Language of the Law 120–22, 325–66 (1963).

further force and effect." And no self-respecting lawyer will sign a "cease letter."

It is reckless for a style manual to propose that lawyers abandon traditional legal doublets and triplets when there is no authoritative statement about which ones are necessary and which ones are superfluous. Lawyers today are the same risk-averse professionals who originally created these doublets and triplets out of caution, and they do not want to risk a court challenge. The purification of the legal language, if it ever comes, should not come from the parties, but from legislatures and courts, with academic input. Still, don't be afraid to omit the obviously superfluous.

Pairs of words where one includes the other, such as *authorize and require*, or *request and demand*, are also redundant. Instead of tossing in both words, use the broader or the narrower, as the context requires. Choose your meaning deliberately. A gaseous verbosity such as "is hereby vested with power and authority and it shall be his duty in carrying out the provisions of this act to" can be reduced to one word: *may* (or *must*).

(4) Examples in Everyday Use

Lawyers are not alone in their weakness for pointless repetition; it is common in all walks of life:

again and again	once and for all
any and all	one and only
any way, shape, or form	one and the same
basic and fundamental	over and above
compare and contrast	part and parcel
day and age	peace and quiet
dead and gone	pick and choose
each and all	plain and simple
each and every	quick and easy
entirely and completely	really and truly
far and wide	safe and sound
few and far between	separate and apart
first and foremost	through and through
hope and trust	time and (time) again
hopes and desires	total and absolute
in truth and in fact	total and complete
leaps and bounds	trials and tribulations
of any sort or kind	tried and true
on and on	

(5) Conclusion

Although the objective of adding a second word is to reinforce the first, the result of amplification by synonym is the opposite: the statement is weakened. When you find yourself writing one of these tandem phrases out of mere habit, stop and look for the single word (one of the series or a new one) that is clear and strong enough to carry the meaning by itself.

§ 3.7   Avoid Tautologies

Tautology is "a form of redundancy, consisting of the needless repetition of an idea, especially in other words in the immediate context, without imparting additional force or clearness."[57] Tautological phrases are used by unthinking writers who don't recognize that they are expressing the same idea in two ways.

> A real basis in fact [a basis in fact is necessarily real]
> Actual fact; true fact [all facts are actual and true]
> Advance planning [all planning is in advance]
> Consensus of opinion [a consensus is an agreement of opinion]
> Contributing factor [a factor always contributes to a result]
> Mutual respect for each other [if it is mutual, it is for each other]
> A panacea for all ills [a panacea is a remedy for all ills]
> With the consequent result that [all results are consequent]
> Surrounding circumstances [circumstances are surrounding conditions]
> Mutual friends [mutual implies a relation between two or more persons or things—A is to B as B is to A].

"Mutual benefits" (obligations, abettors, or respect) makes sense. But because it takes two to make a friendship, to say that A and B are mutual friends is no more than to say they are friends. To say that they have a mutual friend in C is meaningless; they have a common friend, or a friend in common.

Here are some common tautological phrases:

above and beyond	ask a question
accidental mistake	at a later date
actual experience	basic essentials
actual fact	basic fundamentals
add an additional	basic necessities
added bonus	basic principles
advance warning	boarding process

---

[57]   Bergen & Cornelia Evans, A Dictionary of Contemporary American Usage (1957).

both equally
both. . . as well as. . .
brief moment
but nevertheless
circle around
close proximity
close scrutiny
combine together
connect together
continue to remain
cooperate together
current status
current trend
die of a fatal blow
direct confrontation
disappear from sight
during the course of
during the daytime
during the year of
eliminate entirely
emergency situation
end result
English language
equally as
eradicate completely
established pattern
estimated roughly
every single person
exactly similar
exactly the same
extra bonus
false pretense
fatal murder
fellow colleague
first conceived
first introduced
first of all
flawless perfection
foreign imports
forever and ever
free gift
free of charge

further, as a second requirement
future forecast
future plans
gather together
general consensus (of opinion)
general public
give all possible assistance that I can
healing process
integral part
interact with each other
invisible to the eye
join together
joint cooperation
just exactly
kneel down
lag behind
later time
litigation process
local residents
major breakthrough
mass media
meet with each other
merge together
mix together
mutual agreement
mutual cooperation
my own opinion
natural life
negotiation process
never before
new innovation
new recruit
old adage
old cliché
old proverb
on the other hand, however
over and over
over-exaggerate
paid the total amount in full
past experience
past history
past records

period of time

personal belongings

plan ahead

point in time

postpone until later

potential hazard

pre-planned

premeditated before acting

present time

previous experience

prior approval

prior criminal record

prior record

protest against

rate of speed

reason why

recur again

reelect for another term

refer back

reflect back

remaining balance

remand back

repeat again

return again

revert back

safe haven

same exact

same identical

scrutinize carefully

specific example

still remain

subject matter

subtle nuance

successful completion

sudden outburst

summarize briefly

surrounded on all sides

surviving widow

sworn affidavit

temporary reprieve

the basis of the claim rests on

the exception is limited only to

the reason is because

the reason was due to

the resultant effect

throughout the entire

time period

totally devoid of

true fact

unconfirmed rumor

underlying assumption

unexpected surprise

unexpected twist

usual custom

variety of different items (issues)

various different

whether or not

while at the same time

whole entire

write down

written instrument

Starting a phrase with an unnecessary determiner is an easy way to create a tautological phrase:[58]

absolute guarantee

absolutely certain

absolutely clear

absolutely essential

absolutely necessary

absolutely sure

complete monopoly

completely destroyed

completely full

completely surrounded

final completion

final conclusion

final destination

final outcome

final result

---

[58]   See § 3.4, Eliminate Unnecessary Determiners and Modifiers.

Tautologies are also found in phrases like "red in color" and "young in age." To say that a person is "young in appearance" may be meaningful, but to say that he is "young in age" is to say that he is young. Below are other examples of "tautological phrases of specification" or "redundant category":

accurate manner	narrow in width
appreciate in value	of a cheap quality
area of sociology	of a compelling kind
at a low speed	of a different sort
at an early period	of an immoral character
at an early time	of an uncertain condition
beautiful in appearance	of a scientific nature
cheap in cost	of a strange type
earlier in date	round in form
earlier in time	round in shape
extreme in degree	routine fashion
few in number	square shaped
friendly in character	tall in height
heavy in weight	trial court level
in a confused state	unusual in nature
in an effective way	weather condition
large in size	

We sometimes see the adjective *successfully* tacked on to a verb (such as *avoid, conquer, prevent,* or *withstand*) that itself expresses success:

The witness successfully withstood cross-examination.

Did the writer think it necessary to make clear that the witness did not withstand cross-examination unsuccessfully?

It is a waste to say that something is "objective rather than subjective," "valid rather than invalid," or "the majority rather than the minority rule." Using both a positive and negative way of expressing the same idea is as unnecessary as "guilty rather than not guilty," or "thirsty rather than not thirsty."

Some redundancies are the result of carelessness—failure to notice that the word already appears in the sentence:

In determining whether a complaint states a cause of action, affidavits are not relevant to such determination.

Ignorance of foreign languages may also lead to redundancy:

Chai tea

Latina woman

Madrassa school

Matinee performance

Sahara Desert

Sierra Mountains

Sharia Law

The Rio Grande River

Even those that have become accepted usage are still redundant.

Inattentive use of acronyms also leads to redundancy:

ABS braking system [Antilock Braking System braking system]

ATM machine [Automated Teller Machine machine]

CD disc [Compact Disk disk]

CPU unit [Central Processing Unit unit]

DVD disk [Digital Video Disc disc]

DVR recorder [Digital Video Recorder Recorder]

EIN number [Employer Identification Number number]

FISA Act [Foreign Intelligence Surveillance Act act]

GATT agreement [General Agreement on Tariffs and Trade agreement]

GPS system [Global Positioning System system]

HIV virus [Human Immunodeficiency Virus virus]

LCD display [Liquid Crystal Display display]

MRI images [Magnetic Resonance Imaging images]

NAFTA agreement [North American Free Trade Agreement agreement]

PDF format [Portable Document Format format]

PIN number [Personal Identification Number number]

RAM memory [Random Access Memory memory]

SAT test [Scholastic Aptitude Test test]

SIN number [Social Insurance Number number]

UPC code [Universal Product Code code]

Whole clauses or sentences are sometimes repetitious.

This is a comparatively minor point, and one that is of little importance.

The intention of the parties is found by looking to the instrument to determine what was intended.

Psychiatrists agree that one way to avoid mental illness is to have a healthy mind.

The last-quoted sentence is more sententious than repetitious. Sometimes the sententiousness is not so obvious; the statement may even seem learned, until we think about it.

If an idea can be expressed in one sentence, say it and move on. Don't say it again in different words. Inexperienced writers ignore this advice. After wording an idea one way, they think of another way to put it, which they then add. Second thoughts are sometimes better, and there's no reason why you should not promptly get them down before you forget. But don't keep both. As you review your work, choose between them, or, better yet, combine them into one, using the most effective words and phrases of each. "The idea," said Bryan Garner, "isn't to say something as many ways as you can, but to say it once as well as you can."[59]

§ 3.8   The Passive Voice Is Verbose

The passive voice is often ambiguous and weaker than the active voice.[60] It is also wordier.

In the active voice, the subject does the action—the agent does something to someone. In the passive voice, the subject is acted upon—someone does something to the subject.

The lawsuit was filed by the plaintiff.	The plaintiff filed the lawsuit.
The plaintiff was ordered by the judge to stop.	The judge ordered the plaintiff to stop.

In these examples, the passive voice is two words longer than the active. The passive voice also takes longer to process because it defies the expected sentence order of someone doing something to someone else. In a one-sentence document, most readers will not notice the difference, but in a long text the constant use of passive voice saps the vitality of your prose and wears down the reader's attention.

The active voice is more concise, precise, and vigorous; it is also easier to read. But the passive voice is not grammatically wrong, nor is it to be avoided at all costs—sometimes the passive voice is just what you need.[61]

§ 3.9   Not All Repetition Is Pointless

Sometimes clarity and precision conflict with conciseness. As opposed to other writers, lawyers cannot leave room for the reader to openly interpret a legal text. Clarity and precision always take

---

[59]   Legal Writing in Plain English 56 (2013).

[60]   See §§ 5.11, The Passive Voice May Be Ambiguous and 6.5, The Passive Voice is Weak.

[61]   See § 7.15, The Passive Voice May be Just What You Need (discussing legitimate uses of the passive voice).

precedence over conciseness—you need only eliminate unnecessary clutter from your text.

Learn to detect the point when clarity and precision become repetition. "Don't annoy your readers by over explaining," cautions William Zinsser, "by telling them something they already know or can figure out. Try not to use words like *surprisingly, predictably* and *of course*, which put a value on a statement before the reader encounters it. Trust your material."[62] "Sometimes verbiage springs from excessive caution, a determination to be clear and explicit no matter how labored the language. This admirable motive can lead to obscuring the main point to be made."[63]

Conciseness is always a viable alternative to verbosity:

If it must be written, it can be shorter . . . the fewer words that accomplish the purpose is brevity enough, whether the word count is high or low. Beyond that the words are worthless, to be systematically rooted out whether they be many or few. The antidote for verbosity is not haphazard brevity, which sometimes succeeds in achieving the paradoxically bad: language too short and too long at the same time.[64]

A literary master like Ernest Hemingway might forge a career by leaving an iceberg of meaning unspoken. Permitting the core message to go unsaid is not an option for legal writers, who must announce each step in their syllogisms, address each relevant fact, and counter each argument. But a soft gradient separates the essential from the extraneous—a legal writer must develop the judgment for optimum line-drawing.

Start by erring on the side of clarity, and learn to pare down aggressively as you review your text and as your expertise grows. Then delete everything that does not affect substance or nuance.

Say it clearly; say it once—if you can say the same thing in two good ways, pick the best one.

True brevity of expression consists in everywhere saying only what is worth saying, and in avoiding tedious detail about things which everyone can supply for himself. This involves correct discrimination between what is necessary

---

[62]   On Writing Well 91 (2006).
[63]   John Halverson & Mason Cooley, Principles of Writing 190 (1965).
[64]   David Mellinkoff, The Language of the Law 405 (1963).

and what is superfluous. A writer should never be brief at the expense of being clear, to say nothing of being grammatical.[65]

But here, as elsewhere in writing, there are no absolutes. Deliberate repetition can lend emphasis, eloquence, rhythm, aesthetic, and balance.[66]

> It is all too tempting for a defendant to second-guess counsel's assistance after conviction . . . , and it is all too easy for a court, examining counsel's defense after it has proved unsuccessful, to conclude that a particular act or omission of counsel was unreasonable.[67]

Even wordiness may serve a purpose: "readers don't like flab, but neither do they like a style so terse that it's all gristle and bone."[68] The goal is not to delete "every conceivable bit of wordiness from your writing. If you do, your writing will become sparse and lifeless."[69]

Even verbiage that is redundant or unnecessary may have a purpose. The lawyer who includes a direction that the testator's debts be paid knows that it is unnecessary. But the lawyer may have learned that clients expect the express provision and may ascribe an omission to ignorance or carelessness. Confronting such preconceptions, counsel may decide to be wordy.

In an instrument appointing an agent, the drafter must use words that encourage a timid agent to act, while assuring third parties that the agent has the necessary authority. This can be done by a broad "necessary and proper" clause. Another way is to use multiple specific empowerments. Thus, a power of attorney will usually confer power not merely to "receive any of my property" but "to receive and take possession of my property in whatever form, including without limitation, any or all money, stocks, bonds, securities, goods, chattels, land, buildings, and other property belonging to me."

---

[65] Arthur Schopenhauer, On Style [1851], in Lane Cooper (ed.), The Art of the Writer 229 (1952).

[66] See §§ 2.5, Don't be Afraid to Repeat a Word, 6.11, Use Reiteration Deliberately, and 8.5, Reiteration.

[67] Strickland v. Washington, 466 U.S. 668, 689 (1984) (O'Connor, J.).

[68] Joseph M. Williams & Joseph Bizup, Style: Lessons in Clarity and Grace 132 (2017).

[69] Anne Enquist, Laurel Oates & Jeremy Francis, Just Writing 109 (2017).

§ 3.10   Repeating and Realleging Facts Is Pointless

(1) The Formula (Incorporation by Reference)

The talismanic practice of repeating and realleging facts in each count of a pleading is particularly dreadful:

> Each and every allegation set forth in paragraphs 1 through 60 of this Complaint is hereby repeated, reiterated, and realleged with the same force and effect and incorporated by reference as if fully set forth herein at length and in detail.

Most pleaders use a shorter but equally exasperating formula for "incorporation by reference." If a pleading contains ten counts, the plaintiff mechanically repeats the formula ten times, incorporating all previous paragraphs, whether relevant or not.

It is common to justify the practice by arguing that "realleging by reference saves the story from redundancy and tedium."[70] This explanation is centuries old: "In framing a second or subsequent count for the same cause of action, care should be taken to avoid any unnecessary repetition of the same matter, and by an inducement in the first count, applying any matter to the following counts, and by referring concisely in the subsequent counts to such inducement, much unnecessary prolixity may be avoided."[71]

The practice, however, is useless. If the objective is to avoid repetition, the solution is not to reiterate the facts through an inherently repetitive formula. The story would be even less redundant and less tedious if parties did not reallege facts previously alleged in the same document.

Yet some legal writing books explicitly teach the practice of incorporation by reference. Most transcribe complaints with the offending formula, validating it. Formbooks perpetuate the formula. Books that don't teach it don't offer a complaint, or present simple complaints with only one count, or do not number the paragraphs.

---

[70] Elizabeth Fajans & Mary R. Falk, Untold Stories: Restoring Narrative to Pleading Practice, 15 J. Legal Writing Institute 3, 28 (2009). See also Wright & Miller, 5A Fed. Prac. & Proc. Civ. § 1326 (2017).

[71] See 1 Chitty's Pleading 396–399 (1819) (English book once widely used in the United States). See also Phillips v. Fielding, 2 Hen. Bla. 122, 132 (1792) (American case praising incorporation by reference as a means of streamlining documents).

(2) The Old Rule (the Need to Reallege All Facts in Each Count)

The practice of incorporation by reference can be traced back more than four centuries, possibly many more. It allowed efficient writing when the formulaic common-law pleading rule in England (later transplanted to the United States) substantially restricted the joinder of claims in a proceeding. In the limited circumstances in which a party could join claims, each count had to be "separately stated." This meant that each count had to contain a complete and independent cause of action. Each count had to be its own pleading, as each count was considered a separate lawsuit.

In practice, this meant that each count had to allege all facts and elements of the cause of action on which it was based. If one fact happened to be an element of two or more counts, it had to be alleged in each—defects and omissions in one count could not be supplied by the allegations in another. The rule also applied to responsive pleadings asserting more than one defense.[72]

Although this requirement seems a frivolous technicality for modern legal minds, violating this fundamental rule led to severe consequences: incomplete counts were dismissed for failure to state facts sufficient to constitute a cause of action. And the rule was rigidly applied: pleadings were strictly construed, interpreted against the pleader, and could not be amended.

This formalistic common-law pleading rule requiring each count to contain all facts remained in effect in the United States even after 1850, when the states adopted codes of civil procedure and created the then-modern code pleading. In New York, for example, the rule survived in the Field Code of 1848;[73] in the Throop Code of 1877;[74] and in the Rules of Civil Practice of 1921.[75] Only in 1963 did New York abolish the duty to plead self-contained

---

[72] See Currie v. Henry, 2 Johns. 433, 437 (1807); Hughes v. Moore, 11 U.S. 176, 190 (1812); Nelson v. Swan, 13 Johns. 483 (1816). See also William W. Hening, The American Pleader 33–38 (1811); James Gould, Principles of Pleading 171 (1832); Watkin Williams, Principles and Practice of Pleading 99 (1857).

[73] NY Code of Procedure § 167 (1848, as amended in 1849); Benedict v. Seymour, 6 How. Pr. 298 (1862) and Landau v. Levy, 1 Abb. 376 (1855)). See also William Wait, The Code of Procedure of the State of New York 271–72, 305–06 (1875). See also [Proposed] NY Code of Civ Pro § 663 (1850).

[74] NY Code Civ Pro §§ 483, 507, and 517 (1877).

[75] NYCPR 90 (1921).

counts, with the enactment of the current Civil Practice Law and Rules.[76]

(3) The Exception to the Old Rule (Permission to Incorporate by Reference)

To avoid needless repetition, however, the old common-law pleading rules in England and in the United States and most state codes developed an exception: they allowed a party to incorporate into a count allegations contained elsewhere in the document.

Incorporation by reference has been the practice in common law and code pleadings for more than four centuries. The earliest known precedent is an ambiguous English case from 1590.[77] The practice continued in the following centuries in England and in the United States.[78]

It was not necessary to write a full sentence or paragraph as lawyers do now—pleaders could simply use words like *said, same, as above stated*, or *aforesaid*, as long as the matter referred to was clearly identified.[79] The current *repeat, reiterate, and reallege* formula, transcribed above, was conceived towards the end of the

---

[76] NY CPLR 3014 (2017).

[77] See Barnes v. May, Cro. Eliz. 240 (1590).

[78] See Tindall v. Moore, 2 Wils. 114 (1760); Baldwin v. Elphinston, 2 Bla. Rep. 1037 (1775); Phillips v. Fielding, 2 Hen. Bla. 122, 131–32 (1792); Stiles v. Nokes, 7 East 493, 502, 506 (1805); Crookshank v. Gray, 20 Johns. 344, 344–48 (1823); Griswold v. National Ins. Co., 3 Cow 96 (1824); Loomis v. Swick, 3 Wend. 205, 205–07 (1829); Porter v. Cumings, 7 Wend. 205 (1831); Cantebury v. Hill, 5 Steward & Porter 224 (Al. 1833); Nestle v. Van Slyck, 2 Hill 282, 286 (1842); Freeland v. McCullough, 1 Den. 414, 425 (1845); Williams v. Richmond, 9 How. 522 (1854); Sinclair v. Fitch, 3 E. D. Smith 677, 688–89 (1857), Xenia Branch Bank v. Lee, 7 Abb. 372, 386–87 (1858); Baldwin v. U.S. Telegraph Co., 6 Abb. N.S. 405, 425 (1867); Anderson v Speers, 8 Abb. N.C. 382 (1879); Reiners v. Brandhorst, 59 How. Pr. 91 (1879); Bigelow v. Drummond, 90 NYS 913 (1904); Maxwell Steel Vault Co. v. National Casket Co., 205 F. 515 (1913). See also 1 Chitty's Pleading 395–96 (1812); Saunders's Pleading 417 (1828); I Abbott & Abbott's Pleading 114 (1875); Pomeroy's Remedies § 442 (1876); Baylies's Pleading 47–50, 70–71 (1890); Bryant's Pleading § 137 (1894); Shipman's Pleading § 252–54 (1895); Phillips's Pleading § 123, 202–04 (1896); Ames's Pleading 16–17 (1905); I Abbott's Brief Upon the Pleadings 33–6 (1904); Pomeroy's Remedies § 336 (1904); I Nichols's Pleading and Practice 926–27 (1904); Gould's Pleadings 357 (1909); I Sutherland's Code Pleading and Practice § 193 (1910); Simkins's, Federal Equity 279 (1916); Shipman's Pleading § 78–9 (1923); Clark's Code Pleading § 37 (1928); 3 Carmody's Pleading and Practice § 893 (1931); Phillips's Pleading § 320–21 (1932); 3 Carmody-Wait's Cyclopedia of NY Practice 449–50 (1953); 12 Nichols-Cahill's Annotated NYCP Acts 204–06 (1956 & Supp. 1962); Joseph H. Koffler & Alison Reppy, Common Law Pleading § 24 (1969).

[79] See § 2.8, Words to Watch (discussing *said, same*, and *aforesaid*). This explains in part the legal profession's addiction to these words that now sound stilted.

nineteenth century and has endured substantially unaltered for more than a century.[80]

Despite having been a fundamental common law rule for centuries, the first written statute to expressly allow incorporation by reference was the New York Rule of Civil Practice of 1921: "the allegations contained in a separately numbered paragraph of one cause of action, counterclaim or defense may be incorporated as a whole in another cause of action, counterclaim or defense in the same pleading by reference without otherwise repeating them."[81]

(4) The Modern Perspective (No Need to Reallege Facts in Each Count)

The whole thing sort of made sense in the legal mindset of the sixteenth to nineteenth centuries. But this fossilized technique has no place in modern pleadings.

More than half a century ago, in 1963, New York expressly released pleaders from this ancient obligation: "prior statements in a pleading shall be deemed repeated or adopted subsequently in the same pleading whenever express repetition or adoption is unnecessary for a clear presentation of subsequent matters."[82] This was an evolution of the previous pleading practice of repeating and realleging. But instead of deeming the statements repeated, the statute should have provided that there was no need to repeat statements. Despite the rule, however, New York lawyers are still addicted to the practice of repeating and realleging, routinely incorporating statements by reference.[83] Old practices die hard.

Federal procedure, however, has not caught up with New York's 1963 innovation. In a pointless provision that has survived unamended since 1938, Rule 10(c) condones the practice of incorporation by reference: "a statement in a pleading may be adopted by reference elsewhere in the same pleading or in any other pleading or motion." This rule is inconsistent with a modern procedural system that allows flexible amendments and liberal

---

[80]   See Marietta v. Cleveland, 52 Misc. 16 (1906). The language was brewed in the practice of the previous decades. See, e.g., Bogardus v. N. Y. L. Ins. Co., 101 N.Y. 328 (1886) and Treweek v. Howard, 105 Cal. 434 (1895). But see Clinkett v. Casseres, 200 NYS 178 (1923) (not accepting, without explanation, a similar language, possibly because it was not sufficiently specific).

[81]   NYCPR 90 (1921).

[82]   See NY CPLR 3014 (2017). See also 3 Weinstein, Korn & Miller, NY Civil Practice §§ 3014.04–3014.07 (2017); 3B Carmody-Wait, NY Practice 2d § 27:44 (2017).

[83]   See 3 Weinstein, Korn & Miller, NY Civil Practice § 3014.07 (2017).

joinder of claims. Most important, it is incompatible with a system that does not adopt the old common-law pleading rule that each count must be stated completely and independently under penalty of dismissal.[84]

The Federal Rules mindlessly adopted the exception (incorporation by reference) without having adopted the rule (each count must contain all facts and elements of the claim). Rule 10(c) was mimicked in state procedural rules, replicating the error throughout the country. A commentator proposed relaxing the application of Rule 10(c) along the same lines as the New York rule, but concluded that "good pleading practice requires that express incorporations should be used to avoid any ambiguity and any risk."[85] No, it doesn't.

Lawyers unquestioningly repeat the formula today, never stopping to think if they have to. "It doesn't hurt," they say, but it's an empty recitation, and its omission will not affect the outcome of the case. When the courts abolish this silly practice, no one will miss these pointless paragraphs cluttering our complaints.

§ 3.11 Rewrite[86]

> *You never know what is enough until*
> *you know what is more than enough.*
> William Blake (1757–1827)[87]

The advice to cut out unnecessary words is not easy to take. Although we may not fancy ourselves great writers, once we have composed something, we quickly come to love it. As a mother loves her child, we love this brain child of ours. We cannot easily bring ourselves to carve out parts of it. We certainly cannot expect to do it in the warm flush of writing, while still glowing with the pride of authorship. So, let your work get cold, then read it the next day or the next week. As you read it, forget that it is yours; pretend you are instead its intended recipient, reading it for the first time.

---

[84] The possibility of adopting statements by reference to a previous pleading or motion, however, may be useful, particularly in multiparty litigation. See Wright & Miller, 5A Fed. Prac. & Proc. Civ. § 1326 (2017). See also Zuzul v. McDonald, 98 F. Supp. 3d 852, 869 n.15 (M.D. N.C. 2015) (incorporating by reference to previous pleadings); Hinton v. Trans Union, LLC, 654 F. Supp. 2d 440 (2009) (same).

[85] See Wright & Miller, 5A Fed. Prac. & Proc. Civ. § 1326 (2017).

[86] See § 4.12, Simplifying is Painstaking Work (discussing the importance of reviewing one's prose) and Chapter 9, Conclusion (same).

[87] The Marriage of Heaven and Hell (1790).

Read your text dispassionately and even critically, and improvements will usually suggest themselves. As you cut, remember that you are not hurting the composition, but only your parental pride of authorship. As Joyce Carol Oates advises, editing your own work requires you to be "[s]ympathetic but merciless!"[88] Only by a conscious and resolute act of will can you attain the detached attitude needed to carve out unsparingly every bit of fat from your own text.

In an earlier draft of the last sentence, the last clause read, "to root out ruthlessly every luxuriating verbal weed." That sounded mighty fine when I wrote it, but it went out under the spur of Samuel Johnson's rule: "read over your compositions, and when you meet with a passage which you think is particularly fine, strike it out."[89] This advice, directed at a particularly verbose and flamboyant writer, was later developed by Arthur Quiller-Couch. After saying that "extraneous ornaments" were not style, he concluded, "[w]henever you feel an impulse to perpetrate a piece of exceptionally fine writing, obey it—whole-heartedly—and delete it before sending your manuscript to press. *Murder your darlings.*"[90]

The advice to cut verbal deadwood is only a specification of a broader admonition: rewrite. Justice Louis Brandeis was right: "there is no such thing as good writing. There is only good rewriting."[91] This statement dispels the misconception that good writers do not need to review their work and that as they write "the words just fall into place."[92] The opposite is true: "rewriting is the essence of writing well: it's where the game is won or lost."[93]

Rewriting, therefore, is not the mechanical task of catching misspellings and tweaking words here and there. Rewriting is an intellectual task of the same magnitude as writing. Rewriting is not something you do when you have finished writing: rewriting is thinking, rewriting is writing.

---

[88] https://www.huffingtonpost.com/2013/07/18/joyce-carol-oates-writing_n_3617152.html.

[89] Boswell's Life of Johnson 258 (1866).

[90] On the Art of Writing 281 (1916).

[91] Charles W. Pierce, The Legal Profession, 30 The Torch 5, 8 (1957) (quoting Louis D. Brandeis).

[92] William Zinsser, On Writing Well 84 (2006).

[93] Id. at xii, 83. See also Joseph M. Williams, Style. Ten Lessons in Clarity and Grace vi (1997) ("The serious part of writing is rewriting.").

As you review your text, don't think only about what you can add; think also about what you can delete: syllables, words, phrases, sentences, paragraphs, everything that is not essential must be removed to tighten up your style.[94] Conscious of verbal fat in early drafts, good editors aspire to cut the text by at least ten percent at each review. This tightens up the prose and creates room for adding relevant information.

It is easier to be wordy than concise. Being concise takes more than time and effort; it takes dedication and attention to detail. After having written a long letter, Blaise Pascal famously apologized: "if I had more time, I would have written a shorter letter."[95]

No one writes so well that a critical eye cannot find ways of saying things more concisely and precisely. As you reread your work, you may find that the arrangement is poor or that a sentence needs to be clearer, smoother, or more readable. You may find adjectives and adverbs you used to add force, but that you now see are merely exaggeration. You may find nouns qualified by adjectives but determine, after consulting a thesaurus, that you can replace the phrase with a more expressive or descriptive noun. A word may not carry quite the nuance you want and need to be replaced by one that carries your meaning better.

If possible, have someone else read your draft, and never be defensive against criticism. You can never read your text with the needed detachment "because you wrote the thing. You've been backstage. You've seen how the rabbits were smuggled into the hat."[96]

Rewriting is not an act; it is not even a process. Rewriting is an attitude. You will never detect all issues or conceive all possible improvements in one pass. You will have to reread your text several times—sometimes only after removing one layer of problems will you be able to see others. And you will add new problems as you eliminate old ones.[97] It's an endless job: "you might need to read your text several times before you can consider it passable: The vicious circle stops only when I find myself restoring the earlier version of a sentence I 'improved' last time around. I've reached the

---

[94]   See Gary Provost, Make Your Words Work 286 (2001).
[95]   Lettres Provinciales (1657).
[96]   Margaret Atwood, in Write (2012).
[97]   See Claire Kehrwald Cook, Line by line 137 (1985).

point of diminishing returns."[98] That's how experienced writers approach writing.

> Knowing when you are done, of course, is something that comes with time and experience, and everyone has a different perspective on the end of the editing process. . . . When I know I've spent a considerable time on editing, when I've taken all or most of the steps I've outlined here, when I'm not finding any more mistakes, when I'm satisfied with the thrust of the writing, and—most importantly—when I'm so sick of the project that I can't bear to read another word, then I know I've reached the penultimate edit. After giving myself a break, I have to force myself to go through the document one last time. If, on that reading, I don't change anything, then I'm done. If I do make changes, then I read the document through again and again until I don't make a change, and then I stop.[99]

If it strikes you that this approach increases your workload, your instincts are on point.[100] "Writing is hard work. A clear sentence is no accident. Few sentences come out right the first time, or even the third time. Remember this in moments of despair. If you find that writing is hard, it's because it is hard."[101] Dorothy Parker encapsulated the contradiction of the writing struggle: "I hate writing, I love having written."[102] Maya Angelou felt the same: "Nothing so frightens me as writing, but nothing so satisfies me."[103] Writing well takes commitment, but it can be fun too.

Plato, it is said, rewrote the first paragraph of *The Republic* about twelve times. If his first drafts needed reworking, ours do too.

---

[98] Id. at 137.

[99] Ian Gallacher, A Form and Style Manual for Lawyers 192 (2005).

[100] But see Charles R. Calleros, Legal Method and Writing 306-07 (2014) (discussing the economic limitations on multiple revisions, including the client's resources and the value of the claim).

[101] William Zinsser, On Writing Well 9 (2006).

[102] The Sayings of Dorothy Parker (1992).

[103] See Lawrence Toppman, Maya Angelou: The Serene Spirit of a Survivor, in Jeffrey M. Elliot, Conversations With Maya Angelou 140, 145 (1989).

Chapter 4

SIMPLICITY

Make everything as simple as possible, but not simpler.
Albert Einstein (1879–1955)[1]

§ 4.1   Introduction

The main objective in writing is to make yourself understood.[2] Simple, everyday words are more likely to convey meaning than unusual and pretentious ones, and more likely to sound sincere. "If [people] would only say what they have to say in plain terms," quipped Samuel Taylor Coleridge, "how much more eloquent they would be!"[3] Plato knew that as well: "beauty of style and harmony and grace and good rhythm depend on simplicity."[4]

Even in poetry, where readers expect luxuriant verbiage, poignant emotion can be evoked with simplicity. A. E. Housman saluted soldiers who died in war almost wholly in one-syllable words:

> Here dead we lie / Because we did not choose
> To live and shame the land / From which we sprung.
> Life, to be sure, / Is nothing much to lose,
> But young men think it is, / And we were young.[5]

"It is quite possible," said Arthur Schopenhauer, "to be at once simple and sublime."[6] "[E]very really great writer tries to express his thoughts as purely, clearly, definitely, and shortly as possible. Simplicity has always been held to be a mark of truth; it is also a mark of genius."[7]

---

[1]   This famous Einstein quote may be a paraphrase of a more complex statement. See On the Method of Theoretical Physics 10 (1933) ("it can scarcely be denied that the supreme goal of all theory is to make the irreducible basic elements as simple and as few as possible without having to surrender the adequate representation of a single datum of experience."). See Alice Calaprice, The Ultimate Quotable Einstein 384–85 (2011).

[2]   John Dryden, Preface to Fables, Ancient and Modern (1700).

[3]   On Style [1810], in Lane Cooper (ed.), The Art of the Writer 180 (1952).

[4]   The Republic, Book III.

[5]   More Poems, XXXVI, in The Collected Poems of A. E. Housman (1940).

[6]   On style [1851], in Lane Cooper (ed.), The Art of the Writer 229 (1952).

[7]   Id. at 223.

A good writer can use simple, concise, understandable language, even if writing about the theory of relativity. Einstein agreed: "All my life I have been a friend of well-chosen, sober words and of concise presentation. Pompous phrases and words give me goose bumps whether they deal with the theory of relativity or with anything else."[8]

The lawyer, more than other professionals, frequently ignores this rule. It is a mistake, however, to assume that important legal discussions must take place in a boring, long-winded, jargon-laden style. The fear of appearing inappropriately colloquial has resulted in equally inappropriate dullness.[9] Abstract legal issues can be treated with lively, concrete, simple words, as when Holmes compared negligent and intentional torts: "even a dog distinguishes between being stumbled over and being kicked."[10]

Achieving a simple style is no simple matter. You can only say something simply and clearly if you understand it well. Clarity of thought, especially about complicated matters, takes hard mental labor. Do not start writing without first expending the effort necessary to understand the principles you are trying to explain and their application to the problem. The ponderous and abstract words and phrases that we use when our thinking is unclear may seem profound. But the reader who looks below the surface will discover that the water is murky not because it is deep but because it is muddy.[11]

Some legal writers deliberately employ opaque jargon under the delusion that their ideas will seem more learned if cloaked in obscure and pretentious prose. But ostentatiously displaying vocabulary sacrifices clarity, emphasis, and conviction. Of all vanities, this is surely one of the most self-defeating. Ignoring this admonition, one constitutional scholar dared to open a book with the following paragraph:

> From time to time with varying tempo the call goes around to "get government out of business" . . . . Probably no problem of such political and economic proportions has suffered so much from anamorphosis and has been so constantly subjected to acetic enfilade. Before we can hope to decorticate the issue of its partisan and selfish aspects we must bring our

---

[8]   Alice Calaprice, The Ultimate Quotable Einstein 120 (2011).

[9]   David Mellinkoff, The Language of the Law 29 (1963).

[10]   The Common Law 3 (1881).

[11]   See § 7.2, Master Your Subject.

minds to orthoptic viewpoint of the political nature and function of government.[12]

Words or phrases that the reader does not understand are what Stuart Chase called "semantic blanks."[13] What comes through to him can only be something like this:

> Probably no problem of such political and economic proportions has suffered so much from blah-blah-blah-blah-blah and has been so constantly subjected to blah-blah-blah blah-blah-blah.

And the reader is left not only uninformed but resentful. Throwing words at him that he doesn't understand implies that he should be able to understand them. If he doesn't, his self-esteem is hurt. And a wounded reader—even if pinked only in his pride—is a resentful one. Heed Arthur Schopenhauer's advice and "use common words to say uncommon things."[14]

Studies of the readability of collective bargaining agreements showed that more than 90% were at a readability level of high school or college graduates.[15] Yet, at the time of the study, only 24% of American adults had completed high school or had some college education. Most of these agreements, therefore, were difficult for the average worker to understand. They were "above the danger line of reading difficulty."[16] Unless written in language that workers understand, these agreements may foment more grievances, disputes, and strikes than they prevent.

Simplicity of style has nothing to do with simplicity of the ideas presented. Never talk down to your reader—any reader, whether a bench of appellate judges or the least learned client. The reader who has difficulty comprehending pretentious jargon and technical phrases could probably grasp complex concepts if you explain them in plain English. If you cannot do so, you probably do not comprehend them yourself.

The issues discussed in this chapter may be encapsulated in the general principle of simplicity: "whatever is translatable in . . .

---

[12]   James Barclay Smith, Studies in the Adequacy of the Constitution 1 (1939).

[13]   The Tyranny of Words (1938).

[14]   On style [1851], in Lane Cooper (ed.), The Art of the Writer 226 (1952).

[15]   See Joseph Tiffin & Francis X. Walsh, Readability of Union-Management Agreements, 4 Personnel Psychology 327 (1951).

[16]   Robert Gunning, The Technique of Clear Writing 22 (1968).

simpler words of the same language, without loss of sense or dignity, is bad."[17]

§ 4.2   Use Short, Simple Words

George Orwell gave us the first rule for attaining simplicity: never use a long word when a short one will do.[18] This was also the advice of the Fowlers, who proposed additional rules to promote simplicity and other essential qualities of style: prefer the familiar to the far-fetched, the concrete to the abstract, the single word to the circumlocution, and the Saxon to the Romance.[19]

Legal language is known for its pedantry and mystification, and law students assume that legal writing is characterized by big, fancy words. There is an element of soundness in the notion. Legal writing is formal writing and should avoid colloquialisms and slang. But do not confuse formal with stuffy: a lawyer need not shun simple, everyday words and look for pompous polysyllables. Instead, "only use words that you're certain your reader will know and will understand without conscious thought."[20]

Below is a list of overused, pretentious, or stuffy words, along with their simple, familiar, short equivalents in parentheses.

abutting (next to)	alleviate (ease)
accomplish (do)	allocate (divide)
accord (give)	alter (change)
accordingly (so)	alternatively (or)
accurate (right)	ambit (scope)
acquiesce (agree)	ameliorate (improve)
acquire (get, buy)	amicable (friendly)
additional (extra)	anticipate (expect)
address (discuss)	antipathy (dislike)
adjustment (change)	apparent (clear)
advantageous (helpful)	application (use)
advert (refer, mention)	apportion (divide)
affluent (rich)	appreciable (many)
aggregate (total)	approximate(ly) (about)
albeit (although)	apprise (inform)

---

[17]   Samuel Taylor Coleridge, Bibliographia Literaria 147 (1864).

[18]   Politics and the English Language (1946).

[19]   H.W. Fowler & F.G. Fowler, The King's English 1 (1908). See also Herbert Spencer, The Philosophy of Style (1884).

[20]   Ian Gallacher, Legal Communication and Research: Lawyering Skills for the Twenty-First Century 131 (2015).

ascertain (make sure, determine)

as per (in accordance with)

assent (agree)

assimilate (absorb)

assist (help)

attain (reach, gain)

attempt (try)

attributable to (because of)

authorize (let, allow)

automobile (car)

aver (claim)

belated (late)

beneficial (helpful)

bestow (give)

cease (stop)

cognizant (aware)

commence (begin, start)

commitment (promise)

compensate (pay)

complete (finish)

comprise (form)

conceal (hide)

concerning (about)

conjecture (guess)

consequence (result)

consequently (so)

consolidate (combine)

constitute (make up)

consummate (bring about, complete)

contain (have)

contemplate (plan, intend)

convene (meet)

counterfeit (false)

currently (now)

decease (die)

deed (action)

deem (consider)

demise (death, collapse)

demonstrate (show)

demur (object)

depart (leave)

deplete (empty)

desirous (want, wish)

desire (want, wish)

designate (appoint, name)

desist (stop)

deteriorate (get worse)

detrimental (harmful)

disburse (pay)

discontinue (stop)

donate (give)

dwell (live)

dwelling (house)

effectuate (bring about, carry out)

eliminate (remove, strike out)

elucidate (clarify, explain)

employ (use, hire)

employment (work)

encounter (meet)

encumbrance (burden)

endeavor (try)

endorsement (support)

engender (cause)

enjoin (order)

ensue (follow)

envisage (foresee)

enumerate (list)

equitable (fair)

erroneous (wrong)

eschew (avoid)

evince (show)

excluding (except)

exclusively (only)

execute (sign)

exhibit (show)

expedite (hasten, hurry)

expeditious (fast)

expend (spend)

expenditure (cost, expense)

expertise (ability)

expiration (end)

explicate (explain, clarify)

extend (offer)

facilitate (make easy, help)

feasible (possible)

finalize (complete, finish, end)

firstly (first)

foregoing (previously mentioned)

forthwith (promptly)

frequently (often)

fundamental (basic)

furnish (give)

furthermore (further)

henceforth (from now on)

hitherto (before)

implement (carry out)

inasmuch as (because)

indebtedness (debt)

indemnify (repay)

in case (if)

inception (start)

indicate (show)

indication (sign)

individual (person)

inform (tell)

ingenious (clever)

inimical (harmful)

initiate (begin, start)

injunction (order)

in lieu of (instead of)

innocuous (harmless)

inquire (ask)

inquisitive (curious)

instant (this)

instanter (immediately)

institute (begin)

interrogate (question)

intimate (imply)

locality (place)

location (place)

locate (find)

magnitude (size)

maintain (keep, continue)

manner (way)

maximum (most)

minimum (least)

modify, modification (change)

monies (money)

multiple (many)

municipality (city, town)

necessitate (require)

nevertheless (but, yet)

notification (notice)

notify (inform, tell)

notwithstanding (despite)

numerous (many)

objective (aim, goal)

observe (see)

obtain (get)

occasion (cause)

occupation (job)

occur (happen)

oftentimes (often)

operate (run)

opine (say)

optimal (best)

originate (start)

particulars (details)

perforation (hole)

perform (do)

permit (allow, let)

pertain (refer)

peruse (read)

portion (part)

possess (have)

pray (request)

preclude (prevent)

precursor (forerunner)

predisposition (tendency)

presently (soon)

preserve (keep, maintain)

principal (main)

prior to (before, earlier)

proceed (go)

procure (get, obtain)

profound (deep)

proliferate (spread)

prophylactic (preventative)

proscribe (forbid)
provide (give)
purchase (buy)
purported (claimed)
pursuant to (under)
recollect (remember)
regarding (about)
relocate (move)
remain (stay)
remainder (rest)
remuneration (wages, salary, pay)
render (make, give)
represent (is, are)
request (ask)
require (need)
requisite (needed)
reside (live)
respecting (about)
retain (keep)
sans (without)
save (except)
scrutinize (examine)
skepticism (doubt)
secure (get, obtain)
selection (choice)

signify (mean)
solely (only)
solicit (request)
state (say, tell)
style (name)
subsequent(ly) (after, next)
substantiate (prove)sufficient (enough)
summon (call)
surmise (guess)
terminate, termination (end)
transmit (send)
transpire (happen)
unbeknownst (unknown)
unto (to)
upon (on)
utilize, utilization (use)
vacuous (empty)
validate (confirm)
variation (change)
vendor (seller)
verify, verification (check)
vessel (ship)
visualize (imagine)
whereas (because, since)
whilst (while)

The phrases below are also stuffy:

afford an opportunity (allow)
experience has taught that [omit]
further affiant sayeth not [omit]
in order to insure (to make sure)
in process of preparation (being prepared)
is predicated on the assumption (assumes)
raise the question (ask)
the case at bar (this case, here)
the instant case (this case, here)
with a minimum of delay (as soon as possible)

None of the formal expressions listed is wrong. At times, for one reason or another, the simpler term will not serve, and the formal polysyllable will fit perfectly.

You must search obsessively for the right shade of meaning. But if you fall into the habit of always choosing the formal, without reason and without thinking, your style will become that much more ponderous. Even when a simple word is at hand, some writers pass it by to reach for a grander one. They reject *see* and choose *visualize* or *envisage*. They reject *use* in favor of *utilize* or *utilization*. When the only word that comes to mind is too short for their fancy, they make a big word out of it by brute force. Thus *analysis* becomes *analyzation*. You should adopt the opposite default rule: only use a fancy word if a simpler one won't do.

Devotees of the turgid style favor -*wise* almost as much as -*ize*. *Taxwise* has a certain usefulness, but a speaker should be just too wised up to say, as Senator Birch Bayh said in 1975, that "energywise, economywise and environmentalwise, we have become obsessed with the problems." This is a maladroit way of saying "we have become obsessed with the problems of energy, the economy, and the environment." Why add a *wise* to the word? Moreover, using so many words that sound alike tends to make your style dull and monotonous. Yet politicians don't learn: in the 2016 presidential debate, Donald Trump quipped, "the inner cities of our country . . . are a disaster educationwise, jobwise, safetywise, in every way possible." He might as well have concluded, "in every wise possible."

Cousins to the words ending in -*ise* and -*wise* are those ending in -*ive* such as promotive, supportive, and eradicative. The chair of a presidential election campaign said that a cabinet ought to be composed of people who are qualified, "but who are totally supportive of the President." "Who support the President" would be simpler. But simplicity is exactly the quality that people who issue such statements do not want; they want to sound pontifical.

Yet, as Ernest Weekley said, "[t]he key to an effective style . . . is simplicity. Most of the bad writing that prevails today is due to the attempt to write 'well.' "[21]

When you were first exposed to legal writing, you were probably surprised by the amount of jargon. At first you likely despised it because these words stood between you and the message. You probably found them old fashioned, unnecessary, and pretentious, and empathized with Fred Rodell's rebuke: "the [legal] language . . . seems almost deliberately designed to confuse and muddle the ideas it purports to convey."[22] With time, however, and

---

[21]   Cruelty to Words 59 (1931).
[22]   Woe Unto You, Lawyers! 125 (1957).

much effort, you learned the words, accepted them, and eventually grew fond of them. It took you years to learn their meanings, and even longer to be able to use them with confidence. Now that you've mastered them, it seems only fair that you display your ability to "write like a lawyer." After all, you might think, this is what distinguishes legal writing from lay writing.

But you would be wrong. The principle of simplicity, said David Mellinkoff, requires that legal English coincide with everyday English, unless there is reason for a difference.[23] This is not a novel concept: Cicero said much the same 2,000 years ago.[24] Just as a self-respecting mathematician would not use 12/48 instead of 1/4 just to seem more erudite, says Bryan Garner, you should not say *obtund* when the verbs *dull* and *blunt* come more readily to mind.[25] A touch of professional humility will go a long way in gaining simplicity.

§ 4.3   Avoid Jargon When Writing for Laypersons

When writing to the legal community, as in an office memorandum or a brief, technical terms are appropriate and necessary to communicate an idea precisely and efficiently. Every profession, science, or trade has its own terms of art, a shorthand to describe concepts that do not exist outside the specialized field and for which there is no name in ordinary English.

Lawyers cannot operate adequately without terms like estoppel, laches, deposition, impleader, injunction, misdemeanor, plaintiff. Or ordinary words appropriated by the law, like relevance, venue, consideration, service. Or lingo like *Daubert* motion, Warren Court, cert. Or acronyms like UCC, TRO, JNOV. A lawyer can import a complex argument just by mentioning a case (*Erie*), a judge (Scalia), or a Rule (12(b)(6)).

You would invite ambiguity and wordiness and irritate the reader if you substituted these useful shorthands with a layperson's English explanation. "Not to use a technical word," said E. L. Piesse, "would be an affectation as noticeable as the over-frequent use of such words where they are not needed."[26]

---

[23]   The Language of the Law vii (1963).

[24]   Cicero [106 BC—43 BC], De Oratore 1.3.12 (55 BC). See also John Franklin Genung, The Working Principles of Rhetoric 110–11 (1900).

[25]   Garner on Language 516 (2009).

[26]   The Elements of Drafting 46 (1987) (updated by J. K. Aitken).

Always consider your audience, however. A technical term that may be the most precise way of expressing a thought to another member of the profession may be lost on a layperson. Sometimes it seems that legal English and English are not the same language. The reader, like the customer, is always right. If the person for whom you are writing cannot understand the message, you have not written clearly. The fact that your words would be clear to someone else is irrelevant. Like an inside joke, a technical term may be offensive to outsiders. So, avoid technical words when writing for laypersons, as in a letter to a client.

If there is no lay term to convey complex and abstract concepts, like proximate cause or issue preclusion, you may use essential technical terms, if explained in plain English. But the unnecessary ones should be avoided, and so should the hereinbefores, hereinafters and theretofores, the saids and the aforesaids, the whomsoevers and the whereases. To anyone with an ear for prose all these polysyllables are dull, heavy, and unnecessary sounds. Many of them have found their way into ordinary English by way of legal instruments—we have contaminated the entire language. Even in strictly professional writing, their use could profitably be reduced. Law students may be impressed with them because they seem professional, and may take them up on the innocent assumption that this is the way lawyers are expected to write. It's not.

Certain Latin terms are still used in formal writing, more by lawyers than by others. At least in writing to lay people, it is better to translate or avoid them:

a fortiori	duces tecum	in re
a priori	ejusdem generis	in rem
ab initio	et al	infra
actus reus	ex parte	inter alia
ad hominem	ex post facto	in toto
ad litem	ex rel	intra vires
amicus curiae	forum non conveniens	ipso facto
animus	idem	lex fori
arguendo	imprimatur	lex loci
contra	in camera	mutatis mutandis
de jure	in forma pauperis	nexus
de minimis	in limine	nolo contendere
de novo	in loco parentis	non sequitur
dicta	in personam	nunc pro tunc

per annum	qua	sua sponte
per diem	quasi	sub judice
post mortem	quasi in rem	sui generis
prima facie	quorum	supra
pro hac vice	ratio decidendi	ultra vires
pro rata	res gestae	vel non
pro se	seriatim	verbatim
pro tempore	sine qua non	

The Latin abbreviations *i.e.* and *e.g.* are also better translated into English: *that is* and *for example*.

Some Latin terms, however, have entered ordinary English, and may be used with educated readers without explanation:

ad hoc	de facto	pro bono
affidavit	modus operandi	quid pro quo
alias	per capita	status quo
alibi	per se	versus
bona fide		

When using Latin or other foreign words or phrases that your reader may not understand, give the definition. But do it unobtrusively, not in a way that implies, "I know you are not well enough educated to translate this, so I'll do it for you." If you use the term *in pari materia*, for example, do not say, "this is a Latin term meaning 'on the same subject matter.'" You can be less obvious by running the definition in with the use of the term:

> Statutes related to the same subject matter (*in pari materia*) are to be construed together.

Certain legal concepts in Latin have no English equivalents:

certiorari	per stirpes	respondeat superior
habeas corpus	qui tam	scienter
lis pendens	quo warranto	scintilla
mandamus	remittitur	stare decisis
mens rea	res ipsa loquitur	subpoena
parens patriae	res judicata	supersedeas

These are terms of art of the legal profession. In writing to laypeople, they may be used but must be explained.

Explaining legal concepts to laypeople can be difficult, whether the shorthand label is a Latin term like res ipsa loquitur or an English one like comparative negligence. But the effort must be made.

§ 4.4   Avoid Gobbledygook

The stock caricature of the lawyer is a person whose every sentence is loaded with legalistic terms. In Carl Sandburg's poem, "The Lawyers Know Too Much," "the higgling lawyers" are guilty of

> Too many slippery ifs and buts and howevers,
> Too much hereinbefore provided whereas[27]

Groucho Marx captured the silliness of law talk in a letter to his lawyer:

> Gentlemen?
> In re yours of the 5th inst., yours to hand and beg to rep., brackets, that we have gone over the ground carefully and we seem to believe, i.e., to wit, e.g., in lieu, that, despite all our precautionary measures which have been involved, we seem to believe that it is hardly necessary for us to proceed unless we receive an ipso facto that is not negligible at this moment, quotes, unquotes, and quotes.
> Hoping this finds you, I beg to remain, as of June 9, cordially yours.
> Regards.[28]

We need not go so far as to say that a lawyer should not sound like a lawyer, but at least we should try not to sound like its stereotype. And you should never fall into David Pratt's trap: "jargon allows us to camouflage intellectual poverty with verbal extravagance."[29]

Gobbledygook was coined by former Representative Maury Maverick to describe "talk or writing which is long, pompous, vague, involved, usually with Latinized words."[30] The term describes a style adopted by government officials more interested in making a statement than in making things happen. It flourishes in law offices too, and includes legalese (legaldygook) and bureaucratese.

Many have satirized this style. A. P. Herbert, exasperated by governmental jargon, governmentalized Lord Nelson's immortal words, "England expects every man to do his duty," as follows:

> England anticipates that, as regards the current emergency, personnel will face up to the issues, and exercise appropriately the functions allocated to their respective occupational groups.

---

[27] Smoke and Steel 85 (1920).

[28] Animal Crackers (1930). See https://www.youtube.com/watch?v=ZuVe3leQQgE.

[29] Dictionary of Quotations in Communications 118 (Lilless McPherson Shilling & Linda K. Fuller, eds. 1977).

[30] The Case Against Gobbledygook, N.Y. Times Magazine, May 21, 1944, at 11.

But Herbert was too good a writer to be able to do full justice to this style, even when he tried. No true practitioner of gobbledygook would allow even so mildly colloquial a phrase as "face up to."

"The language of the law," said Learned Hand, "must not be foreign to the ears of those who are to obey it."[31] The layperson's frustration in trying to understand government regulations or insurance policies has led to protests.[32] In 1978, President Carter ordered that regulations of federal agencies be "written in plain English . . . understandable to those who must comply" with them.[33] In the same year, New York enacted a "plain language law" requiring residential leases and consumer agreements to be written in "non-technical language and in a clear and coherent manner using words with common and everyday meanings."[34] Several states and countries adopted plain legal English laws in the eighties and nineties, increasing readability and reducing verbosity in legal writing.[35]

Recently, the federal rules of appellate procedure (1998), criminal procedure (2002), civil procedure (2007), and evidence (2011) were restyled to make them simpler and clearer without changing their meaning.[36] But there's still much to do.

If we are to avoid gobbledygook, we must recognize its vices:

(1)   It uses round-about rather than direct language;

(2)   It prefers pompous or pretentious to simple expressions;

(3)   It makes excessive use of nouns;

(4)   It has a penchant for compound prepositional phrases;

---

[31]   Is There a Common Will?, 34 Comm. L. League J. 305, 308 (1929).

[32]   See, e.g., Ralph Nader, Gobbledygook, Ladies' Home Journal, Sept. 1977, at 68.

[33]   Exec. Order No. 12044, 43 Fed. Reg. 12661 (1978) (Rescinded by President Ronald Reagan). Presidents Clinton and Obama issued similar plain English enactments.

[34]   N.Y. Gen. Oblig. § 5–702 (2017).

[35]   See Reed Dickerson, The Fundamentals of Legal Drafting 156–81 (1986); Joseph Kimble, Lifting the Fog of Legalese: Essays on Plain Language (2006); id., Writing for Dollars, Writing to Please: The Case for Plain English in Business, Government, and Law (2012).

[36]   See generally Bryan Garner, Guidelines for Drafting and Editing Court Rules (2004) and Joseph Kimble, Seeing Through Legalese: More Essays on Plain Language (2017). See also Lisa Eichhorn, Clarity and the Federal Rules of Civil Procedure: A Lesson from the Style Project, 5 J. ALWD 1 (2008) ("At the stroke of midnight on December 1, 2007, the Federal Rules of Civil Procedure both changed completely and did not change at all.")

(5) It uses passive instead of active voice;

(6) It uses general and abstract rather than specific and concrete nouns.

(7) It is vague.[37]

§ 4.5   Don't Overuse Nouns

You can simplify and strengthen your style by using fewer nouns and more verbs.

There has been a complete absence of any attempt at reconciliation of differences between the parties.	The parties never tried to reconcile their differences.
We inaugurated the practice of making cross-indexes to the files.	We started cross-indexing the files.
For many years prior to my retirement.	For many years before I retired.

Sometimes the density of nouns is too great to allow any meaning to come through.

> In *Durnherr*, the lack of a creditor-beneficiary existence was the detriment to recovery.

Nominalization is the practice of creating a noun out of a verb, adjective, or adverb. The noun is often formed by adding the following suffixes to the verb: *-al, -ance, -ence, -ancy, -ency, -ant, -ent, -er, -ing, -ism, -ization, -ment, -ness, -sion, -tion, -ty*. Thus "capitalize" becomes "capitalization," "consider" becomes "give consideration to," and "this implies" becomes "the implication is."

Nominalization often results in overstuffed phrases consisting of a weak (non-action) verb, a preposition, and a noun, when a verb alone would suffice.

The verb *to be* frequently serves as the weak verb culprit. Note below how a single action verb can replace each phrase:

be a benefit to (benefit)	be aware of (know)
be able to (can, may)	be benefited by (benefit from)
be abusive of (abuse)	be binding upon (bind)
be a failure (fail)	be capable of (can)
be applicable to (apply to)	be dependent on (depend)
be authorized to (may)	be derived from (derive from)

---

[37] See §§ 3.3, Eliminate Wordy and Useless Expressions; 4.3, Avoid Jargon; 4.5; Don't Overuse Nouns; 5.13, Compound Prepositions Are Often Vague; 6.5, The Passive Voice is Weak; 6.7, Use Specific and Concrete Rather than General and Abstract Words.

be desirous of (want)
be determinative of (determine)
be dispositive of (dispose)
be empowered to (may)
be entitled to (may)
be in accordance with (conform)
be in agreement (agree)
be in attendance (attend)
be in compliance with (comply)
be in conformity with (conform)
be indicative of (indicate)
be in dispute (dispute)
be in existence (exist)
be influential on (influence)
be in need of (need)

be in opposition to (oppose)
be in possession of (possess)
be in receipt of (receive)
be in violation of (violate)
be lacking (lack)
be of help to (help)
be of interest to (interest)
be possessed of (possess)
be probative of (prove)
be required to (must)
be suitable (suit)
be supportive of (support)
be unable to (cannot, may not)
be violative of (violate)
be wasteful (waste)

Nondescript verbs, such as *give, get, have,* and *make,* do not effectively convey action either, and are no better than nouns.

give a report (report)
give authorization (authorize)
give consideration to (consider)
give offense (offend)
give permission (permit)
give testimony (testify)
give warning (warn)
have a meeting (meet)
have a negative impact (hurt)
have an influence on (influence)
have a preference for (prefer)
have control (control)
have knowledge of (know)
have the ability to (can)
have the appearance of (appears)
have the capacity for (can)
have the desire to (want)
have the intention to (intend)
have the need of (need)
have the obligation to (must)
have the opportunity to (can)
have the option of (may)

make accommodation (accommodate)
make a decision (decide)
make a payment (pay)
make a promise (promise)
make a recommendation (recommend)
make a reference (refer)
make a statement (state)
make a suggestion (suggest)
make an adjustment (adjust)
make an argument (argue)
make an appearance (appear)
make an application (apply)
make an assessment (assess)
make an assumption (assume)
make an attempt (try)
make an inquiry (inquire, ask)
make an objection (object)
make an observation (observe)
make provision for (provide)
make reference to (refer to)
make use of (use)

Only strong action verbs can bring prose to life.[38] Nominalization is created with any other dull verb:

bear a resemblance (resemble)	exhibit a tendency (tend)
bring a lawsuit (sue)	exhibit resistance to (resist)
cause damage (damage)	file a lawsuit (sue)
cause harm (harm)	file a motion (move)
conduct an investigation of (investigate)	hold a meeting (meet)
come into conflict (conflict)	interpose an objection (object)
conduct an analysis of (analyze)	meet approval (approve)
conduct an examination of (examine)	offer a suggestion (suggest)
deliver a lecture (lecture)	place emphasis (emphasize)
demonstrate deference (defer)	provide a description (describe)
effect service of process (serve)	provide an explanation (explain)
enter into a contract (contract)	provide assistance (assist, help)
enter into an agreement (agree)	provide evidence (prove)
provide guidance (guide)	take action (act)
reach a decision (decide)	take into consideration (consider)
reach a resolution (resolve)	take notice (notice)
reach an agreement (agree)	the design of (design)
render advice (advise)	the use of (use)
submit an application (apply)	write a report (report)

Nominalization robs the sentence of its key verb by converting it to a noun, burying the action and draining the sentence of its vitality: "[p]ersons and what they do, things and what is done to them, are put in the background."[39] Nominalization tends to produce longer sentences and more abstract ideas. Your style becomes static, indirect, and impersonal, and your writing, dull and difficult to read. Helen Sword calls them "zombie nouns" because they "cannibalize active verbs, suck the lifeblood from adjectives and substitute abstract entities for human beings."[40]

Prefer action verbs over zombie nouns made out of buried verbs—your text will be easier to read and more concise, concrete, and vigorous.

Confirmation of the offer was obtained.	The offer was confirmed.
Reversal of the judgment was handed down.	The judgment was reversed.

---

[38]   See § 6.4, Use Action Verbs.

[39]   H.W. Fowler, A Dictionary of Modern English Usage 5 (2d ed. 1965).

[40]   Zombie Nouns, The N.Y. Times Opinionator Blog, July 23, 2012.

The compilation of the statistics was done last year.	The statistics were compiled last year.
The judge made a recommendation for the parties to reach a settlement.	The judge recommended that the parties settle.
The handling of the leaks should have been conducted with greater transparency.	They should have handled the leaks more transparently.
Ecosystem destabilization can be the consequence of invasion.	Invasion can destabilize ecosystems.
An analysis of the blood was conducted.	The lab analyzed the blood.

Some of the examples above could be further improved by using the active voice.[41]

The noun addict often uses a noun when a simple adjective or adverb will do.

in a negligent manner (negligently)	of an indefinite nature (indefinite)
in height (high)	of an unusual kind (unusual)
in length (long)	of great importance (important)
in size (big)	

Even two-letter prepositions can be encumbered with nouns.

as a means of (to)	in order to (to)
by means of (by)	in the event that (if)
by virtue of (by)	no later than (by)
for the purpose of (to)	provided that (if)
in an effort to (to)	so as to (to)
in case of (if)	subject to (if)

Using too many nouns produces a heavy style, and may introduce ambiguity, grammatical errors, and semantic blunders in your prose:

> The secret of the attainment of a cultivated literary style is difficult and elusive. The observation of the style of those judges endowed with a gift of literary expression may be a helpful suggestion.

"The secret" is "difficult"? "The observation" may be a "suggestion"? You obtain a correct grammatical structure, simplicity, and vigor by cutting out nouns:

> A cultivated style is an elusive goal, difficult to attain. It helps to observe the style of judges who have the gift of literary expression.

---

[41]   See §§ 3.8, The Passive Voice is Verbose; 5.11, The Passive Voice May Be Ambiguous; 6.5, The Passive Voice is Weak.

Nominalization is also wordy and for that reason alone should be avoided.[42]

§ 4.6   Prefer Concrete to Fuzzy Nouns; Avoid Vogue Words

Vogue words include both neologisms and old words with new meanings that suddenly become trendy. They are used by those who want to show they are "in the know." Because they are new, they have not acquired precise meaning. "Ready acceptance of vogue words," said H. W. Fowler, "seems to some people the sign of an alert mind; to others it stands for the herd instinct and lack of individuality."[43] Some of these vogue words catch on precisely because they are vague, so they have an appeal for the lazy and fuzzy-minded writer.

Basis is a favorite. Its literal meaning is a base or foundation, but people addicted to the word often forget it, and speak of a "fragmentary basis" or a "fleeting basis." A New Jersey prosecutor reported that the number of cases pending "cry out for a third judge to sit in [this] County on a rotating basis between the criminal and the civil side." But who wants a dizzy judge?

Writers use *basis* to avoid simple words, but in search of false elegance they reach awkward and unnecessary verbiage. With nothing to prove, experienced writers use simple, concise wording.

The plant is working on a 24-hour basis.	The plant is working 24 hours a day.
These arrangements are on a temporary basis.	These arrangements are temporary.
We are located here on a temporary basis.	We are here temporarily.
Damages are assessed on a case-by-case basis.	Damages are assessed case by case.
The company used the same vendor on a regular basis.	The company regularly used the same vendor.

Sometimes it is impossible to tell just what the phrase means.

We are trying to put the organization on a legal basis.

---

[42]   See § 3.3, Eliminate Wordy and Useless Expressions.

[43]   H.W. Fowler, A Dictionary of Modern English Usage 684 (2d ed. 1965). See also Garner's Modern English Usage 949–50 (2016).

Based on is equally woolly. Moreover, it is sometimes used in a way that is not only unclear, but also ungrammatical.

> Based on the preceding two decisions, it is apparent that the courts have been unable to decide whether the law intended to make this practice illegal.

Based on should read *from*.

Low forms of gobbledygook like *case* and *instance* are often mere stuffing.[44]

This is the only instance of a pro-bitcoin holding in Ohio.	This is Ohio's only pro-bitcoin holding.
The verdicts were for large amounts in most instances.	Most of the verdicts were for large amounts.

Position is often empty.

Our position will be more favorable.	We will be better off.
Our position in regard to the claim for damages is that this should	We think that the claim for damages should

So is *situation*.

We would like to be informed in regard to the present situation.	Please keep us informed.
The situation in regard to revenues is alarming.	The revenue shortage is alarming.

Breakdown (statistical, not mental) is popular with certain writers who think it sounds more scientific than "division" or "classification." When used in referring to things that can actually break down, either mentally or physically, the word is not only pretentious and insensitive but inept:

> The breakdown of mental patients into psychotic and nonpsychotic
> The breakdown of motors according to
> A population broken down by gender

Ceiling is used to mean maximum or limit. While not objectionable, frequent repetition may lead a writer to forget that it is a metaphor and to speak of "increasing" the ceiling. One may raise or lower a ceiling, but "increasing" gives no clear picture of the operation being described.

---

[44] See § 2.8, Words to Watch (discussing *aspect, case, factor, involve,* and *practically*).

Some people have become so accustomed to using the word *level* that they are incapable of saying that something was done locally, nationally, or throughout the state; it must always be "on the local level," "on the national level," or "on the state level."

Other stuffed-shirt words include:

conflate	involve	reinvent
constructive	matrix	resonate
dialectic	meaningful	rubric
dialogue (as verb)	mode	scenario
dimension	myriad	streamline
disconnect (as noun)	output	sustainability
empower	overall (for complete, total)	synergy
eschew	paradigm	upside
ethos	parameter	ubiquitous
facilitator	plethora	unpack (for explain)
foment	postmodern	validation
framework	proactive	viable (for feasible, practical)
holistic	proposition (for plan, proposal)	
impact		vis-à-vis
implement (as verb)	quantum	wellness
interface	reaction (for impression, opinion)	

Most of these words are vogue in some senses and acceptable in others. This is especially true of buzzwords borrowed from science, technology, or academia.

The vogue words of today are the faddish clichés of tomorrow, although some of them endure. Vogue words allure people who think them fashionable terms for the newest concepts but fail to recognize that overuse quickly robs them of the freshness they might have once had.[45]

§ 4.7   Avoid Outmoded Wording

A writer should develop an ear for wording. Words that are too new to be standard are beneath the dignity of formal prose; those that are too old are archaic, and their use is pretentious. In reading old cases one may pick up certain words and phrases and fail to notice that they are no longer in use. Examples of archaisms include:

---

[45]   See § 6.10, Avoid Clichés and Platitudes.

albeit	inasmuch	to wit
behoove	monies	unto
betoken	oft times	verily
erstwhile	partake	viz.
foregoing	peruse	whence
forthwith	save (for except)	whensoever
henceforth	thence	whilst
hitherto	thenceforth	witnesseth

Writing that echoes the literary fashions of a past age sounds insincere. But the writer is usually not insincere, just a bit quaint.

If you do not want to be tacky, avoid words starting with *here-*, *there-*, and *where-*, and not ending there:

hereafter	thereabout	whereas
herebefore	thereafter	whereat
hereby	thereat	whereby
herein	therefor	wherefore
hereinabove	therefrom	wherein
hereinafter	therein	whereof
hereinbefore	thereof	whereon
hereof	thereon	whereupon
hereto	thereout	wheresoever
heretofore	thereover	wherewith
hereunder	therethrough	
hereunto	thereto	
herewith	theretofore	
	thereunder	
	thereunto	
	therewith	

They are usually ambiguous and always unnecessarily pompous legalism.

§ 4.8   Avoid Euphemism and Genteelism

Writers sometimes avoid the simple, direct term for fear it is too blunt. Tact may require using language that is less direct and less precise, so we use a euphemism. This is justified when done to avoid vulgarity, but not when done to evade facing stark reality. Unpleasant statements of facts may be set forth dispassionately, and not softened merely to save emotional distress. And euphemism is never acceptable if the objective is to deceive the reader.

An area for special care involves choice of words to use to refer to people who face challenges. Concern for human dignity has, throughout history, led to changes in what is considered appropriate terminology for such situations. We periodically generate new terms—what might be called sociological euphemisms, and are sometimes called political correctness.

The jobless are now unemployed; illegal aliens are undocumented immigrants; the poor are people with low income or the underclass. The former insane asylum was an improvement on the old lunatic asylum, and is now called mental hospital, psychiatric hospital, or merely hospital. These buildings house not inmates and guards, but patients and attendants.

An example of this evolution involves words historically used to address mental disability. Terms like idiot, imbecile, moron, lunatic, retarded, insane, and feeble-minded were accepted and widely used as terms of art in society and in old decisions.[46] As these terms became pejorative, they were replaced by mentally retarded, then handicapped, both of which in turn became pejorative and were replaced with special needs, mentally disabled, developmentally disabled, and intellectually or cognitively impaired or challenged.

Avoid defining a person by his or her disability, as in "she *is* disabled" or "she *is* a disabled person." Instead, use "people-first language": "she is a person *with* a disability." The word "disabled" itself may eventually become disfavored and differently-abled may slowly take its place, although it still sounds artificial.

Or one may shift the attention to those without disability, calling them temporarily able-bodied. The shift in terminology reflects the view that disability is created not from an impairment of the person but from barriers imposed by a discriminatory environment that unfairly favors the able-bodied. This view of disability is known as the social model of disability, as opposed to the now outdated medical model of disability that focused only on the person's medical deficits.[47]

---

[46] See Atkins v. Virginia, 536 U.S. 304 (2002) (Scalia, J. dissenting) (discussing the eighteenth century common law distinction between idiots, imbeciles, and lunatics); Penry v. Lynaugh, 492 U.S. 302 (1989) (O'Connor, J.) (same). See also Cleburne v. Cleburne Living Center, 473 U.S. 432 (1985) (challenging zoning ordinance referring to people with intellectual disabilities as "feeble minded.").

[47] Arlene S. Kanter, The Law: What's Disability Studies Got To Do With It or An Introduction to Disability Legal Studies, 42 Colum. Hum. Rts. L. Rev. 403 (2011).

Some suggest that you consult members of the relevant community to determine how they prefer to be addressed. This is often poor advice. One member does not speak for the entire community. It is your responsibility to research the appropriate terminology.

Language tracks progress in thinking. The progression from the older and cruder to the more refined ways of thinking and therefore of talking is reflected in the progression of usage. Once a change is generally accepted, the new word is no longer a euphemism, but neutral, until it is overworked and abused, becomes objectionable, then offensive, and in need of its own euphemism. The process of refining the language goes on—dropping words that have absorbed negative meaning and creating fresh replacements—until we address the real issues behind the words and refine ourselves.

Genteelism refers to euphemisms taken to an extreme in a misguided effort to avoid offense. Euphemism was carried to an extreme in the reign of Queen Victoria, when all legs were limbs (even chicken legs), breasts were bosoms, and only horses sweated (men perspired and young ladies got all glowy). All these are now outmoded genteelisms.

But there are still people for whom the homely incidents of life are too coarse to mention in polite company. Genteelism rejects the ordinary word that first comes to mind and substitutes a synonym that is thought to be "less soiled by the lips of the common herd, less familiar, less plebeian, less vulgar, less improper."[48] In their vocabulary, stink becomes smell and smell becomes odor. They do not take a job; they accept a position. The truly genteel never help, ask, or want; they assist, inquire, and desire.[49] Man and woman are, for their taste, not elegant enough labels for members of the human species; they prefer gentleman and lady. It is easier to "let someone go" than it is to fire a single parent, and even easier to downsize. When they need to use the toilet, they look for a restroom. Even dignifying words like death and dying are too melancholy to be allowed. The kin of the committedly genteel therefore never die: their departed always pass away.

Genteelisms can be objectionable when they: (1) are roundabout ways of expressing the thought, taking more time to

---

[48]   H.W. Fowler, A Dictionary of Modern English Usage 222 (2d ed. 1965).

[49]   Id.

write and to read than the plain words for which they stand; (2) require the reader to translate the circumlocution into the direct meaning; (3) are ambiguous; or (4) cheat reality. By trying to "pretty up" the image, they blur or discolor it, sometimes with the objective of deceiving the reader.

But don't take this section's advice too far, cutting all niceties from your prose. A gruff tone does little to advance your cause. As your experience probably proves, you are more persuasive if your audience likes you. Be sensitive and avoid alienating your reader— walk the line between telling the truth plainly and conveying your message harshly.

§ 4.9   Prefer Saxon over Romance Words

Romance words are usually longer, more abstract, and more pretentious. Their frequent use may impart a ponderous tone to one's style. Saxon words (with Germanic origins) are usually shorter, their sounds sturdier, and their meanings more familiar.

After the Norman Conquest in the eleventh century, the Saxons were the conquered peasants. The Normans were the overlords, the refined class. Abstract and technical subjects were discussed by the ruling classes, who spoke Norman-French and read Latin.[50] The peasants talked of simple things, but their words endured.

Scholars, therefore, have advised to prefer the Saxon word to the Romance.[51] But many English words of Romance (Latin) origin are now just as ordinary as Saxon (Germanic) ones, and some are just as vigorous, like beef, bill, brave, bribe, face, fact, vote, and veto. Even the Fowlers did not take their own advice rigidly. They couched it in terms of proportion: "the writer whose percentage of Saxon words is high will generally be found to have fewer words that are out of the way, long, or abstract."[52] In a later work, H.W. Fowler was even more equivocal: "conscious deliberate Saxonism is folly, . . . the choice or rejection of particular words should depend not on their descent but on considerations of expressiveness, brevity, euphony or ease of handling."[53] So the general rule to

---

[50]   See § 3.6, Avoid Doublets and Triplets.

[51]   H.W. Fowler & F.G. Fowler, The King's English 1 (1908). See also Herbert Spencer, The Philosophy of Style 12–15 (1884).

[52]   H.W. Fowler & F.G. Fowler, The King's English 1 (1908).

[53]   H.W. Fowler, A Dictionary of Modern English Usage 537 (2d ed. 1965).

"prefer the simple or familiar to the more pretentious" does not always translate to "prefer the Saxon to the Romance."

Moreover, it is impractical to follow the rule to prefer Saxon over Romance words. Most people nowadays could not choose between commence and begin, cease and stop, assist and help, purchase and buy, render and make, by identifying the one as Romance (or Latin) and the other as Saxon (or Germanic).

This chapter focuses on simplicity, but simplicity is not the only aim in writing. When other ends are more important, Romance or other elaborate words may be appropriate. A long Romance word may serve for its sonorous or majestic effect, or for conveying an important emotion, or simply for the rhythm its syllables impart to a sentence. Lincoln's "four score and seven years ago" had better cadence than "eighty-seven years ago," even though it sounds affected (the longer phrase is just as Saxon as the other). The line between the felicitous and the overblown is so fine that only a writer with a good ear for the sound of words can make sensible choices. This inner ear can be developed by listening to how words sound, even though they are not intended to be spoken aloud.

Without the Norman Conquest and the Renaissance, English would be an almost monosyllabic language.[54] We are fortunate, therefore, to have words stemming from both Latin and Germanic roots. By choosing between them, our writing becomes precise, vibrant, and nuanced.

Otto Jespersen praised the richness of English synonyms derived from foreign influences: because Romance and Saxon words are not perfect synonyms, they allow a writer to express subtle shades of meaning. Juvenile is not the same as youthful, portion as share, miserable as wretched, edify as build, conceal as hide, felicity as happiness, solitary as lonely, aid as help, dress as clothe. The same thing happens with homicide, murder, and killing; magnitude, greatness, and size; masculine, manly, and virile; and feminine, womanly, and womanish. Although both legible and readable mean clear to read, legible also applies to handwriting while readable means that the text is worth reading. Sometimes the Romance word has a more limited, special, or precise sense than

---

[54]   See Otto Jespersen, Growth and Structure of the English Language 6 (1905); Ernest Weekley, Cruelty to Words 49 (1931).

the English: identical and same, science and knowledge, sentence and saying, occult and hidden.[55]

The wide array of synonyms in English also gives flexibility to obtain the most attractive rhythm to a sentence. "Intermingling Saxon words with Latin ones," says Bryan Garner, "gives language variety, texture, euphony, and vitality."[56] We can also get emphasis by a change of pace: we can enrobe the product of our cogitation in sonorous Latin polysyllables judiciously selected for their pontifical tone, and then clinch it with a short Germanic punch line.

With the infusion of European and Latin American immigrants in the United States, a revival of Romance words has made our language even richer and more international. In 2015, over 56 million United States residents identified themselves as Hispanic.[57] When you want to be more easily understood by Europeans, Latin Americans, and one-sixth of the U.S. population, follow the opposite advice: use words with Romance roots. But if you want to write sharp prose, choose Saxon wordstock.

§ 4.10 Should You Write the Way You Talk?

In urging lawyers not to sound pompous, we sometimes suggest that they would develop a more natural style if they would write as they talk. Within limits, you should follow this advice.

We write to make spoken words permanent. No matter how far the written text may depart from speech, it still maintains a voice.[58] Indeed, "prose is the literary evolution of conversation, as Poetry is the literary evolution of singing."[59] "Good writing," says Bryan Garner, "is simply speech heightened and polished."[60] It aims for the simplicity and buoyancy of good conversation: a conversational style.

One screenplay writer said, "I do everything in my power to make my writing not look like writing."[61] This advice is also applicable to legal writers. Before committing something to paper,

---

[55] Growth and Structure of the English Language 139–40 (1955).

[56] Garner on Language and Writing 515 (2009).

[57] https://www.census.gov/newsroom/press-releases/2016/cb16–107.html.

[58] John Franklin Genung, The Working Principles of Rhetoric 119 and 126–28 (1900).

[59] John Earle. English Prose 171 (1890).

[60] Legal Writing in Plain English 63 (2013).

[61] See Ben Yagoda, Elmore Leonard's Rogues' Gallery, N.Y. Times Magazine, Dec. 30, 1985, at 20.

query whether you'd ever speak it: see if it's simple, direct, unpretentious. If you would not say it out loud, don't write it. Read your prose aloud to see whether it says what you want it to say.[62] The written text is to be read, but also to be heard, if only by our inner ears.

Yet we cannot write exactly the way we talk: "those who write as they speak," said Buffon, "even though they may speak well, write badly."[63] In talking, we can repeat ourselves and use loosely organized, disjointed, and fragmentary phrases that would be intolerable in print. We also use other contrivances besides words. We use our voices for intonation, emphasis, pauses. We laugh, shout, whisper. We use our arms and hands to gesture; we use facial expressions; we lean forward and back or move about.

Speaking involves personal interaction between the parties. This is true not only of conversation, but also of addressing an audience: a good speaker is attuned to the audience, and they interact with one another. A speaker veers and tacks, responding to the listener's reactions. The sentences may be incomplete, long, and even rambling, with parenthetical interjections, but intonation enables listeners to follow without difficulty. A similar sentence in print, without the guiding voice, might be utterly confusing. Read a reporter's transcription of spoken English, and you will quickly see that no one would write that way.

A speaker can repeat himself and still achieve variety in expression by stressing a different word or phrase the second time or by varying the inflection or the tempo. Even the speaker who reads from a manuscript without departing from it projects personality through voice and body language.

The written page provides none of this help. Writing must make what impression it can on the reader without assistance from the writer's presence. As a one-way communication, a writer works with no opportunity to right the wayward reader's course. When we read in print a speech that we also heard delivered, we realize just how much personal presence contributed to the meaning. The most fiery and moving oratory often seems flat and pallid in writing. Yet nothing has changed; only the magnetic personality of the speaker is missing.

---

[62]   George Jacob Holyoake, Public Speaking and Debate 228 (1896).
[63]   Discours sur le Style [1753], in Lane Cooper (ed.), The Art of the Writer 149 (1952).

This difference explains why a dictated letter is likely to be a literary failure. A document intended to be absorbed through the eyes and not through the ears must be composed in its own way. It must have a style that is comprehensible without intonation (bold or italics are typically the device of those who try to imitate oral style in writing).[64] It must move smoothly and rapidly; the eye runs over the words at two or three times the normal talking speed. The speaker can pause or slow down to give an audience time to grasp or think through the point, or to feel it emotionally. But the writer has no control over the speed at which the reader's eyes move. All a writer can do is to use more punctuation and more words to phrase and perhaps rephrase the thought, so as to force the reader to give it the time it deserves.

Similarly, a speech that was written, and never tried out orally, is likely to sound stilted. As Charles James Fox put it, a speech that reads well is a bad one when spoken.[65] The inexperienced speaker who has carefully polished a speech through several rewritings may be surprised to find upon delivery that it does not sound right. The natural way of writing is not the natural way of speaking. Never undertake to prepare in writing something to be delivered orally without speaking it out loud: passages that look solid on the page often fall flat when spoken.

The best writing is not exactly like talk, but it seems to be.[66]

§ 4.11 Match Complexity to the Task

A lawyer must develop several levels of formality in writing: the highest for technical instruments such as deeds, statutes, and pleadings, followed closely by briefs, through opinions and office memoranda, to letters addressed to clients who are also friends. The lawyer must remain on the proper level, without injecting stuffy legalism into a friendly letter or dropping a discordant colloquialism into formal discourse. An unexpected shift distracts the attention of the reader from the substance and reflects unfavorably on the writer.

Many idiomatic expressions acceptable in speech and in informal writing may be out of place in a brief:

---

[64]   See § 6.2, Avoid Ineffective Techniques to Emphasize.

[65]   See Thomas Moore, II Memoirs of the Life of the Rt. Hon. Richard Brinsley Sheridan 12 (1858).

[66]   Robert Gunning, The Technique of Clear Writing 11 (1973).

a good deal (much)	get used to (become accustomed)
a piece of cake (easy)	pretty well (fairly well)
call it a day (stop)	screw up (make a mistake)
get off work (finish work)	spill the beans (reveal a secret)
get out of the way (avoid, escape)	under the weather (sick)

But colloquialism can have a place in formal legal writing. Suggesting that legal writers might make occasional use of colloquialism (not slang), Bryan Garner advised: "[i]n a profession whose writing suffers from verbal arteriosclerosis, some relaxation . . . is in order."[67] To do this well, however, you must develop a refined ear for the sound of words.

Similarly, the rule against using a fancy word when the simple will do does not require pedestrian vocabulary. "[A] skilled writer," said Steven Pinker, "can enliven and sometimes electrify her prose with the judicious insertion of a surprising word."[68] Just don't pick fancy polysyllables by default to impress your reader.

In addressing laypeople, a lawyer may sometimes want to impart a tone of extreme formality or magisterial impressiveness, as in a letter threatening a delinquent debtor with dire consequences. Even if the words are beyond the recipient's comprehension, the style may be effective. The Latin words of a Catholic mass may resonate more deeply precisely because they are incomprehensible.

Legal writing has purposes other than merely to inform. Law is a command, and imposing patterns of behavior on others is not easy. To make its legal commands impressive, the legal culture has employed formalism and ritual to give weight to its sanctions. Archaic and stately phraseology is more imposing than familiar language.

A lawyer must strike the precise balance of simplicity, clarity, and precision for the intended audience, calibrating "the degree of specialization in her language against her best guess of the audience's familiarity with the topic."[69] Even judges are generalists and not necessarily familiar with all areas of the law. Abuse of

---

[67]   Garner's Dictionary of Legal Usage 174 (2011).

[68]   The Sense of Style 22 (2014).

[69]   Steven Pinker, The Sense of Style 69 (2014).

specialized terminology, acronyms, and assumptions may confuse the best legal minds.[70]

But never "confuse clarity with condescension . . . . The key is to assume that your readers are as intelligent and sophisticated as you are, but that they happen not to know something you know."[71]

§ 4.12 Simplifying Is Painstaking Work

Achieving a simple style is no simple matter. Nothing in law is simple: simplicity is a human creation, the product of the work of writers with uncompromising determination to communicate an idea. It requires painstakingly revising early drafts, consistently changing long words to short, abstract words to concrete, round-about wordings to direct ones. It means replacing *raise the question* with *ask*, *stated* with *said*, *employ* with *use*. Each change may seem inconsequential. Standing alone, it probably is. But the cumulative effect of many little prunings is appreciable.[72]

Students often assume that their first formulation will be too simple, and that in reworking it they should strive for loftier prose. Some crude colloquialisms may find their way into one's first draft and need to be eliminated, but more likely to appear are the kind of inflated phrases criticized in this chapter. Many of them are already so habitual by the time we get to law school that we can only hope to eradicate them by mindful awareness.

A word that the reader ignores conveys no message except that you know tricky words. Even if the reader looks for the word in the dictionary, the damage is done: she was distracted and the flow of your argument was disrupted. And she may never find her way back to your text.

Do not worry that writing with simple words will make your prose look simplistic. People notice abuse of fancy words, but not their absence: in a simple text, the reader will only notice, undistracted, the message you are trying to convey.[73] You should impress your reader with the quality of your argument, not with the sophistication of the words you were able to pluck from a

---

[70] Douglas E. Abrams, Effective Legal Writing 97–104 (2016).

[71] Steven Pinker, The Sense of Style 69–70 (2014).

[72] See § 3.11, Rewrite (discussing the importance of reviewing one's prose) and Chapter 9, Conclusion (same).

[73] Eugene Volokh, Academic Legal Writing 149 (2016).

thesaurus.[74] William Penn said, "[s]peak properly, and in as few words as you can, but always plainly; for the end of speech is not ostentation, but to be understood."[75] What he meant was, "write to express, not to impress."

Simple style does not mean using the first word that comes to mind, but the best one for the purpose, not loose, slipshod allusions, but clear-cut ones. Finding words twice as big as the thought requires is easy. What is hard is to come upon the one word that will look tailor-made for the thought.

The right word may not quickly come to mind. Two or three words may occur to you, but none quite fit. This is when you need a thesaurus. Look up every word that comes close. From the synonyms listed, you will almost certainly find the word you want. The shade of difference in meaning may be so slight as to be almost imperceptible, yet it may be decisive.[76]

A simple writing style is achieved the same way a dancer finally comes to do a difficult step with apparent ease—by rigorous practice.

---

[74]   Id.

[75]   William Penn [1644–1718], Fruits of Solitude 135 (1901).

[76]   See § 2.3, Use a Thesaurus and a Dictionary.

Chapter 5

CLARITY

[T]he virtue of style is to be clear.
Aristotle (384 BC–322 BC)[1]

Have something to say, and say it as clearly as you can. That is the only secret of style.
Matthew Arnold (1822–1888)[2]

War is what happens when language fails.
Margaret Atwood[3]

If it's slovenly written, then it's hard to read.
Maya Angelou (1928–2014)[4]

§ 5.1   Introduction

"Most of the disputes in the world," said Lord Mansfield, "arise from words."[5] Words are, indeed, the source of misunderstandings.[6]

"The trouble with ambiguity," said Monroe C. Beardsley, "is that it may disrupt communication without either party knowing that communication has been broken down."[7] Frequently, they only realize when it's too late.

Ambiguous language is responsible for innumerable lawsuits. In conducting those lawsuits, lawyers often write briefs containing

---

[1]   On Rhetoric. A Theory of Civic Discourse 221 (transl. George A. Kennedy 1991).

[2]   As quoted in George William Erskine Russell, Collections and Recollections 136 (1898) ("People think I can teach them a style. What stuff it all is! Have something to say, and say it as clearly as you can. That is the only secret of style"). Arthur Schopenhauer had said something similar 35 years before, but it was Arnold's quote that became famous in the United States. Schopenhauer said, "The first rule . . . for a good style is that the author should have something to say; nay, this is in itself almost all that is necessary." On style [1851], in Lane Cooper (ed.), The Art of the Writer 223 (1952).

[3]   The Robber Bride 43 (1993).

[4]   Maya Angelou: How I Write, The Daily Beast, April 10, 2013.

[5]   Morgan v. Jones, 98 Eng. Rep. 587, 596 (1773). This idea was explored in John Locke, An Essay Concerning Human Understanding c. 9,10,11 (1690).

[6]   Antoine de Saint-Exupéry, Le Petit Prince 80 (1943).

[7]   Thinking Straight 163 (1956).

further ambiguities. Paraphrasing Ernest Weekley, there is a certain impertinence in submitting to a busy court sentences that have to be read twice before their meaning can be detected.[8] Justice Ginsburg, with a certain amount of authority on this topic, agrees: "[K]eep it simple, never write a sentence that has to be read again to be understood."[9]

But being clear is not a given. You must cultivate a burning desire toward clarity. For too many lawyers, however, this is not a priority: "too much legal writing," quipped David Mellinkoff, "looks like it was dropped, not written."[10] Yet good writers agree with Ludwig Wittgenstein: "[e]verything that can be thought at all can be thought clearly. Everything that can be said can be said clearly."[11]

The chapter on precision discussed causes of (semantic) ambiguity, including ignorance of the correct meaning of words and carelessness in choosing them. The chapter on simplicity addressed ambiguity created by misplaced complexity. Here we will discuss how to put words together to enable the reader to grasp their meaning with minimum effort. We will examine common causes of dense prose, including defects in sentence structure, misplaced modifiers, and pronouns without clear antecedents. Other causes of (syntactic) ambiguity and rambling prose are discussed in the chapter on organization.[12]

§ 5.2   Think About What You Are Saying

Much fuzzy writing is the result of fuzzy thinking. The writer may know the subject but may not be thinking about how to best express the idea. There's no substitute for clear thinking.[13] "[G]enerations of writers . . . have hidden their ideas not only from their readers but sometimes even from themselves."[14] Before writing, advise George Orwell, think what you are saying and how you will say it:

---

[8]   Cruelty to Words 61 (1931).

[9]   A Conversation with Justice Ruth Bader Ginsburg, 25 Colum. J. Gender & L. 6, 26 (2013).

[10]   Sense and Nonsense 91 (1982).

[11]   Tractatus Logico-Philosophicus 4.116 (1921).

[12]   But see § 5.15, Use Ambiguity Strategically.

[13]   See § 7.3, Writing is Thinking.

[14]   Joseph M. Williams & Joseph Bizup, Style: Lessons in Clarity and Grace 3 (2017).

A scrupulous writer, in every sentence that he writes, will ask himself at least four questions, thus: What am I trying to say? What words will express it? What image or idiom will make it clearer? Is this image fresh enough to have an effect? And he will probably ask himself two more: Could I put it more shortly? Have I said anything that is avoidably ugly?[15]

Consider the impact of incautious use of negatives in the following sentences:

> It could not have been done except at a prohibitive cost.

This seems to say both that it could have been done and that the cost would have prohibited its being done.

> We make no such claim. Much less do we claim . . . .

How much is less than none?

> The court did not allow recovery on the ground that it did not want to extend the liability of companies supplying necessary public services.

The reader is not sure whether the court denied recovery on the ground mentioned, or granted recovery on some other ground.

Careless, blundering wording may lead you to say things you do not intend:

> The term "third party beneficiary" refers to that type of contract in which two people contract for some kind of performance to be rendered to a third person.

The writer here says something she does not mean—that a "third party beneficiary" is a "type of contract."

> He testified that he remembered being in the lobby when he saw a young woman carrying a baby and her husband enter.

One remembers sights like that.

> Under the law, the board must approve any award recommended by the arbitrator.

The writer does not mean that the board must approve. She means that "before an award can become final the board must approve it," or that the award "does not become final unless approved by the board."

---

[15]　Politics and the English Language (1946).

Guard against slipping into what we call "retroactive construction":

> The doctor persuaded the deceased to submit to the operation.

Did the doctor manage to persuade a corpse? Because the writer has been referring to the person as "the deceased," she mistakenly uses that term in describing something that happened before the person died.

Such fumbling approximations of what we are trying to say frequently show up in first drafts—this is how we talk extemporaneously. You should not feel guilty when you find such blunders in your writing. You deserve blame, however, if you fail to find them because you do not read your early drafts critically.

§ 5.3   Follow the Expected Sentence Order

For Jonathan Swift, "proper words in proper places make the true definition of a style."[16] Select precise words, arrange them coherently, and the reader will understand your message: the sequence of the words is almost as important as their meaning.

The expected sentence order is: (1) subject, (2) verb, (3) object. Write your sentences mostly in this order, except when you want to obtain a particular effect, such as variety of sentence patterns or emphasis on a certain word or phrase.[17]

Do not begin sentences with participles or subordinate clauses unless you have a reason to do so. In each of the examples below, the writer failed to follow normal sentence order by starting with "There have been" and "Because," instead of with the subject of the sentence.

There have been many solutions to this problem advanced.	Many solutions to this problem have been advanced.
Because a rule is old does not prove it is sound.	A rule is not sound merely because it is old.

Thoughtful writers sense how the reader will experience their text and make a conscious effort to present the subject in a way that minimizes the reader's effort. Arthur Schopenhauer was insightful:

---

[16]   A Letter to a Young Clergyman [1721], in Lane Cooper (ed.), The Art of the Writer 138 (1952).

[17]   See § 6.12, Put Words to be Stressed at the Beginning and the End of Sentences. See also § 7.7, Sentence Structure and Organization (encouraging variation in sentence structure).

"thought . . . follows the law of gravity [in] that it travels from head to paper much more easily than from paper to head; so that [the writer] must assist the latter passage by every means in his power."[18] The cost of failing to heed this advice is not only a tired reader, but a weakened message. Every reader has limited time and energy: "[t]he more time and attention it takes to receive and understand each sentence, the less time and attention can be given to the contained idea; and the less vividly will that idea be conceived."[19]

A writer must expend substantial energy to craft the clearest possible statement. Herbert Spencer laid out a rule for selecting from among alternatives: "the relative goodness of any two modes of expressing an idea may be determined by observing which requires the shortest process of thought for its comprehension."[20] Choose the alternative that is invulnerable to misinterpretation yet easy to process.

Legal writing frequently calls for complex sentences and qualifying phrases. Adhering to normal sentence order helps make them clearer and is not likely to oversimplify your style: "[l]egal readers appreciate appropriate variety, but they do not appreciate variety at the expense of clarity."[21]

§ 5.4   Put Modifiers with the Word or Phrase Modified

A fundamental technique to avoid ambiguity is to "put all modifiers as close as you can to the words they modify, and keep them away from other words you don't want them to modify."[22]

Careless placement of modifiers often causes ambiguity:

> The game warden filed four complaints, charging illegal fishing in Judge Padgett's court.

In this sentence, it takes time to realize that the illegal fishing did not occur in court.

---

[18]   On style [1851], in Lane Cooper (ed.), The Art of the Writer 231 (1952).

[19]   Herbert Spencer, The Philosophy of Style [1852], in Lane Cooper (ed.), The Art of the Writer 239 (1952).

[20]   The Philosophy of Style [1852], in Lane Cooper (ed.), The Art of the Writer 259 (1952).

[21]   Anne Enquist, Laurel Oates & Jeremy Francis, Just Writing 96 (2017).

[22]   Monroe C. Beardsley, Thinking Straight 166 (1956).

"In every sentence," said Herbert Spencer, "the sequence of words should be that which suggests the constituents of the thought in the order most convenient for the building up of that thought." This requires that the words and expressions most nearly related in thought be brought closest together—modifiers of the subject with the subject, modifiers of the verb with the verb, modifiers of the object with the object. Spencer explained:

> The longer the time that elapses between the mention of any qualifying member and the member qualified, the longer must the mind be exerted in carrying forward the qualifying member ready for use. And the more numerous the qualifications to be simultaneously remembered and rightly applied, the greater will be the mental power expended, and the smaller the effect produced. Hence, other things equal, force will be gained by so arranging the members of a sentence that these suspensions shall be at any moment the fewest in number; and shall also be of the shortest duration . . .[23]

Legal propositions may have to include a number of modifying phrases or clauses.[24] Fitting them all into a sentence without making it clumsy or unclear is sometimes difficult. Usually, the best places to put these phrases and clauses are (1) before the subject or (2) after the predicate. Conditions or exceptions modifying the subject should generally be placed before the subject. Those qualifying the predicate should generally be placed after the predicate. A short modifier of the subject may be placed (3) after the subject; but a long string of modifiers may make the sentence hard to follow because the whole thought is kept hanging until we reach the verb. The least desirable place to put modifiers is (4) between the verb and its object or predicate noun.

The complaint was, in the court's opinion, both in form and in substance, seriously defective.	In the court's opinion, the complaint was seriously defective in form and substance.
A petition by property owners protesting the board's order of June 17, calling for reassessment was filed yesterday.	Yesterday, property owners filed a petition . . .

---

[23]   Philosophy of Style [1852] 22–23 (1915).

[24]   See §§ 6.8, Do Not Qualify Unnecessarily and 7.6, Say One Thing at a Time.

When a direct object is long, however, an indirect object may sometimes be placed before the direct object.

The lessor conveyed all the minerals of whatever kind that lay on or below the surface of the tract to lessee.	The lessor conveyed to lessee all the minerals . . .

"The lessor conveyed all the minerals to lessee" is the proper and normal sentence order. But when one word or phrase in the sentence carries with it a long string of qualifying words, as "minerals" does here, it is better to get the indirect object, "to lessee," into the sentence before starting the long clause describing the minerals.

Clumsy word order impairs reading efficiency by requiring the reader to exert undue mental effort.

> In *Buchannon*, the promisee procured money to prosecute a claim to a will which would benefit his wife.

What would benefit the wife—the will, or prosecution of the claim?

> The exclusion of implied warranties under the common law was more readily accomplished than under the UCC.

The subject under discussion is "the exclusion of implied warranties," not "the exclusion of implied warranties under common law." This exclusion, the writer wants to say, was more readily accomplished under common law than it now is under the UCC; "under common law" therefore belongs after "is more readily accomplished."

> The exclusion of implied warranties was more readily accomplished under the common law than it is under the UCC.

Rearranging a sentence often improves it:

The court's holding that the lessee's right to use the underground tunnels was terminated when the coal was exhausted is inconsistent with the holding that the estate in the coal is perpetual in *Attebery v. Blair*.	The court's holding that the lessee's right to use the underground tunnels was terminated when the coal was exhausted is inconsistent with the holding in *Attebery v. Blair* that the estate in the coal is perpetual.
There was probable cause to believe that an illicit still was being operated only after there had been an illegal trespass by the federal agents.	Only after there had been an illegal trespass by the federal agents was there probable cause to believe that an illicit still was being operated.

Even judges may on occasion arrange words so carelessly that they fail to say what they intended. For example, Justice Murphy began a dissenting opinion by saying:

> It is disheartening to find so much that is right in an opinion which seems to me so fundamentally wrong.[25]

What disheartened the Justice was not to find so much that was right in the opinion, but that the conclusion was wrong:

> It is disheartening to find an opinion containing so much that is right come to a conclusion that seems to me so fundamentally wrong.

Clumsy word order impairs reading efficiency and creates ambiguity:

> When Brown was arrested by Sheriff Ramsey, on May 10, the sheriff testified she told Brown the reason for her arrest.

What happened on May 10?

> Unfortunately, the operators have taken advantage of this provision but our organization has not.

The writer did not really regard it as unfortunate that the operators had acted. What she meant to say was:

> The operators have taken advantage of this provision, but unfortunately our organization has not.

A misplaced modifier might make a statement ludicrous:

> The federal officers arrived at the conclusion that a felony was being committed by the odor of toxic chemicals.

An offensive odor, even if toxic, is not a felon.

> There are millions of children who do not go to school in Asia.

Yes: yours and mine, among others. But what the writer meant was,

> Millions of children in Asia do not go to school.

A common form of misplaced modifier is the dangling participle. When a participle—the verb with the *-ing* ending— begins a sentence, it must modify the subject of the main clause. If the subject noun is placed in some subordinate position, or is omitted entirely, the participle is left dangling.

> Notwithstanding its many shortcomings, this court has adopted the Missouri rule.

---

[25]   Wolf v. Colorado, 338 U.S. 25, 41 (1949).

The writer does not mean that the court had shortcomings, but that the rule did. To make this sentence clear, the writer should either (1) keep the participle construction but make the rule the subject ("Notwithstanding its many shortcomings, the Missouri rule has been adopted by this court"), or, to avoid the passive voice, (2) leave the main clause as it stands but abandon the participle construction ("This court has adopted the Missouri rule, notwithstanding its many shortcomings"). A shorter, sharper, simpler sentence would be, "this court has adopted the Missouri rule, despite its many faults."

> Overcome with emotion, the defendant's eyes filled with tears.

The defendant's eyes were not overcome with emotion; he was.

> Having borne him two sons, Mrs. Abney and her husband were hoping that this would be a girl.

Without disparaging Mr. Abney's contribution to the birth of his sons, he was not an equal partner in bearing them. (See how easy it is to dangle a participle? We just did it.)

> The brief quotes from the dissenting opinion in a case of statutory rape by Judge Blank.
>
> Defendant harassed Ms. Bates while she was walking in the park in a most offensive manner.

Single words as well as phrases and clauses are sometimes misplaced. Adverbs are especially likely to get lost, and certain adverbs more than most. *Only* is perhaps the most footloose. Unthinking writers tend to put it next to the verb whether it belongs there or not. *Both, even, alone, at least,* and *merely* are other words often mislaid. Usually the best place for these and similar modifiers is immediately before the element they modify.

The following sentences have different meanings:

> *Only* Officer Jones heard the suspect's confession.
> Officer Jones *only* heard the suspect's confession.
> Office Jones heard *only* the suspect's confession.
> Office Jones heard the *only* suspect's confession.
> Officer Jones heard the suspect's *only* confession.
> Officer Jones heard the suspect's confession *only.*

Sometimes the difference is merely a shade of meaning.

Modifiers preceding or following a series are likely to create ambiguity. Suppose a regulation says that it applies to "all domestic corporations or partnerships engaged in intrastate commerce."

Does it apply to all domestic corporations, or only those engaged in intrastate commerce? All partnerships engaged in intrastate commerce, or only domestic ones?

It is difficult to detect ambiguity caused by your own misplaced modifiers because you know what you want to say and read your own sentences "with the inflection and emphasis that bring out the meaning you intend."[26] That is why you must revise your text from a reader's perspective.[27] The outsider's viewpoint takes time (and experience) to acquire, so build some three-day rests into your editing process whenever you can.

Sometimes efforts to rearrange a poorly constructed sentence will be futile; the revision is no better than the original. The likely reason is that you clung too closely to the original, changing only words here and there, when the defect lay in its basic structure. Ask yourself whether you are violating one or more of the guidelines laid down in this book. Does the sentence follow normal sentence order? Does it attempt simultaneously to make two or three statements that would be better made in two or three sentences instead of one? Are modifiers next to the words they modify? To craft a properly organized sentence, consider starting from scratch.

§ 5.5   Be Sure Pronouns Have Clear Antecedents

You make writing less clumsy by using pronouns to avoid repeating nouns. To strengthen your prose, you may use personal pronouns (I, we, he, she, it, they, me, us, him, her, them), demonstrative pronouns (this, that, these, those, such) or relative pronouns (which, who, whom, that). But carelessly used, pronouns can cause trouble.

Studies in cognitive psychology have confirmed what experienced writers and stylists have always known—that the ambiguity generated by pronouns without clear antecedents will distract and slow the reader down in processing the information, forcing him to reread the text to grasp its meaning.[28]

---

[26]   Claire Kehrwald Cook, Line by Line: How to Edit Your Own Writing 12 (1985).

[27]   See §§ 3.11, Rewrite (discussing the importance of reviewing one's prose), 4.12, Simplifying is Painstaking Work (same), and Chapter 9, Conclusion (same).

[28]   Anthony Sanford, Simon Garrod, A. Lucas & R.J. Henderson, Pronouns Without Explicit Antecedents? 2 J. Semantics 303–18 (1983); Mante S. Nieuwland, Marte Otten, & Jos J.A. Van Berkum, Who are You Talking About? Tracking Discourse-level Referential Processing with Event-related Brain Potentials, 19 J. Cognitive Neuroscience 228 (2007); Ruth Filik, Anthony J. Sanford, & Hartmut Leuthold, Processing Pronouns without Antecedents: Evidence from Event-Related Brain

We may laugh at the person who writes, "in answer to your question, I gave birth to a boy, weighed ten pounds. I hope *this* is satisfactory." But lawyers are often guilty of the same mistake. They discuss a case or a rule of law, and then start a new sentence with *this*: "this is also true when . . . ." The reader may not be able to discover whether *this* refers to an entire preceding paragraph or only to a specific thing or idea previously mentioned. Sometimes, it seems to refer to something not mentioned at all.

> There has been dissatisfaction with what appears to be a tendency on the part of courts not to disturb Board findings. *This* has been true even where such findings are based on questions of mixed law and fact.

What "has been true"? The writer meant that the *tendency* existed (was true). But the words say that the *dissatisfaction* existed. One way to avoid falling into this error is to avoid using *this* as a demonstrative pronoun, and to use it instead as an adjective by adding the noun identifying what is referred to: *this* tendency or *this* dissatisfaction.

A book on brief writing argued for brevity in the following words:

> It is a pity that so many, often justifiably, consider lawyers to be "slaves of verbosity." Actually, *such* should not be the case.[29]

What should not be the case? Does the writer mean: (1) it should not be a pity (but a good thing, perhaps?) that many people consider lawyers to be verbose; (2) lawyers should not be verbose; or (3) people should not consider them to be?

This text was rewritten in subsequent editions:

> Many persons consider lawyers to be "slaves of verbosity." *This* is unfortunate, for lawyers ought to be the masters of words rather than their slaves.[30]

The revised construction is clearer and easier to process, but it still violates the rule against pronouns without clear antecedents: it is still unclear what is unfortunate.

The word *it* is particularly easy to misuse. This nimble little word often feels so convenient that writers fail to make clear what *it* refers to.

Potentials, 20 J. Cognitive Neuroscience 1315 (2008) ("Pronouns that do not have explicit antecedents typically cause processing problems.").

[29]   Edward D. Re, Brief Writing and Oral Argument 24 (1957).

[30]   Edward D. Re & Joseph R. Re, Brief Writing & Oral Argument 5 (2005).

In order to exclude the warranty of merchantability, *it* must be mentioned expressly, and if in writing, *it* must be conspicuous.

The word *it* in this example, both times used, refers grammatically to "the warranty of merchantability." But the writer meant to say that the exclusion must be mentioned expressly, and if in writing, the exclusionary provision must be conspicuous.

He, she, him, and *her* often appear without clear antecedents.

Defendant killed the deceased when she thought she was raising her gun to shoot her.

Who thought who was going to shoot whom?

Similar to the fault of using pronouns without clear antecedents is that of using nouns with demonstrative adjectives that lack referents, as by referring to *this* item when no such item has been mentioned.

From the dicta in *Daly v. Palmer*, it might seem that a choreographic work would be held registerable as a dramatic composition, but *this* hope was quickly dispelled.

No hope had been previously mentioned.

The defendant was indicted for unlawful possession of cocaine. *This* indictment was based on evidence obtained by a search warrant improperly issued.

Because the writer has said that the defendant was indicted, she felt free to refer to "this indictment." She should have said, "the indictment . . ."

The majority view is found in *Lill v. Gleason*, 92 Kan. 754, 142 P. 287 (1914). *This* court declares that . . .

Because he has cited a Kansas case, the writer assumed (if he was thinking at all) that "this court" is sufficient to refer to the Supreme Court of Kansas.

The Company must bargain with the union for a period of one year. At *this* time, if the situation still exists, the company may file a petition for determination of representation.

At what time? For referring to a past or future occasion, *at that time* is better; *at this time* can then be reserved for referring to the present. In the above sentence, it would be better to say "If the situation still exists after one year, the company . . ."

Some of these sentences might be clear in their context or with careful rereading. But a mere hope that context will provide clarity should never allow a writer to settle for an ambiguous sentence: each sentence should be clear independent of the context.[31]

To avoid distracting, slowing, or confusing your readers, follow Claire Kehrwald Cook's advice: "Reference-of-pronoun errors are easy to spot if you're willing to look for them. Just trace every pronoun back to the word it replaces and make sure that the antecedent is an appropriate part of speech appropriately placed and uniquely qualified to do the job."[32]

But you should not be concerned with this level of detail too early in the drafting process, or it will slow your progression. Wait until you review the final draft.[33]

A pronoun that confuses or slows the reader defeats its purpose—it is better to repeat the noun and be clear than to be succinct and ambiguous.

§ 5.6   Avoid Ambiguity by Association

Accidentally placing two important words next to one another may lead the reader down a false trail.

> Federal laws directed at the control of an evil thought by Congress to require regulation have been upheld.

When we have "an evil" followed by "thought," we end up with "an evil thought." The writer, knowing what she meant, may not notice that the words are subject to "ambiguity by association," as we may call it, but the reader may be momentarily confused.

This kind of ambiguity can result when an introductory word may be read as one of a series that follows:

> To police officers, migrants, protesters, and vagrants are suspicious characters.

Instead, energize your verb and build in a buffer:

> Police view migrants, protesters, and vagrants as suspicious characters.

---

[31]   See § 5.16, Do Not Rely on Context to Cure Ambiguity.

[32]   Line by Line: How to Edit Your Own Writing 98 (1985).

[33]   Id. at 104–05 (1985). See §§ 3.11, Rewrite (discussing the importance of reviewing one's prose), 4.12, Simplifying is Painstaking Work (same), and Chapter 9, Conclusion (same).

§ 5.7   Use Hyphens to Join Compound Adjectives

Compound adjectives (compound modifiers or phrasal adjectives) are formed when two or more words are used to modify a noun. To avoid ambiguity, join them with a hyphen to show that they are to be read together as one word.

> The program is designed to help small business owners.

"Small-business owners" would make clear that it is not a program for short people. Below are other ambiguous compounds where inserting a hyphen would help:

a general rule making process	a man eating shark
a heavy metal detector	a small state senator
all too common mistake	a violent weather conference
a long haired man	our work oriented curriculum
a long term contract	the court appointed experts

Even if the meaning of the compound adjective is not ambiguous or can be ascertained in the context, a hyphen may lead to faster reading, better flow, and easier comprehension.[34] In legal writing style, consistency is key to obtaining clarity and precision.

§ 5.8   Avoid Double Negatives

Avoid double negatives; they confuse and slow down the reader.

> We do *not deny* that *im*moral works should *not* receive copyright protection.

> *No* valid *dis*tinction can be drawn between this case and *Wolf v. Colorado* on the ground that here the evidence has *not* already been brought under control of the state.

Even a United States Supreme Court Justice may on occasion produce a glut of negatives:

> This is *not* to say, however, that the prima facie case may *not* be met by evidence supporting a finding that a *lesser* degree of segregated schooling in the core city area would *not* have resulted even if the Board had *not* acted as it did.[35]

Insecure writers use double negatives in the false belief that their use makes writing sound sophisticated. Instead, their use adds unnecessary complexity. Seeking to sound elegant, lawyers

---

[34]   See Joan Ames Magat, Hawking Hyphens in Compound Modifiers, 11 J. AWLD 153 (2014).

[35]   Keyes v. School Dist. No. 1, 413 U.S. 189, 211 (1973) (Brennan, J.).

abuse the formula *not un-*. They say, "not unaware" instead of "aware"; "not unusual" instead of "usual"; "not unlike" instead of "like."[36]

Writers who abuse the negative may lose track of their message. The worst abuse results from adding a redundant negative in a subordinate clause, making the sentence say the opposite of what the writer intended.

> We would *not* be surprised if investigation did *not* ultimately prove the signature to be a *forgery*.

> I do *not* know how many times I have*n't* checked this item.

> We do *not* contend that *no* case may *ever* arise in which an *exception* to the rule would *not* be justified.

You obtain negation with prefixes like a-, dis-, il-, im-, in-, ir-, mis-, non-, un- (atypical, disconnect, illegal, impossible, incorrect, irrational, misjudge, nonessential, uncertain) and with words with negative connotation (absent, avoid, deprive, deny, fail, false, ignore, lack, never, preclude, rarely, reject, seldom, without). When scanning for double negatives, therefore, look deeper than *no* and *not*.

To avoid ambiguity, convert double negatives into affirmative statements. To obtain forcefulness, translate a negative statement into affirmative.[37]

The use of a double negative is acceptable, however, when it conveys a specific meaning or you need a less forceful statement: "not uncomfortable" does not mean the same as "comfortable;" "not deny" is weaker than "confirm." Use it deliberately.

§ 5.9　Distinguish Between the Conjunctive and the Disjunctive

If either fact A or fact B produces a legal result, do not say that the law requires A *and* B.[38] The error is obvious, but it may not be apparent when swathed in many words.

Even courts occasionally trip over the distinction between *and* and *or*. In an old New York case, the trial court instructed the jury that a mere false belief would not excuse a woman accused of murdering her child "unless it was the result of some mental

---

[36]　See George Orwell, Politics and the English Language (1946).

[37]　§ 6.6, Make Assertions in the Affirmative.

[38]　See § 2.8, Words to Watch, (discussing *and, or* and *and/or*).

disease which prevented her from knowing the nature and quality of the act and that it was wrongful." On appeal, this instruction was held to be erroneous; it should have been made clear "that a defect of reason which inhibited a knowledge *either* of the nature and quality of the act *or* that the act was wrong excused a person from criminal liability."[39] In states recognizing both the right-and-wrong and the irresistible impulse test of insanity, courts sometimes carelessly say that the test is ability to distinguish between right and wrong *and* ability to resist the impulse.[40]

Whether to use *and* or *or* may in some situations be difficult. Suppose a law licensing cleaners and dyers defines a cleaning establishment as "any place where cleaning and dyeing is done." Use of the word *and* requires that both be done. Substituting *or* would cover places where either is done, but might be interpreted to exclude places where both are done. The safe way to cover all the possibilities is to say "any place where cleaning or dyeing, or both, are done."

§ 5.10   Avoid the *Former* and the *Latter*

Former and *latter* refer to the first and the last of two things previously mentioned. They should never be used when more than two things are involved. They may substitute for subjects like arguments, theories, and points of view, especially those without snappy names or short descriptive labels. To recall their meanings, use an alliterative mnemonic: former is first and latter is last.

But *former* and *latter* are stiff and break the flow of the argument: they invite the reader's eye to travel back, when it should be encouraged always to move forward.[41] Avoid them.

The two significant dates are 2012 and 2017, the former because it is the date when the act was passed and the latter because it is the date when it was held unconstitutional.	The two significant dates are 2012, when the act was passed, and 2017, when it was held unconstitutional.

If you use these terms, make sure that they are close to their referent and are easily understood, or the reader will be forced to

---

[39]   People v. Sherwood, 3 N.E.2d 581 (N.Y. 1936).

[40]   See Howard v. United States, 232 F.2d 274 (5th Cir. 1956); State v. Beckwith, 46 N.W.2d 20 (Iowa 1951); Com. v. Smith, 97 A.2d 25 (Pa. 1953); Weihofen, Mental Disorder as a Criminal Defense 75 (1954).

[41]   Robert Graves & Allan Hodge, The Reader Over Your Shoulder: A Handbook for Writers of English Prose 197 (1943).

search back to understand your reference. To preserve the sanity of your audience and your own dignity, do not ever use them in speech.

If the two subjects are events that occurred at different times it is advisable to make *former* refer to the earlier in time as well as first mentioned, and *latter* to refer to the later in time and second mentioned.

Former and *formerly* occasionally confuse writers, including the *New York Times* reporter who wrote:

> Leon H. Keyserling was a former government economist.

Has Keyserling ceased to be a former government economist? No, he still is.

§ 5.11   The Passive Voice May Be Ambiguous

The passive voice is wordier and weaker than the active voice.[42] It may also be ambiguous. Instead of saying that someone did something, you say that something was done and may leave it unclear by whom. "When Congress writes a statute in the passive voice," said Justice Thomas, "it often fails to state who must take a required action. This silence can make the meaning of a statute somewhat difficult to ascertain."[43]

> A defendant *shall be given* credit toward the service of a term of imprisonment for any time he has spent in official detention prior to the date the sentence commences . . .[44]

"Given" by whom? Arguably by the Attorney General, who has historically computed federal sentences. Use of the active voice would have saved the reader and the Supreme Court from having to figure that out.[45]

White nationalist talk show host Harold Turner was charged with threatening to murder three federal judges (Easterbrook, Bauer, and Posner). Defendant argued that his statement could not be a threat because he only used the passive voice—he wrote that the judges "deserve to be killed," not "I will kill them." Despite the uncertainty about who intended to harm the judges, the Court of Appeals determined that Turner was guilty of making the threat.

---

[42]   See §§ 3.8, The Passive Voice is Verbose and 6.5, The Passive Voice is Weak.

[43]   U.S. v. Wilson, 503 U.S. 329 (1992). See also Anita S. Krishnakumar, Passive-Voice References in Statutory Interpretation, 76 Brooklyn L. Rev. 934 (2011).

[44]   See 18 U.S.C. § 3585(b) (1984) (Sentencing Reform Act).

[45]   U.S. v. Wilson, 503 U.S. 329 (1992) (Thomas, J.).

In dissent, Judge Rosemary S. Pooler agreed with the passive voice argument.[46]

Ambiguity, however, is not always a vice; sometimes it is deliberate.[47] In these and in other situations, the passive voice is a useful tool.[48]

Be consistent: do not shift without reason from active to passive voice.

Plaintiff signed the contract on March 1 and it was mailed to defendant the same day.	Plaintiff signed the contract on March 1 and mailed it to defendant the same day.

§ 5.12   Identify Who Is Making the Assertion

Presenting an assertion without identifying the asserter may lead to ambiguity. This happens when, for example, a writer does not make clear whether she is speaking for herself or attributing the assertion to someone else:

> The decision fortifies the proposition advanced by some writers that the only effective restraint on the commerce power resides in the political processes rather than the judicial process. The term "interstate commerce" no longer presents a constitutional problem, but only raises a problem of statutory construction to determine the scope of federal regulatory power authorized by Congress in any particular statute.

In the second sentence, is the writer speaking for himself, or merely enlarging on "the proposition advanced by some writers"?

During negotiations with a labor union over pay rates, an employer was asked to supply certain financial information. The employer's attorney wrote an opinion containing the following paragraph:

> The union has stated that the information requested is necessary for administering the existing contract and for bargaining in good faith. For these purposes, they need to know your net profit for last year, the number of hours worked by each of your employees, and their total pay.

The second sentence was intended merely to state the union's position—not the lawyer's own. But the client may read it literally, and resent her own lawyer's saying something that she strongly feels is wrong.

---

[46]   U.S. v. Turner, 720 F.3d 411 (2d Cir. 2013).

[47]   See § 5.15, Use Ambiguity Strategically.

[48]   See § 7.15, The Passive Voice May be Just What You Need (discussing legitimate uses of the passive voice).

§ 5.13   Compound Prepositions Are Often Vague

The chapter on conciseness pointed out that compound prepositional phrases are wordy.[49] Sometimes they are also ambiguous.

> The appellant argues that she was incompetent to stand trial *in view of* an earlier adjudication as insane by a Florida court in 2017.

In view of confuses the statement so that we do not know what appellant argued: (1) that the earlier adjudication conclusively established appellant's incompetency at the time of trial; (2) that it created a rebuttable presumption of such incompetency; or (3) that it was evidence tending to show such incompetency.

Other prepositional phrases, such as *with reference to, as to,* and *in this connection,* often create ambiguity:

> The seller must know the purpose to which the goods are to be put, and the buyer must rely on the seller's judgment *as to* the selection of the goods.

> Besides the problem of whether a deliverer is an independent contractor, other questions have come before the Board *in this connection*.

> The sales contract was signed *with reference to* the oral agreements made by the parties.

§ 5.14   Present Statistics Clearly

Statistical data can help communicate your message, if presented clearly. Data that may be hard to comprehend when presented in one way may be quite plain when presented in another. But burying copious statistics in the text is bad practice. Do not write:

> In Wobegon state courts, 32% of the defendants whose bail was fixed at $500 could not raise bail. When bail was set at a higher amount, the proportion of offenders who could not post bond rose. When the bail was $1,000, 50% could not raise bail; when the amount of bail was $1,500 to $4,000, 67% could not post bond; and when the amount was $5,000 or over, 87% could not post bond.

Instead of putting this information in a solid paragraph, the data may be set out in a table. But long tables are difficult to read—the reader will probably skip them—and may not demonstrate the trend or point you want to make. So present your position both ways: state the crucial point briefly and then support it with a table.

---

[49]   See § 3.3, Eliminate Wordy and Useless Expressions.

Use statistics with discrimination, depending on your message and audience—they should be "sprinkled like pepper, not smeared like butter."[50]

§ 5.15   Use Ambiguity Strategically

For Arthur Schopenhauer, "[n]othing is easier than to write so that no one can understand; just as, contrarily, nothing is more difficult than to express deep things in such a way that everyone must necessarily grasp them."[51] Perhaps he overlooked an even more demanding task: writing with "calculated ambiguity."

We must be careful not to overstate the importance of precision and clarity in legal writing. In certain situations, they are unnecessary; in others, they are undesirable and even incompatible with the writer's objectives. Excessive precision conflicts with conciseness, and may lead to verbosity and ambiguity. Excessive clarity may make reaching agreement impossible when the parties' positions are close but not aligned.

Many contract clauses, legislative enactments, and appellate opinions are intentionally left ambiguous: a more precise statement would have killed the deal. The art of writing strategically with "calculated ambiguity" or "precise imprecision" is as important as the skills of precision and clarity, for an imperfect agreement may be better than none. Only inadvertent or deceitful ambiguity is a vice; if the intentional ambiguity is calculated to address the needs of the situation, it is a virtue.

A lawyer will often have legitimate reasons for using ambiguous language. Your client might benefit from a description of his tardiness as "a few weeks," when the delivery was thirty-seven days late. Or you may not want to take a clear position or make a firm commitment, thinking it wiser to express only a vague assurance that you will take some favorable action, or a vague threat to do something adverse.

> Unless this account is paid within the next ten days, it will be necessary to *take appropriate action.*

The writer could have found more specific wording—"start legal proceedings" or "bring suit," for example. Using the vaguer

---

[50]   Gary Provost, 100 Ways to Improve Your Writing 85 (1985).

[51]   On style [1851], in Lane Cooper (ed.), The Art of the Writer 222 (1952).

wording indicates the writer does not want to make a specific threat at this time.

When a lawyer is unsure of a legal position's soundness, she may want to state it in vaguer terms.

> *In view of the fact that* payments had been so *erratic,* my client exercised his right to cancel the contract.

"Because" would be more precise and concise than "in view of the fact that." And "erratic" does not state a legally recognized objection to the way payments had been made. But perhaps counsel was not sure that the way payments had been made gave legal cause for cancellation, or it was too soon to know whether the manner of payment was the best legal theory to support her client's cancelling. The lawyer therefore preferred neither to state baldly what the deficiency was, nor to use a word asserting that it was the cause. "In view of the fact that," a phrase that suggests a broad-minded perspective, therefore, replaces a narrower word implying a causal relation.

Seems or *it seems* is a phrase often useful for hedging. *It appears* has a different connotation: "*seems* is applied to that which has an aspect of truth and probability . . . *appear* suggests the giving of an impression which may be superficial or illusory."[52] This does not mean that you should avoid *appear*: superficiality or illusoriness may sometimes be exactly what you want to suggest. Your opponent's argument, you may want to say, "appears, until one examines it, to have some validity."

It seems to me adds nothing except to focus the spotlight on the writer instead of the subject. Never interject yourself needlessly between your writing and your reader.

Posing a question commits a writer less than suggesting an answer, no matter how tentatively.

When you have to keep your cards close to your chest, craft strategically sparse documents.

Because the passive voice is sometimes less clear than the active, it may be useful where ambiguity is desired. In saying that certain dishonorable acts have been committed, we may not want

---

[52]   The Random House College Dictionary 1191 (1982).

to name the actor. By using the passive, we avoid pointing the finger at any particular person.[53]

> Certain rumors have been circulated.
> The gun was fired at close range.
> Mistakes were made.

You may also manufacture ambiguity through nominalization, a technique that allows you to omit the agent, the object of the action, or both.[54]

Courtesy drives much ambiguity and verbosity into legal writing. When your answer is a refusal or other disappointment, a vague or long-winded expression is usually less harsh than a bluntly direct one. Although the indicative mood is usually preferred in legal writing, consider using the subjunctive for a refusal. "It would seem that we cannot find an agreeable compromise," is wordier and muddier than its blunt counterpart, but it stings less. A disappointing response could start politely with a point of agreement before addressing the denial. This approach is particularly common in letters.

Even when clarity is a prime requirement, ambiguity may be called for on occasion. Although the legislative drafter should normally strive to make the meaning clear, occasions may call for deliberate vagueness—specificity can raise doubts or opposition and precipitate a fight that would jeopardize the project. Or the legislature may lay down only a broad policy, leaving courts or administrators the task of shaping the finer contours of the law. The Federal Trade Commission Act, for example, uses a broad concept in forbidding "unfair methods of competition," leaving it to the Commission to determine what practices are considered unfair. Justice Brandeis later explained the reason for adopting this device:

> Experience with existing laws had taught that definition, being necessarily rigid, would prove embarrassing and, if rigorously applied, might involve great hardship. Methods of competition which would be unfair in one industry, under certain circumstances, might, when adopted in another industry, or even in the same industry under different circumstances, be entirely

---

[53] See §§ 5.11, The Passive Voice May Be Ambiguous and 7.15, The Passive Voice May be Just What You Need.

[54] See § 4.5, Don't Overuse Nouns.

unobjectionable. Furthermore, an enumeration, however comprehensive, of existing methods of unfair competition must necessarily soon prove incomplete, as with new conditions constantly arising novel unfair methods would be devised and developed.[55]

Drafters must tread a fine line between unnecessary or unintended ambiguity on the one hand and embarrassingly naked clarity on the other. Collective bargaining agreements, for example, are frequently negotiated by representatives on both sides whose prestige is at stake. Face-saving is an important interest which can be served by ambiguous statements. Or the parties may not be able or willing to spell out the details of how a general principle should be implemented, preferring to leave the specific questions unresolved—perhaps hoping they will not arise during the life of the agreement.[56] The employer's right to discharge, for example, is typically restricted in general terms, such as that employees are not to be discharged except for "cause" or "just cause." The general term must suffice because it is impossible to foresee all the situations that might justify discharge.

Judicial opinions are sometimes deliberately imprecise, and on rare occasions blatantly so. Justice Frankfurter, in one of his dissents, acknowledged, "I am not unaware that there is an air of imprecision about what I have written. Such is the intention."[57] Imprecision may be better than a mere illusion of exactness, especially where bright line rules could produce injustice.

The Founding Fathers thought it unwise to give specific answers to questions that they knew would arise under the Constitution. Article IV, section 3, provided that "new States may be admitted by Congress into this Union." This wording gave no answer to a question sure to arise: were new states to be admitted as equals, or was Congress to have power to attach conditions to admission? The delegates debated this question, but in the end rejected an addendum that "the new States shall be admitted on the same terms as the original States." They left the question unresolved, and so it remained for more than a hundred years.[58]

---

[55]　F. T. C. v. Gratz, 253 U.S. 421 (1920) (Brandeis, J., dissenting).

[56]　Shulman, The Settlement of Labor Disputes, 4 Record of N.Y.C.B.A. 12 (1949).

[57]　Braniff Airways v. Nebraska, 347 U.S. 590, 609 (1954).

[58]　Coyle v. Smith, 221 U.S. 559 (1911).

The Constitution is one of the most successful examples of the surprising durability of vague language. To this day, the Supreme Court continues to redefine flexible expressions like cruel and unusual punishment, due process of law, equal protection, necessary and proper, probable cause, unreasonable search and seizure.

"If there is vagueness in your writing," advises Deborah E. Bouchoux, "make sure it is intentional."[59]

§ 5.16   Do Not Rely on Context to Cure Ambiguity

A sentence may be ambiguous for several reasons, including poor word choice, clumsy word order, or the use of a pronoun without clear antecedent. The first is semantic and the others are syntactic ambiguities.

Careless writers caught composing ambiguous sentences may become defensive, arguing that the meaning is clear in context and that any criticism is unfair. Context may disambiguate many ambiguous sentences, but writing an inadvertently ambiguous sentence hoping it will be understood in context is not the hallmark of a superior writing style. "You know what I meant" is a last resort argument: it is unlikely to persuade the audience, repair your credibility, or win the case.

A sentence should be clear independent of context: forcing readers to consider context is an imposition that slows them down and distracts attention from the message. Or worse, readers may get the context wrong. The more you ask your readers to do, the less they can focus on your idea.

Often, too, the context does not help. Judging from the amount of litigation on ambiguous clauses, reliance on context only invites trouble. Moreover, those who write using context as a crutch tend to be careless in all their constructions. So it pays to be constantly alert: do not put yourself in a position that needs to be saved by context, by a reasonable or attentive reader, or by luck. Always write clearly.

But "writing clear is not just hard: it is almost an unnatural act. It has to be learned, sometimes painfully."[60] Your text will always seem clear to you, because when you read it your mind reads

---

[59]   Aspen Handbook for Legal Writers 91 (2017).

[60]   Joseph M. Williams & Joseph Bizup, Style: Lessons in Clarity and Grace 196 (2014). See also James C. Raymond, Writing (Is an Unnatural Act) (1980).

exactly what you wanted it to say. From your perspective, it even says things it does not say explicitly. This is "the curse of knowledge," an inability to empathize with the audience:

> The better you know something, the less you remember about how hard it was to learn. . . . Anyone who wants to lift the curse of knowledge must first appreciate what a devilish curse it is. Like a drunk who is too impaired to realize that he is too impaired to drive, we do not notice the curse because the curse prevents us from noticing it.[61]

The difficulty in writing effectively is that the text must be clear to someone else, someone who does not know what you know. The text will not clarify itself—you will have to work hard on it, through several rounds of revisions, with intellectual empathy for your reader. If you want others to understand your message, you have to read and critique your text, as if it were written by someone else.[62]

Good legal writers go beyond writing merely to be understood; they make sure they cannot be misunderstood.[63]

---

[61]   Steven Pinker, The Sense of Style 57–76, esp. 61 (2014).

[62]   See §§ 3.11, Rewrite (discussing the importance of reviewing one's prose), 4.12, Simplifying is Painstaking Work (same) and Chapter 9, Conclusion (same).

[63]   Quintillian (35 AD–100 AD), Institutes of Oratory § 8.2.24 (95); *In re* Castioni, 1 QB 149, 167–68 (1891).

Chapter 6

FORCEFULNESS

A well-constructed sentence should be able to carry a stress on any of its words and should show in itself how these stresses are to be compounded.
William Empson (1906–1984)[1]

§ 6.1   Introduction

The subject of most legal writing is complex and demands a reader's concentrated attention. But readers tire and stop paying attention. Writing thus becomes a psychological campaign, an exercise in holding the reader's interest. The writer must continually spur the reader on, now tickling his fancy with a neat turn of phrase, now stirring or shocking him with a moving or vivid word, constantly stimulating him to think more keenly, see more clearly, or feel more strongly. A vigorous style is particularly important for lawyers, who need to make the impact on the reader strong and indelible.

Before considering how forcefulness can be attained, let's make clear how it cannot.

I.   How Not to Do It

§ 6.2   Avoid Ineffective Techniques to Emphasize

In speaking, we can use devices to gain forcefulness that are not available in writing, such as pauses, gestures, and raising or lowering the voice.

Thoughtless writers, deceived by the abundance of tools in modern word processors, abuse typographic techniques, such as highlighting words, phrases, even whole sentences. But force is not conveyed by mechanical gimmickry such as underlining, bold, capital letters, or italics. This is bad writing, a practice that is artless and usually ineffective. Instead, forceful writing results from nuanced word choice, sentence structure, and organization. You may use typographic techniques in early drafts to call attention

---

[1]   Seven Types of Ambiguity 34 (1955). See also John Franklin Genung, The Working Principles of Rhetoric 129 (1900).

to what you need to emphasize, but you should eliminate them as you edit.[2] When sparingly used in a finished draft, however, italics may offer an acceptable way to highlight a specific word or phrase.

No emphasis is gained by the use of exclamation points, either individually or in a string!!! An exclamation point is a crutch used by insecure writers looking for an easy way to emphasize an otherwise feeble statement. "Cut out all these exclamation points," advised F. Scott Fitzgerald. "An exclamation point is like laughing at your own joke."[3] Intensity will emerge from the message and from the artful choice and arrangement of words, not from decorative punctuation.

Attention is not effectively directed to a statement by saying, "it is important to bear in mind"; "we should like to point out"; "it cannot be overemphasized"; or "it is to be noted."[4] A lawyer who wants to convey the idea that a conclusion clearly follows must present the material in such a way that the reader will inevitably come to that conclusion, and not merely say that it is clear. If the conclusion is clear, if the element is essential, if the statement is important, the reader need not be told. If it is not clear, the extra descriptors will not convince anyone and may hurt your credibility. Don't demand that the reader take your word that something is clear, reasonable, or essential; demonstrate it with facts and arguments. Show, don't tell.

§ 6.3   Intensifying Adverbs and Adjectives Weaken Your Prose

Insecure writers routinely use intensifying adjectives to strengthen nouns and adverbs to strengthen verbs: *very, clearly, certainly*. But this abuse leads to verbosity and weakens the message: a "threat" is scarier than a "very serious threat" and an "extremely serious and urgent" emergency is less dire than a catastrophe. "The adjective that exists solely as decoration," said William Zinsser, "is a self-indulgence for the writer and a burden for the reader."[5]

---

[2]   Ian Gallacher, A Form and Style Manual for Lawyers 91–92 (2005).

[3]   Quoted in Sheilah Graham & Gerold Frank, Beloved Infidel: The Education of a Woman 198 (1958).

[4]   See § 3.5, Eliminate Throat Clearers.

[5]   On Writing 70 (2006).

Adjectives and adverbs are indispensable parts of speech; they can lend character and color to your style.[6] They are valuable when you want to characterize the situation you are talking about, but not when you merely want to intensify the degree. It is proper to refer to a "financial crisis," a "procedural point," a "patient judge," but when you find yourself writing about a "serious crisis," a "very important point," or an "alarming increase," it is time to push delete. "The adjective," said Voltaire, "is the enemy of the noun."[7]

Lawyers overuse exaggerated adjectives and adverbs in the mistaken belief that they add strength to arguments:

absolutely	fullest	plainly
certainly	highest	profoundly
clearly	incontrovertible	surely
completely	inevitably	totally
deepest	irresistible	undeniably
definitely	necessarily	undoubtedly
essential	obviously	unthinkable
exceedingly	perfectly	utterly
extremely		

These terms are hollow and their use is ineffective. Any intensifying effect quickly wears off, leaving them as weakeners, not strengtheners. Omitting an intensifier will usually not affect the meaning; in most situations, the message will be stronger without it. Do not weaken your prose with intensifiers.[8]

Be particularly vigilant about words ending in -*ly*. Hunt them down like vermin until their population is under control.

> I find the arrangement of the opinions to be terribly unimportant.

This was written by a law professor. *Terribly* is a poor word to modify *important*; it is worse for modifying *unimportant*. Was the writer really terrorized by the unimportance of the arrangement? This question may strike you as bickering; any sensible reader, you may say, understands that the writer was not using *terribly* to mean "exciting terror." Yes, but any sensible person reading these

---

[6]   See, e.g., Virginia Tufte, Artful Sentences: Syntax as Style 91–109 (2006).

[7]   Quoted in Arthur Schopenhauer, On style [1851], in Lane Cooper (ed.), The Art of the Writer 228 (1952).

[8]   See § 3.4, Eliminate Unnecessary Determiners and Modifiers. Contradictorily, lawyers also have a tendency to hedge, qualifying even the most uncontroversial statements. See § 6.8, Do Not Qualify Unnecessarily.

words will understand that this writer does not always mean what he says. It is better to build the opposite kind of reputation.

> Four witnesses testified that the foreman's account was accurate in every particular.

The reader's suspicion is aroused by such an extreme claim. Did all four witnesses really testify that the account was accurate "in every particular"? If they did, weren't they overdoing it, and aren't we justified in wondering whether they themselves were being accurate in their testimony?

Exaggeration destroys the reader's confidence not only in the particular statement but also in everything else that is said. A lawyer has a special responsibility to be trustworthy and reliable. If you hope to gain respect, avoid reckless superlatives and unrestrained generalizations, or run the risk of being perceived as a person not to be trusted.

When you feel that a noun is not strong enough, instead of trying to intensify it by adding an adjective, find a stronger noun that will get the effect you want without any qualifier. If *accident* doesn't seem sufficiently powerful, don't call it a *terrible accident*. Look for a stronger synonym for *accident*, such as *disaster*, *catastrophe*, *calamity*, or *tragedy*. Express intensity through meaning, not through a veneer of modifiers.

> grave error (blunder, botchery, bungle, folly, failure)
>
> great malice (hatred, malevolence, spitefulness, venom, spite, cruelty, hostility, viciousness)
>
> great pain (agony, anguish, torment, misery, affliction, torture)
>
> great wrong (evil, iniquity, outrage, villainy, wickedness)
>
> very large (huge, enormous, gigantic, massive, immense, vast, comprehensive, colossal, monumental)
>
> very negligent (heedless, mindless, rash, reckless, careless, sloppy, inconsiderate)
>
> very painful (excruciating, agonizing, harrowing, traumatic, tortuous)
>
> very poor (destitute, indigent, bankrupt, impoverished)
>
> very sad (heartbroken, melancholy, mournful, somber, sorrowful, bitter, bereaved, grieving, disheartened, depressed, crestfallen)
>
> very simple (elementary, straightforward, facile)
>
> very strong (potent, powerful, compelling, persuasive, forceful, substantial, mighty, unyielding)

In 1770, Sir George Savile made blunt accusations against fellow members of the House of Lords. Lord North tried to soften his words the next day by saying that he was sure "Sir George had spoken in warmth." "No," said Savile, "I spoke what I thought last night, and I think the same this morning. Honorable members have betrayed their trust. I will add no epithets, because epithets only weaken. I will not say they have betrayed their country corruptly, flagitiously, and scandalously; but I do say they have betrayed their country, and I stand here to receive the punishment for having said so."[9]

Certain adjectives look too small and lonely to some writers to stand unaccompanied by an adverb. These writers never describe a thing as merely *far* or *near*, *long* or *short*; it must always be *very far*, *quite near*, *fairly long*, *relatively short*.

The most overused adverb is *very*. In its original meaning of *truly* this was a word of some force, but it has become so worn out from overuse that it no longer adds anything but clutter. When you find yourself using it, consider whether it would be missed if deleted. Usually you can strike it without a loss. To say that a point is *very clear*, a speech *very good* or *very convincing* and its defects *very few*, does not add anything to the same statements without *very*. On the contrary, *clear*, *good*, *convincing*, and *few* are stronger without the qualifying adverbs. "Never use the word, 'very' ", said William Allen White. "It is the weakest word in the English language; doesn't mean anything. If you feel the urge of 'very' coming on, just write the word, 'damn,' in the place of 'very.' The editor will strike [it] out . . . , and you will have a good sentence."[10]

Writers sometimes use intensifiers in ways that suggest they do not know what they mean. They say *literally* when they mean *figuratively* ("we were literally thrown out of court"). They will say that one thing is *incomparably better* (or worse) than another, and then proceed to compare them. They use comparatives with qualities that have no degrees, as *very essential*, *most perfect*, *partly identical*, or *more unique*. These are as inane as *very dead*.

If you say, "it is impossible to contend . . ." in answering an opponent who does so contend, you are obviously wrong. If you mean that the contention is illogical or unsound, say so. *Unthinkable* is another intensifier that typically overshoots the mark. Things that are truly unthinkable can hardly be talked about. So when writers call something that they are thinking and

---

[9]   George Otto Trevelyan, The Early History of Charles James Fox 199 (1880).

[10]   Seattle Daily Times, Oct. 18th, 1935, 37. See http://quoteinvestigator.com/2012/08/29/substitute-damn/.

talking about *unthinkable*, we know that they do not mean what they say.

Saying that something is *undoubtedly* true suggests doubt. Introducing a sentence with "to tell the truth" or "to be frank" merely prompts the question, "Haven't you been, so far?" The lead-in "I am sure that" is so often used to bolster an assertion the writer is unsure about that we have come to expect anything introduced by these words to be questionable. To say that a contention is clearly unsound, that it has been practically overruled, or that no reasonable person would accept it, is likely to lead a critical reader to question and perhaps reject it. There is a streak of contrariness in all humans that prompts us to reject peremptory assertions. Judges and lawyers are trained to be more skeptical than most.

"I am only too glad" is weaker than "I am glad." (This peculiar use of *too* is not only weak but fatuous). The same can be said of *not too*, as in, "his feelings toward defendant were not too friendly," or "the decision is not too clear." When you say, "this kind of misrepresentation is not to be taken too lightly," you imply that it may be taken somewhat lightly. Omit *too*.

Comparatives are weaker than unqualified statements. "Let us die to make men more free" is weaker than "let us die to make men free."

Sometimes these supposed strengtheners weaken the statement to the point of carrying the opposite meaning from that intended. If you want to tell your client not to be alarmed over certain developments, you do not add reassurance with the word *unduly*. "There is no reason to be unduly alarmed" means that there is reason for a certain amount of alarm but not more than necessary. "With *all due* respect" does not imply more respect than the word *respect* standing alone; it implies less. Since the phrase is usually used to introduce a critical statement, it means, "with all the respect that is due to someone holding such an unsound view."

Restraint is more effective than exaggeration, just as the low growl of a mastiff is more persuasive than the vehement yipping of a terrier. The right noun or verb, unqualified, is more powerful than the wrong one bedecked in superlatives. Deliberate understatement, relying on the reader's intelligence to supply the more appropriate tone, is often more successful in inducing the desired emotional response than overt urging. That's the power of subtlety. It is a matter of credibility, as much as it is of style.

Having dismissed these mistaken devices, let us discuss effective ways for gaining forcefulness. We can group them under two main headings: choosing the forceful word or expression and arranging words for emphasis.

II. CHOOSING THE FORCEFUL WORD OR EXPRESSION

The qualities of precision, conciseness, simplicity, and clarity, discussed in the previous chapters, are not only virtues in themselves, but also means for a more forceful style. One way to make a sentence stronger is to make it shorter, plainer, and clearer. A short word is ordinarily more forceful than a long one, a familiar idiom more than the elaborate or bookish. In the words of Robert Southey, "if you would be pungent, be brief; for it is with words as with sunbeams, the more they are condensed, the deeper they burn."[11]

We can all animate our writing style if we consistently cut down nominalization, use strong action verbs and concrete nouns, and prefer the affirmative over the negative and the active over the passive.

§ 6.4   Use Action Verbs

We have just warned against overusing adjectives and adverbs.[12] We have also said that nominalization makes for an overstuffed, pretentious style[13] and decried the abuse of prepositions and conjunctions.[14] A compelling writing style, however, demands muscular verbs, words of action that infuse your writing with vitality and vigor. Too often, legal writers opt for flabby verbs that enervate their writing.

The verb is the power plant of the sentence; it supplies the energy and the action. Nevertheless, writers often pass over a direct verb and reach for a ponderous noun derived from the verb. Instead of saying, "we have revised the traffic code," weak drafters say, "revisions have been made in the traffic code." Instead of, "by distributing the caseload better, we have markedly improved the court's operation," they say, "better distribution of the caseload has

---

[11]   In Henry Southgate, Many Thoughts of Many Minds 71 (1862).

[12]   See § 6.3, Intensifying Adverbs and Adjectives Weaken Your Prose.

[13]   See § 4.5, Don't Overuse Nouns.

[14]   See § 3.3, Eliminate Wordy and Useless Expressions (discussing "glue words" and "working words").

effected a marked improvement in the operation of the court." The verbs *"distribute"* and *"improve"* are made into nouns, *distribution* and *improvement*, making the sentence more verbose and less forceful.

Some writers will say, "Improvement in the field of pest control was accomplished by the utilization of more effective insecticides." The only verb in that sentence is the weak "was accomplished." The action words have been smothered and turned into polysyllabic nouns: *improvement* and *utilization.* If we turn these words back into verbs, we get a stronger sentence: "Using more effective insecticides has improved our pest control program."

When we say "use verbs," therefore, we don't mean the spineless auxiliary verbs like *be, give, have, hold, make,* and *take,* which seduce you into using nouns that derive from verbs and sap their strength. Use the direct verb itself, a strong verb that does something: not "it was the court's intention," but "the court intended."

be binding upon (bind)	have the capacity for (can)
be in need of (need)	hold a meeting (meet)
be required to (must)	make an attempt (try)
come into conflict (conflict)	make provision (provide)
exhibit a tendency (tend)	provide guidance (guide)
enter into an agreement (agree)	reach a decision (decide)
give authorization (authorize)	take notice (notice)
have knowledge of (know)	take into consideration (consider)[15]

Before a state will be allowed so to impair a person's liberty, it will be required to show a compelling justification.	Before a state may impair a person's liberty, it must show a compelling justification.

Auxiliary (little) verbs encourage making dreary nouns out of real action verbs by adding suffixes like *-ion, -ation, -ment, -ence, -ancy, -ency,* and *-ent.* Thus *examine* becomes "make an examination"; *act* becomes "take action"; *encourage* becomes "give encouragement to"; and *appear* becomes "make an appearance." This process is called nominalization and leads to using abstract nouns instead of saying what somebody did to someone else.[16]

The general response was cynical laughter.

---

[15]   See § 4.5, Don't Overuse Nouns (with an extensive list of nominalizations).
[16]   See § 4.5, Don't Overuse Nouns (discussing nominalization).

> The campus confrontations have faded.
> There is a tendency to use . . . .

These sentences have an eerie quality: they have no people in them, only abstractions. They also have no working verbs, only weak little verbs like *was, have, is*. The working words are all abstract, impersonal nouns: *response, laughter, confrontation, tendency*.

Linguistic theory tells us that such nominalizations are harder for readers to process than equivalent verbs, for two reasons:

(1) Verbal phrases are simpler. Anything that makes a verb less like a verb and more like a noun creates abstraction. And abstract terms are vague.

(2) Readers like personal references, whereas nominalization is impersonal. When talking, we might say, "when you describe a thing, make sure . . . ." In legal writing, we are likely to think that too informal. So we nominalize. We write, "the description of a thing should . . . ." This takes the actor out of the picture, and leaves only an impersonal act with no action. Readers find this harder to visualize; their minds have to work harder to get your message.

Breathe life into cold, dead sentences by adding people. Energize your prose using vivid verbs—get people into the action, doing things. Instead of, "the general response was cynical laughter," say, "the candidates laughed cynically." Instead of, "the campus confrontations have faded," say, "students today no longer organize protests or stage sit-ins." Instead of, "there is a tendency to use," say, "we tend to use," or better yet, "we use." You can get people into even abstract propositions by using the word *we*. Instead of saying "the American concept is," say, "we in America believe," or better, "Americans believe."

Transitive verbs, which aim at an object, are more forceful than intransitive ones.

One form of verb often neglected is the participle—the verb with the *-ing* ending—used as a noun. Participles can often be substituted for nouns.

Upon performance of certain minimum conditions, the lessee may bring a claim.	Upon performing certain minimum conditions, the lessee may bring a claim.
The depletion of the trust by the application of its assets to non-trust purposes constituted a breach.	Depleting the trust by applying its assets to non-trust purposes constituted a breach.

Breathe life into your prose with strong, active verbs. Unless, of course, you don't want to convey action or compose a forceful scene.

§ 6.5   The Passive Voice Is Weak

The active voice is normally more concise[17] and more vigorous than the passive voice, and it leads to more interesting reading. Passive verbs are lazy verbs; they don't do anything. "The verbs you want to use," says Rudolf Flesch, "are those that are in the active business of doing verb work."[18] Arthur Quiller Couch similarly said, "the first virtue, the touchstone of a [muscular] style is its use of the active verb and the concrete noun."[19]

The passive voice is not only weaker and wordier than the active, it may also be ambiguous.[20] It may leave uncertain who the actor is. Even when the actor is known, the passive voice takes the spotlight off of him.

The measure was approved by the President in the State of the Union Address.	The President approved the measure in the State of the Union Address.

Passive piled on passive produces graceless constructions such as the following:

> A favorable atmosphere was hoped to be created.
> The decision was attempted to be taken to the Supreme Court.
> This is the question that is proposed to be discussed.

If you write such a sentence, recast it by identifying the actor (unnamed in the examples above) and by starting with that actor as the subject:

> The proponents hoped to create a favorable atmosphere.
> The defendant attempted to take the decision to the Supreme Court.
> We propose to discuss this question.

You will strengthen your writing style if you consistently prefer the active voice over the passive.[21]

---

[17]   See § 3.8, The Passive Voice is Verbose.

[18]   How to Write, Speak, and Think More Effectively 50 (1951).

[19]   On The Art of Writing 117 (1916).

[20]   See § 5.11, The Passive Voice May Be Ambiguous.

[21]   But see § 7.15, The Passive Voice May be Just What You Need (discussing legitimate uses of the passive voice).

§ 6.6   Make Assertions in the Affirmative

The lawyer who wants to make a strong assertion should put it in the affirmative: tell what happened, not what did not. Telling us that something *is not* only denies the existence of something or its quality; it does not posit anything. Avoid *not*, except when making a denial.

Language is more vigorous, concise, and easier to read when it affirms something. Although a sprinkling of negative sentences might not be noted, and might even bring variety to your prose, their persistent use will sap your writing's vitality.

Negative ideas can often be expressed in positive form, giving them greater forcefulness.

does not accept (rejects)	not honest (dishonest)
does not allow (prohibits)	not important (trivial, insignificant)
does not come to work (misses work)	not many (few)
does not give consideration to (ignores)	not often (seldom, rarely)
does not have (lacks)	not occupied (vacant)
does not include (excludes)	not on purpose (accidentally)
does not know (is unaware)	not opened (closed, unopened)
does not remember (forgets)	not possible (impossible)
does not succeed (fails)	not probable (improbable)
does not take care (neglects)	not the same (different)
not able (unable)	not true (false)
not certain (uncertain)	not until (only when)
not current (outdated)	of no use (useless)

The positive form inside the parentheses, however, still carries a negative connotation, and may lead to a double negative.[22]

I rarely do not go to the office on Sundays.	I often go to the office on Sundays.
In rare cases, courts do not sanction parties who act unethically.	Courts often sanction parties who act unethically.

Whole sentences can be changed from negative to positive.

This provision does *not* apply to lessees who do *not* reside on the premises.	This provision applies only to lessees who reside on the premises.

---

[22]   See § 5.8, Avoid Double Negatives.

No preliminary injunction shall be issued *without* notice to the adverse party.	The court may issue a preliminary injunction only on notice to the adverse party.[23]

Here we are discussing ways to achieve forcefulness. There may be times, however, when a lawyer does not want to be forceful or positive—as when there is reason for saying "not unlawful" instead of "lawful."

§ 6.7 Use Specific and Concrete Rather than General and Abstract Words

Legal writing deals with complex analyses that are difficult to comprehend even when well written. Do not make it more burdensome by using fuzzy verbiage. Specific and concrete words are clearer and more precise than general and abstract ones.[24] They are also simpler and stronger, and easier to read.

General words are ineffective not because they are incorrect, but because they are imprecise. What they say is not only true of their target, but also of many other things, making them meaningless. That is why there is no vividness and no force in words like large, small, fast, slow, condition, framework, variable, good or bad, adequate, reasonable, sufficient. Other words are subjective and thus vague: interesting, attractive, inspiring. Abstract words are vague because they are so inclusive that they have no precise boundaries: law, right, wrong, idea, property, equity, reasonable, fair, due process, freedom, justice.

Writing that is stuffed with general nouns is hard to read because it lacks color and life. General nouns call for equally colorless verbs. They never run, jump, grasp, or scratch; they produce, comprise, or refer to. They demand mental effort to translate generalities into concrete propositions. The reader who doesn't invest that much effort finds her eyes moving over words that leave no impression. The reader who does is disappointed.

Lawyers, who must frequently discuss general principles and propositions, are particularly subject to the danger that their discourse may wander to such a high level of abstraction that even legal professionals will find it difficult to follow. Even more than most writers, lawyers should make their writing specific and

---

[23] FRCP 65(a)(1), before and after the 2007 restyling.

[24] See §§ 2.7, Abstract Words are Inexact and 4.7 Prefer Concrete to Fuzzy Nouns; Avoid Vogue Words.

concrete, using examples, details, similes, and metaphors that evoke vivid images. They should talk of automobiles rather than means of transportation, of cars rather than automobiles, and of a red Porsche sedan rather than a car. They should refer not to a noise, but to a crash, roar, shriek, or hum.

In *Schenck*, Justice Holmes conjures a scene of clear and present danger, illustrating the advice:

> The most stringent protection of free speech would not protect a man in falsely shouting fire in a theater and causing a panic.[25]

Avoid sentences like this:

> In proportion as the manners, customs, and amusements of a nation are cruel and barbarous, the regulations of their penal code will be severe.

Instead, write:

> In proportion as men delight in battles, bullfights, and combats of gladiators, will they punish by hanging, burning, and the rack.[26]

The level of forcefulness you want to impart in your prose will depend on the situation. You must develop the technique to write in whatever style is appropriate, and the wisdom to know when to use one or the other. While a defendant would say, "the boy was often beaten by his father," a plaintiff would want to give concrete details: "the father often lashed the boy's back with a leather strap that cut the flesh and left permanent scars."

You should have some tough, hard-hitting words at your command to shock, surprise, or express strong feeling.[27] But you must recognize the line between toughness and crudity—find tough words that are not crude or offensive. And, always, keep your audience in mind.

§ 6.8   Do Not Qualify Unnecessarily

"There is an accuracy that defeats itself by the overemphasis of details," said Justice Cardozo. "The sentence may be so overloaded with all its possible qualifications that it will tumble down of its own weight."[28]

---

[25]   Schenck v. United States, 249 U.S. 47, 52 (1919).

[26]   Herbert Spencer, Philosophy of Style 15 (1884).

[27]   See §§ 2.1, Introduction, 2.3, Use a Thesaurus and a Dictionary, and 5.4, Put Modifiers With the Word or Phrase Modified.

[28]   Law and Literature, 14 Yale Rev. 699, 701 (1925); 52 Harv. L. Rev. 471, 474 (1939).

Inexperienced writers are often hesitant to leave clarifications for a later sentence or paragraph. Perhaps they fear that a hostile reader might argue that a later qualification on a separate sentence does not apply.[29] But there is nothing wrong with deferred specificity; do not feel you must squeeze all qualifications into one sentence.[30]

Qualifications that do not affect your point may be safely omitted without compromising precision. As Clarence Edwin Ayres said, "[a] little inaccuracy saves a world of explanation."[31] You don't want the reader lost in irrelevant details. For Justice Cardozo, "one must permit oneself, and that quite advisedly and deliberately, a certain margin of misstatement. Of course, one must take heed that the margin is not exceeded, just as the physician must be cautious in administering the poisonous ingredient which magnified will kill, but in tiny quantities will cure."[32]

Omitting essential qualifications, however, may have fatal consequences. Exactness must be the lawyer's primary aim. And if constancy in this aim makes the style less than graceful, so be it. As Lord Macmillan put it, "there are few higher intellectual pleasures than . . . expressing an argument . . . in just precisely the right language, so that the thought is . . . poised exactly as we would have it."[33]

The lawyer must exercise judgment about what is material and what is incidental and therefore omissible.[34] First, make sure that all the necessary qualifications are included; later, strike out those that on reflection seem unnecessary.

A related problem is excessive hedging. When you can make an absolute statement, do so. You can hardly make a stronger statement than that something is *always* or *never* so; that every A is always B, or that no X is ever Y. Unqualified assertions like the following are very effective:

> [W]e have been unable to find a single instance of a criminal trial conducted *in camera* in any federal, state, or municipal court during the history of this country. Nor have we found any record of even one such

---

[29]   Peter M. Tiersma, Legal Language 56 (1999).

[30]   See § 7.6, Say One Thing at a Time.

[31]   Science, the False Messiah (1927).

[32]   Law and Literature, 14 Yale Rev. 699, 701 (1925); 52 Harv. L. Rev. 471, 474 (1939).

[33]   Lord Macmillan, Law and Letters, 16 A.B.A.J. 662, 665 (1930).

[34]   See § 6.8, Do Not Qualify Unnecessarily.

criminal trial in England since abolition of the Court of Star Chamber in 1641, and whether that court ever convicted people secretly is in dispute.[35]

Every other state in the union has found it possible to regulate the professions of architecture and engineering without being nearly as indefinite as Arizona. Assuming for the sake of discussion that these professions are constitutionally subject to some regulation, it would be easy to do better than Arizona has done, and hard to do worse.

But lawyers can seldom make absolute statements. We frequently deal with complex situations and nuanced concepts incapable of being expressed accurately without using qualifying clauses that weaken the statement with an equivocating *generally* or *as a rule*. When we think we can, we had better examine each categorical expression to make sure it is really true. More often than not, it will need to be qualified. But because exactness often calls for qualifications, lawyers are likely to reflexively qualify everything they say. They add *it seems*, *apparently*, or *it is indicated that* even into the most innocuous sentences. They timidly back away from saying that B is "as good as" A, and prefer B "compares favorably with" A. They may even say:

> Your report does not *seem to* include a statement of your income for the past year.

Either it does or it doesn't. Omit *seem to.*

Afraid of absolute statements that may be proved wrong, lawyers hedge with words like

apparently	likely	seemingly
appears	may	should
basically	might	somewhat
comparatively	nearly	sort of
could	possibly	substantially
entirely	presumably	tend to
essentially	predominantly	ultimately
fairly	probably	usually
generally	rather	virtually
in part	relatively	would
kind of	seem	

Indirect statements also create weak prose:

> Our company *ultimately* (or *essentially*) follows the *pertinent* regulations.

---

[35] *In re* Oliver, 333 U.S. 257, 266 (1948) (Black, J.).

The sentence is tepid and leaves the reader wondering whether the company complies with all regulations.

Lawyers often overdo caution; we resolve all doubts in favor of keeping every qualification that may or may not need to be expressed. We draft complex legal provisions overburdened with qualifications, cross-references, exceptions, provisos, and footnotes.[36] "Caution and reticence in writing," as Justice Frankfurter said, "make for qualifications and circumlocutions that stifle spontaneity, slow the rhythm of speech, check the play of imagination. . . . Law as literature is restrained by its responsibility."[37]

Popular writers can get a breezier, more colorful style by using looser, more imaginative—but less exact—language. They can make broad, provocative generalizations. "To philosophize is to generalize," said Justice Holmes, "but to generalize is to omit."[38] Lawyers, however, cannot afford to omit very much very often.

"It's not that good writers never hedge their claims," said Steven Pinker. "It's that their hedging is a choice, not a tic."[39] Lawyers may hesitate to be direct because they think circumlocutions are more formal and dignified than plain talk. But dignity does not demand debilitating verbosity. Nor does precision dictate overparticularization.

§ 6.9   Use Figures of Speech

(1) The Alluring Power of Figures of Speech

One of the most vivid ways to make a point is through a figure of speech. Similes, metaphors, and other figures are shorthand, "harnessing the physical world in the service of abstract ideas."[40] They enable us to say more in fewer words, and to do it with vitality and color.

Illustrating a general proposition with a specific symbol is a highly effective stylistic device. Justice Harlan, arguing that the

---

[36] Contradictorily, lawyers also overuse hyperbole. See § 6.3, Avoid Ineffective Techniques to Emphasize.

[37] Law and Politics 103, 106 (1939).

[38] Donnel v. Herring-Hall-Marvin Safe Co., 208 U.S. 267, 273 (1908).

[39] The Sense of Style 45 (2014).

[40] Helen Sword, Stylish Academic Writing 104 (2012).

Constitution forbids distinctions based on race or color, said it was colorblind.[41]

An apt illustration impresses the reader more than anything else you say. We all like analogies, and often accept them too readily and then extend them too far. The figurative analogy is such a delightfully easy device that the writer who discovers it may be tempted to oversimplify difficult concepts. Nothing in law is so apt to mislead, said Lord Mansfield, as a metaphor.[42] The proposition that free speech "would not protect a man in falsely shouting fire in a theater,"[43] for example, may be extended to the proposition that free speech does not protect a person who criticizes government policy in the conduct of a war.

Courts and commentators use figures of speech as shorthand to refer to legal doctrines, rules, and theories. Conflict of laws has a bootstrap doctrine and a center of gravity theory. A contract is a meeting of the minds, it may contain a grandfathered clause, and its boilerplate provisions are a binding agreement that must not be broken. Having returned to the high seas, pirates now also plunder intellectual property. In constitutional law, we refuse to admit into evidence the fruit of the poisonous tree, states are the laboratories of democracy, and we bitterly discuss whether the Constitution is dead or alive.

In civil litigation, ambulance chasers sue deep pocket corporations (who are persons) and engage in forum shopping, expecting a lower court to exercise long-arm jurisdiction when a corporation has minimum contacts, is present in the forum state, or places its products in the stream of commerce. Lawyers sue a parent corporation, may pierce the corporate veil, or go on a fishing expedition to discover a smoking gun. After opening arguments, lawyers ask leading questions on cross examination, and before they rest their cases, they conduct an arm's length negotiation to buy global peace.

First Amendment cases have also given us a host of metaphors: marketplace of ideas; wall of separation between Church and State; chilling effect; fighting words; captive audience; multitude of tongues; schoolhouse gate; the pall of orthodoxy over the classroom; the penumbras of the Bill of Rights; the breathing room for freedom

---

[41] Plessy v. Ferguson, 163 U.S. 537, 559 (1896).

[42] Quoted by Lord Westbury in Knox v. Gye, L.R. 5 H.L. 656, 676 (1872).

[43] Schenk v. United States, 249 U.S. 47, 52 (1919) (Holmes, J.).

of expression to survive; falsely shouting fire in a theater; kindle a fire that may burst into a conflagration; and the fixed star in our constitutional constellation.[44]

It is as if no legal argument can be made or rebuked without a figure of speech. Most rules can be broken down into parts or divided into elements; modern doctrines employ balancing or weighing tests; and one must offer a narrow, strict, or broad construction of a rule, sometimes searching for the spirit of the law.[45] When one party needs to stretch a concept, strengthen a rule, or make a principle more elastic or an exception more flexible, the opponent will accuse him of twisting or straining it. And one cannot make any policy argument that will not eventually open the floodgates for something terrible or put society on a slippery slope to something even worse.

A memorable figure of speech seems to have magical powers. It hypnotizes the mind, seducing the reader and distracting attention from the real issue. As useful as they are to convey thought, they may also distort it: a good catchword can obscure analysis for fifty years.[46] Justice Cardozo felt its risk in legal analysis and cautioned—metaphorically—that "[m]etaphors in law are to be narrowly watched, for starting as devices to liberate thought, they end often by enslaving it."[47]

A good metaphor may hijack reasoning and take on a life of its own. "The trouble with metaphors," elaborated Monroe Beardsley, "is that they have a strong pull on our fancy. They tend to run away with us. Then we find that our thinking is directed not by the force of argument at hand, but at the interest of the image in our mind."[48]

Figures of speech help us understand and explain reality, but they also create reality. Their power can also be invoked to dominate and oppress. The Nazis used metaphors to label their scapegoats. Roman law classified slaves as objects, a metaphor that carried over to the Americas and remained current more than two millennia later. You can do almost anything with the right figure

---

[44] See Haig Bosmajian, Metaphor and Reason in Judicial Opinions (1992).

[45] Michael R. Smith, Advanced Legal Writing 210 (2013).

[46] Oliver Wendell Holmes, Law in Science and Science in Law, 12 Harv. L. Rev. 443, 455 (1899). See also Hyde v. United States, 225 U.S. 347, 391 (1912) (Holmes, J.) ("It is one of the misfortunes of the law that ideas become encysted in phrases and thereafter for a long time cease to provoke further analysis").

[47] Berkey v. Third Ave. Ry., 155 N.E. 58, 61 (N.Y. 1926).

[48] Thinking Straight 245 (1956).

of speech: they are so powerful that they may create an illusion for centuries that a person is a thing and a corporation is a person.

Judges and other people in power impose their metaphors and similes on the rest of us. The effect is intensified in a system of precedents, for their repetition in successive opinions institutionalizes figuratively expressed analysis.[49]

The alluring power of metaphors, therefore, must be identified and actively resisted: metaphors, cautioned Jeremy Bentham, are not reasons.[50] As mere "figurative representation of an idea, [they] cannot possibly capture the true meaning of, and all the dimensions and nuances implicated by, an abstract legal concept."[51] A dissenting opinion warned that "a rule of law should not be drawn from a figure of speech."[52] Yet legal principles, theories, doctrines, and rules routinely derive from figures of speech.

So, lawyers "must look beyond established metaphoric labels."[53] The first step to create, oppose, or accept a metaphor is to be aware of the problem. The Supreme Court fought against their pull in *Nicastro*: "the stream of commerce, like other metaphors, has its deficiencies as well as its utility."[54] Cognizant of the power of metaphors, the Supreme Court felt the need to clarify that they do not supersede the Constitution: "the stream-of-commerce metaphor cannot supersede either the mandate of the Due Process Clause or the limits on judicial authority that Clause ensures."[55]

In another case, Judge Posner grappled with the misuse of the cat's paw theory of employer liability: "this is all a dreadful muddle for which we appellate judges must accept some blame because doctrine stated as metaphor . . . can be a judicial attractive nuisance; because vague judicial terminology . . . confuses judges, jurors, and lawyers alike."[56]

Sometimes, it is difficult to combat a prevailing metaphor with reason alone: you need to conscript an alternative metaphor that

---

[49]   Haig Bosmajian, Metaphor and Reason in Judicial Opinions 18 (1992).

[50]   Principles of Legislation 69 (1864).

[51]   Michael R. Smith, Advanced Legal Writing 206 (2013).

[52]   See McCollum v. Board of Education, 333 U.S. 203, 247 (1948) (Reed, J.)

[53]   Michael R. Smith, Advanced Legal Writing 216 (2002).

[54]   J. McIntyre Machinery v. Nicastro, 564 U.S. 873 (2011) ("The 'stream of commerce' metaphor carried the decision far afield.")

[55]   Id.

[56]   Cook v. IPC Int'l Corp., 673 F.3d 625 (7th Cir. 2012).

will convey the reality more effectively or fairly. The United States has been described as a melting pot, a metaphor unchallenged for more than a century, until it was argued that the best analogy was a salad bowl. For Jesse Jackson, it's neither:

> America is not like a blanket—one piece of unbroken cloth, the same color, the same texture, the same size. America is more like a quilt—many patches, many pieces, many colors, many sizes, all woven and held together by a common thread.[57]

The difference between these images hides deep political relevance: one stresses assimilation, the other, multiculturalism. Similarly, the only viable weapon against the ideology of a living, breathing constitution is a dead constitution.

When you use a figure of speech, do so without apology. Don't hide it behind quotes; don't say you are speaking metaphorically; don't qualify it with "as it were," or "so to speak," or—worst of all—"if you please." Don't say the thing you are discussing is "somewhat like"; say it is "like," or don't say it at all.

(2) Use Similes

The most obvious figure of speech is the simile, which describes one thing by saying that it is like another: "the brain is *like* the hand," said Justice Brandeis, "it grows with using."[58] An effective simile portrays some striking, concrete, or picturesque aspect of the subject. It lends vividness to abstract ideas. Devising a good simile calls for imagination. The comparison should be between objects that are so different that the reader is slightly shocked that things so dissimilar share commonality.

We find pleasure in resemblances we have not seen before. Justice Jackson used simile frequently:

> There is no such thing as an achieved liberty; like electricity, there can be no substantial storage and it must be generated as it is enjoyed, or the lights go out.
>
> We granted certiorari, and in this Court the parties changed positions as nimbly as if dancing a quadrille.
>
> If ever we are justified in reading a statute, not narrowly as through a keyhole, but in the broad light of the evils it aimed at and the good it hoped for, it is here.

---

[57] Address Before the Democratic National Convention, July 18, 1984.

[58] The Curse of Bigness 36 (1965).

> The principle then lies about like a loaded weapon ready for the hand of any authority that can bring forward a plausible claim of an urgent need.[59]

Justice Ginsburg, too, showed just how powerful a simile can be:

> Throwing out preclearance when it has worked and is continuing to work to stop discriminatory changes is like throwing away your umbrella in a rainstorm because you are not getting wet.[60]

(3) Use Metaphors

A metaphor is stronger than a simile: it does not merely compare one thing with another; it identifies the two. The simile pictures and illustrates, creating clarity, but the metaphor has a more striking effect. The ability to create metaphors, said Aristotle, is the surest sign of originality.[61] Especially in the cold and formalistic world of legal writing, a metaphor is a powerful tool.

When we say that nominal damages are a peg on which to hang costs, we are using a metaphor. Abraham Lincoln said that the patent system "added the fuel of interest to the fire of genius." He also used earthy metaphor on responsibility at the polls:

> It is the people's business. The election is in their hands. If they turn their backs to the fire and get scorched in the rear, they'll find they have got to sit on the blister.[62]

In deciding that a pleading satisfied the requirement for heightened specificity, a court said,

> Rule 9(b) is a net designed to catch intrinsically faulty claims, not a trap designed to ensnare claims that merely lack a Zolaesque rigor of detail.[63]

Metaphors take several forms, like taking part of an object for the whole, the thing for its use, the effect for the cause.

> We need more boots on the ground.
> The pen is mightier than the sword.[64]

---

[59] The Task of Maintaining Our Liberties, 39 A.B.A.J. 962 (1953); Edwards v. California, 314 U.S. 160, 186 (1941); Orloff v. Willoughby, 345 U.S. 83, 87 (1953); United States *ex rel*. Marcus v. Hess, 317 U.S. 537, 557 (1943) (dissenting); Korematsu v. United States, 323 U.S. 214, 246 (1944) (dissenting).

[60] Shelby Cty. v. Holder, 133 S.Ct. 2612, 2650, (2013) (Ginsburg, J., concurring).

[61] Poetics, Part XXII (335BC).

[62] 3 The Works of Abraham Lincoln 297 (1908).

[63] McQueen v. Woodstream Corp., 248 F.R.D. 73 (D.D.C. 2008).

[64] Edward Bulwer-Lytton, Richelieu; or The Conspiracy 52 (1939).

Although these figures of speech may be regarded as aspects of metaphor, rhetoricians usually classify them as different. A reference to part for the whole is called synecdoche; effect for the cause, metonymy.

One can build a powerful one-word metaphor. "The bite of law," said Justice Frankfurter, "is in its enforcement."[65] He also spoke of "the slippery slope of due process." Justice Holmes told us that when he began practicing, the law was "a ragbag of details."[66] "Liberty," said Justice O'Connor, "finds no refuge in a jurisprudence of doubt."[67]

The world of figures of speech is vast, and the sophisticated legal writer is advised to master it. Figures of speech are "as much a matter of premeditation as they are of inspiration." Therefore, "good advocates do not just hope that an apt metaphor will occur to them. Instead, they consciously create the proper metaphor to achieve a specific rhetorical effect."[68]

(4) The Dangers of Figures of Speech

But there are dangers. Visualizing a figure of speech sometimes demand more effort from the reader than visualizing facts. Because a figure of speech is a condensed, indirect statement, it must be interpreted. To be effective, therefore, it must be simple and easily understood. If there's any risk that the reader may ignore or misunderstand your reference, make it clear or avoid it.

Figures of speech must be used with discrimination and restraint. A single memorable figure of speech is better than several good ones, and too many mental pictures flashed before the reader in rapid succession become wearying. Metaphors, advised Thomas Haggard with a simile, are like strong seasoning: a dash enhances the flavor; too much ruins the dish.[69]

Failure to pay attention to the literal meaning of metaphors may lead to ludicrous statements:

> Only a handful of spectators
> Our biggest bottleneck

---

[65] Fisher v. U.S., 328 U.S. 463, 484 (1946) (dissenting).

[66] Introduction, in Continental Legal History xlvii (1912).

[67] Planned Parenthood v. Casey, 505 U.S. 833, 844 (1992).

[68] Michael H. Frost, Introduction to Classical Legal Rhetoric: A Lost Heritage 96 (2016) (citing Quintillian).

[69] Rhetoric in Legal Writing, S.C. Lawyer, vol. 8, number 6 at 13 (1997).

Failure to remember the literal meaning also leads to ludicrous mixing of metaphors:

> We build castles in the air, the bubble bursts, and leaves naught but ashes in our hands.
>
> The team has been literally working around the clock.
>
> The record speaks louder than any smoke screen.
>
> Though often the target of storms of criticism, the Supreme Court has been the keystone of our constitutional system.

Storms do not have targets and keystones are not targets of storms.

Justice Harlan expressed fear that a majority opinion "paint[ed] with such a broad brush" that "it may result in a loosening of the tight reins" that courts should hold on enforcement of obscenity statutes.[70] Two good metaphors, badly combined.

Metaphors must evoke a concrete image that serves as a helpful analogy, but mixed metaphors "evoke no clear picture in the reader's minds, and what jumbled mental picture they do create confuse more than they clarify."[71]

Keep your audience in mind. Make sure that your figure of speech involves something your readers can easily understand. Obscure references that require the reader to puzzle out your meaning are distracting. References that require specialized knowledge about history, literature, sports, or other areas may not work. Not only might the message be missed, you might also have a reader who resents being excluded from your inner circle.

Another danger in the use of figures of speech is that they are rarely perfectly aligned with the thought they represent. Lurking beneath an apparently felicitous analogy may be another unintended meaning or connotation that will hijack your message.[72] For example, when you say a criticism is Monday-morning quarterbacking, you want to convey the difficulty of reaching an ideal decision at the time. But you are also admitting

---

[70]   Roth v. United States, 354 U.S. 476, 496 (1957) (dissenting).

[71]   Michael R. Smith, Advanced Legal Writing 234 (2013).

[72]   Monroe C. Beardsley, Thinking Straight 193 (1966). See, more specifically, Julie A. Oseid, The Power of Metaphor: Thomas Jefferson's Wall of Separation Between Church & State, 7 J. ALWD 123 (2010) (discussing how a mere stylistic metaphor developed into a legal doctrine) and Linda L. Bergers, What Is the Sound of a Corporation Speaking—How the Cognitive Theory of Metaphor Can Help Lawyers Shape the Law, 2 J. ALWD 169 (2004) (discussing how mixing two metaphors, corporate personhood and marketplace of ideas, led to a third, corporate speech).

that, as one reviews the situation more calmly, one may take a different course.[73]

Metaphors burn out fast. Language changes, and a once-evocative image no longer has meaning. A hackneyed comparison, faded from overuse, calls up no mental image, but slides unnoticed through the mind or is just annoying. "To wrestle with a problem" no longer makes us think of a wrestling match and "saddled with debts" evokes nothing equestrian. To convey strong feeling, we need strong words. Words that once were strong but are now weak from age and overwork won't do—we need words that have the strength and freshness of youth. Thus the advice to avoid clichés.

§ 6.10 Avoid Clichés and Platitudes

A cliché was once a fresh way of expressing a thought, a good figure of speech. But through overuse it has lost its freshness and perhaps its precise meaning, becoming worn out and stale. A platitude is a commonplace, a banal, dull, or insipid remark. If a cliché is a has-been, a platitude never was—it is and always was "weary, stale, flat and unprofitable,"[74] and when uttered with an air of solemn importance is particularly annoying.

"Born, not made" was an original remark, once. But over the centuries, so many kinds of people have been said to be born, not made, that the expression has long ago lost its vigor. The same can be said of activities that are "more art than science." "To make the supreme sacrifice" was once a moving way to refer to dying for a cause. Today, it is so hackneyed that one may use it sarcastically to evoke derision.

Hundreds of formulaic expressions still pass as currency in our language. Here are some that turn up frequently in legal writing:

Achilles' heel	back to the drawing board
add insult to injury	ball is in your court
agree to disagree	bare bones
all walks of life	beat a dead horse
as luck would have it	beg to differ
at arm's length	be in the same boat
back against the wall	bend over backwards
backhanded compliment	be that as it may
back to square one	better safe than sorry

---

[73] Id. at 194.

[74] Quote from William Shakespeare, Hamlet, Act I, scene 2 (1600).

between a rock and a hard place
bite off more than one can chew
bite the bullet
blessing in disguise
blow the whistle
bone of contention
bottom line (up)
bounce back
break ranks
bright-line rule
broken record
burn bridges
burning question
business as usual
buy into
by the book
call a spade a spade
call it a day
call the shots
can safely say
catch someone off guard
change the tune
chilling effect
chip on someone's shoulder
coin a phrase
cold blood
compare apples and oranges
complete picture
considered opinion
conspicuous by its absence
courage of one's convictions
cross a bridge when come to it
cross the line
crushing blow
curve ball
cut and dry
cut both ways
death by a thousand cuts
dig oneself into a hole
do what it takes
draw to a close
drop in the bucket

due consideration
easier said than done
elephant in the room
eleventh hour
every effort is being made
exercise in futility
fall on deaf ears
find a needle in a haystack
fine line
fit a square peg in a round hole
follow in the footsteps of
force to be reckoned with
foregone conclusion
form over substance
free reign
get one's foot in the door
get the ball rolling
get to the bottom of it
give and take
gloss over
goes without saying
go too far
go to the (other) extreme
grievous error
ground rules
half baked
hands are tied
hands down (off) (on)
hard and fast rule
hard to swallow
have a leg up
have a shot at
have the last laugh
head over heels
heads up
height of absurdity
hired gun
icing on the cake
ill-gotten gains
in a nutshell
in no uncertain manner (terms, way)
in the affirmative (negative)

in the hot seat
in the same boat
incontrovertible fact
inevitable conclusion
it stands to reason
judge a book by its cover
keep one's cards close to one's vest
kill two birds with one stone
know full well
know where someone stands
larger than life
last but not least
law-abiding citizens
lesser of two evils
light at the end of the tunnel
like a ton of bricks
litmus test
long arm of the law
long shot
long-standing authority
look over one's shoulder
make a long story short
make ends meet
make it or break it
make waves
matter of life and death
more than meets the eye
nail in the coffin
needs no introduction
no brainer
no strings attached
not a shadow of doubt
off the hook
old school
on all fours
on a short leash
on the right side of the law
on the same page
on thin ice
open a can of worms
open an old wound
open Pandora's box

out on a limb
pale in comparison
path of least resistance
pay lip service
powers that be
preach to the choir
pull no punches
put all one's eggs in one basket
put one's foot in one's mouth
put the cart before the horse
pure and simple
raise (lower) the bar
read between the lines
red herring
reinvent the wheel
remains to be seen
rest on someone's laurels
rough road
sad but true
sanctity of life
sanctity of marriage
sanctity of the home
scraping the bottom of the barrel
separate the wheat from the chaff
shed light on the subject
silver lining
shoot from the hip
shoot oneself in the foot
shoot fish in a barrel
sink one's teeth into
slam dunk
slap on the wrist
sleep on it
small world
smoke and mirrors
smoking gun
split second
spread like wildfire
spread too thin
stack the deck
state of the art
step in the right direction

step on someone's toes	tip of the iceberg
straight shooter	trial by fire
sugarcoat	tried and true
swallow one's pride	twist of fate
sweetheart deal	two bites of the apple
team player	two-way street
test the waters	up for grabs
the easy way out	uphill battle
the glass is half empty (full)	up the ante
the jury is still out	wait for the dust to settle
thing of the past	wake-up call
think outside the box	wash one's hands
through thick and thin	wear many hats
throw cold water on	when all is said and done
throw in the towel	when push comes to shove
throw the baby with the bath water	witch hunt
throw the book at someone	with a grain of salt
time and (time) again	writing on the wall
time is running out	

Some common expressions do not make sense. "Dead as a doornail" is close to meaningless. "Happy as a lark" is not much better. Nor is "happy as a clam." Others once had meaning that has been lost:

a windfall	in the lurch
at first blush	rack and ruin
at loggerheads	salt of the earth
in one fell swoop	turn the tables

Avoiding clichés is not an absolute rule—sparingly used, they communicate your idea simply, effectively, and powerfully. But do not use them unconsciously. Thoughtless writers flood their writing with clichés, producing a lazy, unoriginal, weak style, when they could have expressed themselves in a fresh way.

Some writers stumble into clichés without thinking about what they mean. They start to say "safe," and "safe and sound" rolls out by free association. They say "pomp" and for no good reason add "and circumstance." That's the trouble with habit; it makes us bring up the same response with little concern for sense, as when we bless sneezing strangers.

A good writer stays away from faded phrases. It isn't easy. They are so pervasive that we echo them without thinking about what they mean, if anything. In infancy, we learn to say words before we understand what they mean; we repeat them without much thinking. The habit persists into later life; we continue to pick up words from others, and because they have become familiar we assume they have meaning. We could eliminate verbiage if we consider what we are saying. And if we would pull out the hackneyed, foolish, and vacuous phrases and use fresh, meaningful words instead, we would add originality, vividness, and vigor to our style.[75]

Nevertheless, a new twist can be given to an old saw. To "think twice before you act" is a cliché. But it can be renovated to sound like new: "this will compel the administrator to think once, if not twice, before acting." "Not worth the paper it's written on" is a drab cliché; but was revitalized when Judge Francis Biddle said that in his court, "the unwritten law is not worth the paper it isn't written on."[76]

Some clichés are so overused that we know the connection before we are told. If we read "after a short illness . . .," we know that someone died. If we see the phrase "not to be rude," we know that something offensive may follow. And what to expect of a sentence that begins, "I'm not a racist, but . . ."?

§ 6.11 Use Reiteration Deliberately

An obvious way of giving emphasis is to repeat a word or phrase that you want to stress. "Repetition," said Walter Raleigh, "is the strongest generator of emphasis known to language."[77]

President Lincoln displayed moral complexity and expert drafting in an 1862 letter outlining his Civil War policies:

> My paramount object in this struggle is to save the Union, and not either to save or to destroy slavery.
>
> If I could save the Union without freeing any slave, I would do it; if I could save it by freeing some and leaving others alone, I would also do that.
>
> What I do about slavery and the colored race, I do because I believe it helps to save the Union; and what I forbear, I forbear because I do not believe it would help to save the Union.

---

[75] See § 4.6, Prefer Concrete to Fuzzy Nouns; Avoid Vogue Words ("the vogue words of today are the faddish clichés of tomorrow.").

[76] See 3 Bouvier's Law Dictionary and Concise Encyclopedia 3377 (1914).

[77] Style 52 (1897).

> I shall do less whenever I shall believe that what I am doing hurts the cause; and I shall do more whenever I shall believe doing more will help the cause.
>
> I shall try to correct errors where shown to be errors, and I shall adopt any new views as fast as they shall appear to be true views.[78]

Other examples of reiteration include:

> [Men] are born into the State, are members of the State, must obey the laws enacted by the State, in time of danger must come to the defense of the State, must, if necessary, hazard their lives for the State.[79]
>
> [The forefathers] knew what emergencies were, knew the pressures they engender for authoritative action, knew, too, how they afford a ready pretext for usurpation. We may also suspect that they suspected that emergency powers would tend to kindle emergencies.[80]
>
> Government of the people, by the people and for the people, shall not perish from the earth.[81]

Somewhat akin to reiteration is the use of several words in place of one. Eliminating unnecessary words is a virtue, but determining whether certain words are necessary may depend on the context. The three words, *but only if* say no more than *if* alone. *If*, however, is a very short word and one that carries no emphasis. In a sentence where the word is likely to be overlooked, and where the writer considers it so important that it should not be, the writer can underscore it for the reader by saying, *but only if*. Similarly, while *but* means the same as *however*, the latter may be preferable for emphasis, simply because it is longer. The issues of repetition and reiteration are also discussed elsewhere.[82]

III. ARRANGING WORDS FOR EMPHASIS

The placement of a word in a sentence or paragraph reflects its forcefulness. To be a good writer, one must develop the ability to estimate accurately the effect of even small changes in the order within a sentence or paragraph.[83]

---

[78]   Letter to Horace Greeley, August 22, 1862.

[79]   Lyman Abbott, The Open Shop, LXXVII The Outlook 633 (July 16, 1904).

[80]   Youngstown Sheet & Tube Co. v. Sawyer, 343 U.S. 579, 650 (1952) (Jackson, J., concurring).

[81]   Abraham Lincoln, Gettysburg Address (1863).

[82]   See §§ 2.5, Don't be Afraid to Repeat a Word, 3.9, Not All Repetition is Pointless, and 8.5, Reiteration.

[83]   John Franklin Genung, The Working Principles of Rhetoric 35 (1900).

§ 6.12   Put Words to Be Stressed at the Beginning and the End of Sentences

Emphasis is largely determined by the placement of words within a sentence, and of sentences within a paragraph. The positions that carry the most emphasis within a sentence are the end and the beginning—this is beach-front real estate. At the beginning, we are attentive to the new thought; near the end we look for its completion. Spend time thinking about how to begin and end each sentence you write and you will be rewarded—rearrange the word order so that emphasis falls where it should.

Barrett Wendell, attempting to express this point, wrote: "be sure that your sentences end with words that deserve the distinction you give them." He then noticed that his sentence violated the rule it laid down; it placed in the positions of distinction the unimportant words "be" and "them," when the most important words were "end" and "distinction." He therefore rearranged his sentence to put these words at the beginning and end respectively: "end with words that deserve distinction."[84]

Sometimes strategic ordering cannot be done without disrupting natural word order. But if you try, you will be surprised to see how often you can find an arrangement that puts the words to be stressed in their proper places. Consider the phrase, "faith, hope and charity, and the greatest of these is charity."[85] The emphasis would be lost if written, "and charity is the greatest of these." Yet no word was added or omitted.

In a sentence made up of elements of different value, they should be arranged to progress from the lesser to the greater.

He is a murderer, a liar and a thief.	He is a liar, a thief and a murderer.
Their only choice was to be killed or to obey.	Their only choice was to obey or be killed.

The middle of a sentence carries the least emphasis. That is usually where to put terms like *however, nevertheless*, and *for example*, unless you want to emphasize them.

However, personal belongings are exempt.	Personal belongings, however, are exempt.

---

[84]   English Composition 102–03 (1918).
[85]   1 Corinthians 13:13.

Nevertheless, the defendant continued with the work.

The defendant, nevertheless,
continued with the work.

For example, a summer cabin is
considered a residence.

A summer cabin, for example, is
considered a residence.

Of course, this rule is subject to
exceptions.

This rule is, of course, subject to
exceptions.

Bury subordinate thoughts—and those you do not want to emphasize—in the middle of a sentence. If you place a harmful fact between two supportive facts, you will lessen the importance of the harmful fact while simultaneously heightening the importance of the supportive facts.

If the thought you want to emphasize is in a grammatically subordinate clause, move it to the end. Compare the shift in emphasis in the following two sentences. Which is the more optimistic? Which the more doubting?

This, if the jury believes it, is a
perfect defense.

This is a perfect defense, if the jury
believes it.

A restrictive phrase or clause, such as one beginning with *at least*, makes a weak beginning and an anti-climactic ending:

Such an interpretation of the
statute would render it grossly unjust, at
least in some cases.

In some cases, such an
interpretation of the statute would render
it grossly unjust.

Phrases or clauses beginning with *not* also make weak endings:

The rule we ask the court to adopt
would promote corporate responsibility,
not recklessness as plaintiff contends.

The rule we ask the court to adopt
would not encourage recklessness as
plaintiff contends, but would promote
corporate responsibility.

As the illustration above shows, ending with a *not* clause may give the greatest emphasis to your opponent's contentions.

Weak words make a weak ending. A monosyllable is usually a weak word to end a sentence:

A creditor beneficiary may recover
also.

A creditor beneficiary may also
recover.

We have had no success so far.

So far, we have had no success.

We have been disappointed ever
since.

Ever since, we have been disappointed.

To put emphasis on a modifier, put it after the term modified:

| He deliberately committed this crime. | He committed this crime deliberately. |

Unemphatic words at the beginning of a sentence get it off to a weak start:

| By such a rule, the court could establish the means by which business people could find what their rights were in such transactions. | The rule would enable business people to find what their rights were in such transactions. |
| Because the judgment was affirmed it does not follow that this contention was sound. | Affirmance of the judgment does not mean that this contention was sound. |

Introductory terms such as *there are, there were,* and *it is* are wordy.[86] They are also weakening, because they are unemphatic and because they often lead to overuse of nouns and weak verbs.

| There are more people killed by relatives or acquaintances than by strangers. | More people are killed by relatives or acquaintances than by strangers. |
| It is the contention of the petitioner that | Petitioner contends that |

In a two-part sentence, the natural emphasis also falls on the end. That's where you should place the more important proposition. An opponent's argument can be minimized by putting it in a subordinate clause and ending with the proposition you want to emphasize. Justice Douglas did this when he said,

> And while a search without a warrant is, within limits, permissible if incident to a lawful arrest, if an arrest without a warrant is to support an incidental search, it must be made with probable cause.[87]

This puts the emphasis on the point he wanted to make: that an arrest without warrant must be based on probable cause. Consider also these two arrangements of the same words:

| The victim, although she testified that her assailant had worn a blue sweater, could not give any description of his features and failed to identify the defendant in the line-up. | Although the victim could not give any description of her assailant's features and failed to identify the defendant in the line-up, she testified that her assailant had worn a blue sweater. |

---

[86] See § 3.2, Eliminate Unnecessary Words (discussing *there are, there is, it is*).

[87] Henry v. United States, 361 U.S. 98, 102 (1959).

The version on the left is more favorable for the defense. The one on the right emphasizes the sweater and would be appropriate for introducing an argument showing, for example, that the defendant was wearing a blue sweater at the time.

Suppose your opponent argued that a certain rule of law established by case A (which you rely on as a precedent) has been weakened or overruled by case B. You want to rebut that assertion and argue that the cases can be reconciled. Which of the three following ways is best for your purpose?

> The two cases can be reconciled, although they differ somewhat on their facts.
>
> Although they differ somewhat on their facts, the two cases can be reconciled.
>
> Although the two cases can be reconciled, they differ somewhat on their facts.

This rule is applicable to short sentences—the end does not carry as much punch in a long one. The reader has been in suspense for so long that by the time she gets there, she is just happy the tension is over. In long sentences, therefore, close the thought quickly and leave developments, justifications, or exemplifications to the end.[88]

Inversion of the natural order of a sentence is an effective way to get emphasis. The normal English sentence order is: (1) the subject, preceded or followed by its modifiers; (2) the verb; (3) the object; and (4) the predicate modifiers.[89] Changing the order emphasizes the word moved from its normal position. Since the normal place for the subject is at the beginning, putting it there gives it no special emphasis. But you can give emphasis by moving it to the end:

> Franklin D. Roosevelt was the greatest man I ever met.
>
> The greatest man I ever met was Franklin D. Roosevelt.

If the end of the sentence is the natural place for a word, it's not emphasized by leaving it there. You can give emphasis by interpolating phrases to build suspense or by moving the key word to the beginning:

> Courage it is that sustains a person.

---

[88]   See § 7.8, Structure Periodic and Cumulative Sentences With Care (discussing cumulative sentences).

[89]   See § 5.3, Follow the Expected Sentence Order.

You can emphasize phrases in the same way:

> With malice toward none; with charity for all; with firmness in the right,
> as God gives us to see the right, let us strive on . . . .[90]

But do not overdo it. Used too much, rearrangement becomes a tedious mannerism and ceases to achieve its purpose.

Emphasize a word by setting it off with an interpolation following it.

> You, being a business person, recognize better than most people the value of a good credit rating.

If you don't want to put emphasis on *you*, it is poor writing to use this form by mere blundering. Thus:

You, being a business person, recognize the value of a good credit rating.	Being a business person, you recognize the value of a good credit rating.

Even subordinate clauses can be improved by putting important words in important positions:

In the absence of a showing of the essential nature of the information you have asked for,	Without a showing that the information you have asked for is essential,

Although the passive voice is generally less forceful than the active voice,[91] the passive may sometimes supply emphasis where you want it. To emphasize the actor's name, put it at the end of the sentence:

> Some labor legislation has been enacted by the states, but the more important controls are those enacted by the Federal Government.
>
> The gun could only have been fired by this woman.

Or you may want to emphasize the deed rather than the doer or the recipient:

> For many are called, but few are chosen.
>
> All four nurses were indicted, but only one was convicted.

When you want to put emphasis on the object or recipient, and cannot do so by putting it at the end, you can move it to the second most emphatic position in the sentence, the beginning:

> The fallacy of defendant's argument was exposed by this Court in *Patton v. Peck.*

---

[90]   Abraham Lincoln, Second Inaugural Address (1865).

[91]   See § 6.5, The Passive Voice is Weak.

In the sentence above, the word to be emphasized is *fallacy*. But it cannot be put at the end, for it is followed by "of defendant's argument." The passive voice allows you to emphasize *fallacy* by putting it at the beginning instead.[92]

The periodic sentence distorts the expected sentence order. Completion of the thought, to prevent the reader's attention from wandering and to heighten the dramatic effect, is suspended through subordinate clauses, adverbial modifiers, and participial or adjective phrases, until the end.[93] That was a periodic sentence.

In periodic and other long sentences, emphasis can be obtained by developing a good ear for sentence rhythm.[94] By observing where the cadence of the sentence causes the verbal emphasis to fall, the writer with a sense of rhythm can use this natural stress to emphasize key words.

The periodic sentence is a device that may tempt lawyers into fine writing. Don't get carried away.

You gain emphasis by building to a climax.[95] Arranging words, phrases, clauses, or sentences in an ascending series continually heightens the reader's interest. Thomas Wolfe used this device in *Of Time and the River:*

> If a man has a talent and cannot use it, he has failed. If he has a talent and uses only half of it, he has partly failed. If he has a talent and learns somehow to use the whole of it, he has gloriously succeeded, and won a satisfaction and a triumph few men ever know.

We like things to wind up with a grand finale. We are disappointed—and a little annoyed—when they end not with a bang but a sputter.

Used sparingly, anti-climax can create emphasis by shocking or amusing your reader with the unexpected or the incongruous, as when Macaulay wrote: "the chief justice was rich, quiet, and infamous."[96]

---

[92] See § 7.15, The Passive Voice May be Just What You Need (discussing legitimate uses of the passive voice).

[93] See § 7.8 Structure Periodic and Cumulative Sentences With Care (discussing periodic sentences).

[94] See § 8.3, Rhythm.

[95] See § 7.16, For Emphasis, Build to a Climax.

[96] Warren Hastings 49 (1885).

§ 6.13   Use Parallel Construction

In a parallel sentence structure, where the pattern or arrangement of words in one sentence is repeated in another, all the elements of the repetition must belong to the same grammatical category. The expressions so balanced are thereby strongly accented, building up cumulative credibility.

> First in war, first in peace, first in the hearts of his countrymen.[97]

Clumsy writers may fail to compose balanced sentences, perhaps because their attention has never been called to the form, or because they mistakenly think they should avoid reiteration. They compose faulty parallelisms such as those in the left-hand column below:

The buyer must be reasonable and act in good faith.	The buyer must act reasonably and in good faith.
In the former situation, the courts have held for the defendant, while in the latter the plaintiff has been successful.	In the former situation, the courts have held for the defendant; in the latter, for the plaintiff.
The filing is not designed to give detailed information, but only that some of the debtor's assets are already encumbered.	The filing is designed to give, not detailed information, but only information that some of the debtor's assets are already encumbered.
Plaintiff contends that she had no duty to exercise the option but that the duty was on the transferee.	Plaintiff contends that the duty to exercise the option rested not on her but on the transferee.

Parallel construction also improves clarity and grammatical consistency.

The amendments include a new penalty clause, additional remedies for individual members, and create a wholly new category of offenses.	The amendments include a new penalty clause, additional remedies for individual members, and a wholly new category of offenses.
The congressional investigation was concerned with two main ends, the first, in aid of legislation, and the second of holding the executive branch of the government to a strict accountability.	The congressional investigation was concerned with two main ends: first, aiding legislation, and second, holding the executive branch of the government to a strict accountability.

As the last example illustrates, punctuation can be called upon to help in enumeration.

---

[97]   Henry Lee, Funeral Oration on the Death of General Washington 14 (1800).

Be consistent when listing items or outlining. Consider the following outline:

(A)   Due process

(B)   Equal protection

(C)   Whether entry without warrant constituted unreasonable search and seizure

(D)   Did the officer have reasonable ground to believe a felony had been committed?

Here, *A* and *B* are mere subject headings. *C* introduces a query with the word *whether*, and *D* is a question. All of them, however, should be put in the same form.

If *C* and *D* are to conform to *A* and *B*, they should be changed to similar short titles, such as "C. Search and seizure" and "D. Arrest without warrant." If the others are to conform to *C*, they should all start with the word *whether*. If they are to conform to *D*, all should be stated as questions. Select the format that serves your purpose.

The writer shifts from one form to another because she feels the subject heading is sufficient for some items, but a fuller statement is needed for others. But usually you can get a fuller statement and still use catch phrases. Thus *C* could be put into parallel construction with *A* and *B* by some such phrasing as "C. Entry without warrant as constituting unreasonable search," or "Search and seizure: entry without warrant." If a certain item does not lend itself to this treatment, the others may have to be conformed to it.[98] But don't let the tail wag the dog: what gives title to a section is its content, not its format or arbitrary rules of parallelism. As a careful reader might have already noticed, not all subtitles in this book are parallel.

Parallel construction is effective not only to gain emphasis but also for other rhetorical purposes.[99]

---

[98]   See § 7.5, Follow an Outline (discussing headings).

[99]   See §§ 7.11, Strive for Continuity, 8.6, Parallel Construction, and 8.7, Antithesis.

Chapter 7

ORGANIZATION

Proper words in proper places
make the true definition of a style.
Jonathan Swift (1667–1745)[1]

§ 7.1   Introduction

Some aspects of your writing may improve after you are in practice. Your vocabulary may increase and you may develop tactful ways to say what you mean without unnecessary bluntness. But a logical mind is the product of rigorous training.

§ 7.2   Master Your Subject

Just as water cannot rise above its source, so you cannot write more clearly than you think. "Thought and speech," said John Henry Newman, "are inseparable from each other. Matter and expression are parts of one: style is a thinking out into language."[2] That is why Arthur Schopenhauer said that "the first rule . . . for a good style is that the author should have something to say; nay, this is in itself almost all that is necessary."[3]

Ambiguity caused by muddled thinking can be avoided by knowing the topic well, by learning to think straight, and by taking time to think carefully. Painstaking care in thinking through what you want to say and how to say it will help you avoid blurry writing, and will lead to clarity, conciseness, and vigor.[4] Most symptoms of writer's block result from poor research, poor organization, and poor planning.

Liberate yourself from the delusion that ideas will come and fall in place if you just start writing. To write clearly you must have gathered your material and arranged it in some sort of order; you must also have thought through the relationship of one part to others, evaluated their relative importance, decided which one or

---

[1]   A Letter to a Young Clergyman [1721], in Lane Cooper (ed.), The Art of the Writer 138 (1952).

[2]   The Idea of a University 276 (1852).

[3]   On style [1851], in Lane Cooper (ed.), The Art of the Writer 223 (1952).

[4]   See § 5.2, Think About What You Are Saying. Imprecision and ambiguity are further discussed on Chapters 2, Precision and 5, Clarity.

two are primary, and worked out a logical plan of presentation. The novice might start writing immediately after finishing the research without first digesting, organizing, and considering the material. But time spent thinking, even before preparing an outline, may be the most worthwhile investment in the project.[5]

The person who has just been collecting data is deep amidst the trees. During the sitting-and-thinking process, the writer should back away to see the forest. To see an object whole, and see it clearly, one must have found the right perspective. Thinking over the principles and rules is a way of getting the subject into proper focus so you can perceive how they group themselves, with some standing forth as dominant and others retiring into the background of mere details. Only when you clearly see what is central can you get your readers to focus on those points, instead of dispersing their attention over a morass of details in which nothing stands out. For Robert Louis Stevenson, if you can group your ideas, you are a good writer.

Mechanically reviewing a series of cases without analyzing them is a common and particularly bad form of writing. Reporting cases without first gaining some perspective imposes the task of integration and analysis on the reader. Without any analytical thread connecting each case to the others (synthesis), you are just taking notes. But this should have been done before the first word was written: it's preparation, not product.

Writing without perspective also leads to uncritically discussing a statute. In a letter to a client, lawyers often merely rephrase the statutory language sentence by sentence, much as an interpreter translates language. This is a shallow and unanalytical mental operation, which calls for a low level reading comprehension, allowing the mind to go wherever the written words lead. A lawyer's function is not merely to translate statutory or contractual jargon into simple English. Writing artfully to clients requires reflection controlled by the purpose of helping the reader understand the problem. To do this, the lawyer must first think through the general meaning of the statute, and then how it bears upon the client's concerns. Only then can the lawyer effectively explain the conclusion to the client.

---

[5]   See § 7.5, Follow an Outline. But see § 7.3, Writing is Thinking.

§ 7.3   Writing Is Thinking

The need to think ahead does not mean that writing merely puts a finished thought to paper.[6] Writing improves thinking because writing is "thinking at its hardest."[7] "Writing," said John Updike, "educates the writer as it goes along."[8] This prompted E.M. Forster to wonder, "how can I tell what I think til I see what I say?"[9]

Richard Posner articulated the connection between deliberating, deciding, and writing a judicial opinion:

> In thinking about a case, a judge might come to a definite conclusion yet find the conclusion indefensible when he tries to write an opinion explaining and justifying it. The reason is that we do not think entirely in words, and certainly not entirely in sentences and paragraphs. Inarticulable or even unconscious feelings and impressions fill in around the sentence fragments that form in our minds as we think about a problem. This silent, incompletely verbalized thinking can be insightful . . . . But it can also be muddy, with the result that when we try to systematize it in sentences and paragraphs that are unmistakable because written down and not just imperfectly remembered, we may find that our confident conclusion is wrong; it "will not write." Reasoning that seemed sound when "in the head" may seem half-baked when written down, especially since the written form of an argument encourages some degree of critical detachment in the writer, who in reading what he has written will be wondering how an audience would react. Many writers have the experience of not knowing except in a general sense what they are going to write until they start writing. A link is somehow forged between the unconscious and the pen. The link is lost to the judge who does not write. The difference between what is merely thought in silence and

---

[6]   See § 5.2, Think About What You Are Saying.

[7]   Roger J. Traynor, Some Open Questions on the Work of State Appellate Courts, 24 U. Chi. L. Rev. 211, 218 (1957) ("In sixteen years I have not found a better test for the solution of a case than its articulation in writing, which is thinking at its hardest.").

[8]   Odd Jobs: Essays and Criticisms xxi (1991).

[9]   Aspects of the Novel 71 (1927). See also W. L. George, Hail, Columbia. The American Scene, CXLII Harper's Monthly Magazine 304 (1921).

what is written down is a reason for having judicial opinions rather than blind announcements of results.[10]

For decades, experienced judges have battled against the opinion that "won't write."[11] Frank M. Coffin said,

A remarkably effective device for detecting fissures in accuracy and logic is the reduction to writing of the results of one's thought processes. . . . Somehow, a decision mulled over in one's head or talked about in conference looks different when dressed up in written words and sent out into the sunlight. . . . [W]e may be in the very middle of an opinion, struggling to reflect the reasoning all judges have agreed on, only to realize that it simply "won't write." The act of writing tells us what was wrong with the act of thinking.[12]

Justice Ruth Bader Ginsburg also shared her experience:

At least once each of the nine terms I have already served on the Court, an opinion writer finds that the conference position, in whole or in part, "won't write," so the writer ends up taking a different view. Similarly, once or twice each term, an opinion circulated as a dissent attracts the majority's approval and becomes the opinion of the Court.[13]

The experience in the Canadian Supreme Court is strikingly similar.[14]

"Committing arguments to paper," summarized Douglas E. Abrams, "can often focus decision making more clearly than

---

[10] Judges' Writing Styles (And Do They Matter?), 62 U. Chi. L. Rev. 1420, 1447–48 (1995). See also Law & Literature 376-77 (2009) ("writing may even be necessary to bring deep intuitions to the surface.").

[11] See Joseph N. Ulman, The Plague of Judicial Opinions, 33 Am. Mercury 345 (1934); Karl N. Llewellyn, On The Why of American Legal Education, 4 Duke B. Ass'n J. 21 (1936); Felix Frankfurter, Remarks in Report of the Cincinnati Conference on Functions and Procedure of Administrative Tribunals, 12 U. Cin. L. Rev. 184, 276 (1938).

[12] The Ways of a Judge. Reflections from the Federal Appellate Bench 57 (1980).

[13] Workways of the Supreme Court, 25 T. Jefferson L. Rev. 571, 526 (2003). See also Edwin W. Patterson, The Role of Law in Judicial Decisions 19 Mo. L. Rev. 101, 117–18 (1954).

[14] See Donald R. Songer, Susan W. Johnson, C.L. Ostberg & Matthew E. Wetstein, Law, Ideology, and Collegiality. Judicial Behaviour in the Supreme Court of Canada 62 (2012).

contemplation or oral discussion."[15] This may give a new meaning to Francis Bacon's maxim, "reading maketh a full man, conference a ready man, and writing an exact man."[16]

But Geoffrey C. Hazard, Jr. has warned, "confusion of expression usually results from confusion of conception. The act of writing can help clarify one's thoughts. However, one should spare the reader having to repeat one's own extrication from confusion. The object is to be clear, not to show how hard it was to be so."[17]

You may have to write freely to discover your meaning. Many accomplished writers sometimes do just that: "I often put the key words and phrases on the screen without knowing their proper sequence and move them around to find what seems the best fit."[18] But recognize your earlier drafts as stepping stones leading toward your finished product. Write so that the reader will not notice how your thought process evolved—write as if your thought was already fully formed and you had a clear plan before you started.

§ 7.4   Writing Is a Peephole Art

"To get your precise message through to a complete stranger," said David Mellinkoff, "with only cold words to break the barrier of isolation, is a small triumph of creative art."[19]

The writer can present to the reader only one word or phrase at a time; the eye cannot take them in any faster. A painter presents the canvas whole, and a viewer can get an impression either by stepping closer and analyzing the details or by standing back and appreciating the whole at one time. But this is impossible with writing. The writer's art is more like that of the motion picture director who must present one frame after another. Both must present their images in an order that the audience can follow and recreate the precise idea in its own mind.

One writer vividly illustrates this concept:

---

[15]   Effective Legal Writing 146 (2016). See also Ryan A. Malphurs, Rhetoric and Discourse in Supreme Court Oral Arguments: Sensemaking in Judicial Decisions 41 (2013).

[16]   Essayes: Religious Meditations: Places of Perswasion and Disswasion (1597).

[17]   Quoted in Tom Goldstein & Jethro K. Lieberman, The Lawyer's Guide to Writing Well 48 (2016).

[18]   Geoffrey C. Hazard, How I write, 3 Scribes J. Leg. Writing 15, 16 (1993).

[19]   Sense and Nonsense 91 (1982).

Word must follow word in an orderly procession; and when the last word has filed into its place, the whole army should be found drawn up so as to present exactly the formation from which it started. Suppose a regiment, massed in the form of a square, is ordered to pass through an opening too narrow to admit more than one [soldier] at a time, and to form upon the other side in the same square formation. As the [soldiers] pass from the one place through the opening into another, so the words must pass from your mind by ear or eye into the mind of another; and as the [soldiers] break off from the square, rank by rank, in a certain order, and fall in again in the same order, so must the words progress from your mind and rearrange themselves in a certain order. Then, when the process is complete, they will be found drawn up in the mind of another, in the same formation as that in which they are drawn up in your own mind.[20]

§ 7.5   Follow an Outline

Orderly presentation calls for a scheme of development, an outline.

The development must march in a straight line. Sentences and paragraphs must follow one another in a sensible and understandable way. Each sentence must be a step, each paragraph a point, closer to the conclusion. If sentences or paragraphs interrupt the flow of development, the reader is distracted; coherence is lost.

We wish that if we just start writing, the material will fall into place as we go. It won't. Lawyers typically work with a confusing mass of refractory and contradictory data. If you start writing without first reducing your material to an orderly argument, your writing will ramble just as your speech would if you spoke extemporaneously on a subject. If your thoughts remain diffused and imprecise, no amount of effort to dress them with artful words will hide the deficiency of substance. But if you have thought through your material, so that principles and conclusions have taken shape in your mind, some sort of outline will have suggested itself. Once you know what you want to say, an orderly way of

---

[20]   Leslie Cope Cornford, English Composition: A Manual of Theory and Practice 172–73 (1900).

presenting it will not be hard to find. So, before you put word on paper, think the problem through.[21]

Time spent on an outline is time saved later. An outline is a map on which you can see the relationship of the parts of your material. A 30-page brief is not easily considered whole. An outline shows whether the several points are in logical order and given proper emphasis, with the most important highlighted, the less important properly subordinated, and the marginally relevant omitted. Making changes after the manuscript is written is awkward: even if this could be done, it's more than just "drag and drop." Moving a point or a paragraph in the completed text is much more trouble than moving a sentence or clause in an outline.

The importance of carefully drawing a plan cannot be overemphasized: Without a plan, said Buffon, "the best writers will wander; the pen running on unguided to form haphazard, irregular strokes and incongruous figures."[22]

If you try to write without an adequate outline, you will find yourself trying to do three things at once. For every issue that presents itself to your mind, you must decide: (1) whether or not to include it; (2) how and where to fit it in; and (3) how fully to develop it. Attempting to make these decisions while writing is likely to disappoint. You should concentrate on the creative effort of putting your conviction on paper without having to think about the logical organization of the material.

Moreover, the stimulation of seeing your argument grow as you write may sweep organization out of your mind and destroy your perspective along with your value judgment. It may lead you to expand a point far beyond its importance in your case. An outline keeps you in line; it helps you balance the relative importance of the various points and maintain the proper tone. It helps you keep a grip on your subject.

You may build your outline with complete sentences, with keywords, or with phrases. Complete sentences are sometimes necessary to help recall what you intended to say. A subheading labeled "procedure" or "due process" is so indefinite that the writer may not remember what she meant. Even if it helps recall the point in a general way, the writer may not recall some of the nuances she

---

[21]   See § 7.2, Master Your Subject.
[22]   Discours sur le style [1753], in Lane Cooper (ed.), The Art of the Writer 149 (1952).

had in mind when she wrote it. Some vague and general topic-words and phrases are so hazy that the writer may not have had anything specific in mind when she wrote them. An outline made up of such indefinite phrases, therefore, is not particularly helpful.

When a writer's ideas are hazy and the outline unfocused, writing becomes an unsatisfying chore. But if you prepare an outline with declarative sentences, you will have to know what you want to say before you write, and then you will have a reminder. As a bonus, when the work is finished, these complete sentences may conveniently serve as the headings. Headings and subheadings are common in legal writing: each point in the argument is given a heading to break down arguments into smaller segments.[23]

But a plan should not be set in stone—it evolves as research and writing progress. If by the time you are done your structure is different from the one originally conceived, you may be tempted to think that the planning was useless. Yet you were only able to build the structure because you planned first.

An inflexible plan is a straightjacket. Everybody recognizes the importance of being prepared, from scouts, to generals, to scientists. "In preparing for battle," said Dwight D. Eisenhower, "I have always found that plans are useless but planning is indispensable."[24] Louis Pasteur had a similar approach to his research: "chance favors only the prepared mind."[25] The secret of fluency is preparation.

A writer with a plan writes differently—right from the start—from a writer who has none, just as a person who knows where she is going follows a straighter and shorter path than a person feeling his way in the dark. The writer who knows where she is going will continually point out the relevance of the information as it is presented, so that the reader always knows what is important. Figure out your plan at the start, adapt it as necessary, and be sure to let your reader in on it.

---

[23] See § 6.13, Use Parallel Construction (discussing parallel constructions in outlines).

[24] Also quoted as "Plans are worthless, but planning is everything."

[25] Conference, University of Lille, December 7, 1854.

§ 7.6   Say One Thing at a Time[26]

For a simple subject, the outline may be very simple. It may consist merely of point one and point two. But many people fail to have even that much order in what they write. As George Pólya said, "[t]he first rule of style is to have something to say. The second rule of style is to control yourself when, by chance, you have two things to say; say first one, then the other, not both at the same time."[27]

Lawyers always have much to say. But the second rule deserves careful attention. When setting forth obligations or undertakings, as in contracts, a sentence should concern only one obligation or undertaking; when setting forth commands, permissions, or prohibitions, as in statutes, a sentence should concern only one command, permission, or prohibition; when making allegations or denials of fact, as in pleadings, a sentence should deal with only one allegation or denial.

Experienced writers know that "the maxim 'one thought per sentence' does not mean 'one sentence per thought.' A complex thought may require two or three sentences."[28]

Here are examples of sentences that try to say two things at the same time:

> Unless all the Arkansas statutes on the subject (and the administrative regulations issued thereunder) are invalid, in which case a refusal by the state courts to restrain the suspension of Hays would eventually be reversed by the Supreme Court, which for the reasons expressed above would not be done, the state court was entirely within its powers in suspending Hays' state permit and his permission thereby to drive over state roads in the capacity of a contract carrier.

> In most cases, an officer of the law is justified in arresting a person without a warrant—and there is no evidence that any warrant had been obtained in this case—only when the officer has reason to believe that a crime is being committed in his or her presence.

The second sentence not only interrupts one thought with another, but does so at a point where the interrupted fragment apparently says something quite different from what the writer

---

[26]   See §§ 5.4, Put Modifiers With the Word or Phrase Modified and 6.8, Do Not Qualify Unnecessarily.

[27]   How to Solve it: A New Aspect of Mathematical Method 172–73 (1957).

[28]   Tom Goldstein & Jethro K. Lieberman, The Lawyer's Guide to Writing Well 247 (2016).

intends. An egregious example of that sort of blunder is the following:

> No other judge of this court has written so much and said so little, whether on criminal law, torts, or procedure, that is not still true and still important.

§ 7.7   Sentence Structure and Organization

Lawyers are notorious for spawning long, tortuous, and obscure sentences. Shorter sentences encourage conciseness and focus, and are clear to the reader.[29] But length itself does not obscure meaning; good writers can compose long sentences that are clear and readable. What muddles legal writing is poor sentence structure and lack of organization.

Whether short or long, simple or complex, a sentence must be properly structured. It must be a closely knit unit of expression, not a mere string of loosely connected clauses. A poor writer who has just enough skill to know that a series of simple sentences will sound unsophisticated may try to avoid that effect by the easy device of connecting two or more simple declarative statements with a conjunction or relative pronoun (*and, but, that, so, which, while, who, whom, whose*).

Defendant had been drinking all evening and sometime after midnight she undertook to drive home.	Defendant had been drinking all evening. Sometime after midnight she undertook to drive home.

The following sentence illustrates an absurdly lengthy sequence strung together with *ands*:

> We most respectfully submit it would be a travesty upon justice, a rape upon the fundamental principles of law *and* in violation of every decision *that* has been rendered by this Honorable Court, *and* an injustice *that* all the spices of Arabia could not cure, *and* would disgrace *and* bankrupt an honest citizen, an honest merchant *and* a blameless family *and* would not tend to enforce the law, *but* would cause hatred *and* disrespect to the law of our State *and* Nation *and* there would be a great injustice inflicted *or* could be inflicted upon a citizen of our state, *and* without extending this argument, *which* could be for many hours, *but* with an abiding confidence in the wisdom of this Court, we consign the future hopes, the tears of the loved ones *and* the laws of our nation to the bosom of this Court.[30]

---

[29]   See § 7.9, Vary the Length of Sentences, Keeping Them Predominantly Short.

[30]   Camp v. State, 89 P.2d 378 (Okla. Crim. 1939) (quoting brief from the defendant).

Failure to perceive the correct structural relationship between ideas leads to loosely constructed compound sentences.

The evidence is not convincing that, even conceding that such a rule had been promulgated, it had been brought to the employee's attention.	Even conceding that such a rule had been promulgated, there is no convincing evidence that it had been brought to the employee's attention.
The company contracted to exclude any person from any part of the plant which was being used for military work if the Secretary asked the company to in writing.	The company contracted to exclude from any part of its plant being used for military work any person named in writing by the Secretary.

The reader trying to follow a long, rambling sentence cannot be sure whether any of its assertions has been completed until the end. Several statements may be so intermingled, with some dependent on or modified by others, that the reader cannot sort them out and keep them all in mind. If they are separated by periods, instead of strung together with *ands*, the reader can handle them one at a time.

> Lack of privity between the promisor and the mortgagee was not overcome, as in the leading case, by an obligation of the promisee to the mortgagee, so as to connect the mortgagee with the transaction so closely that it substituted for privity and, according to the court in *Vrooman*, the plaintiff was denied an action on two grounds: (1) no legal obligation from promisee to third party; and (2) no privity between the latter and the promisor.

Courts do better than the paragraph above, which comes from student work. But sometimes opinions contain sentences which, though grammatically correct, would be clearer if divided into shorter sentences. Even judges sometimes lose themselves in long, rambling sentences:

> The party who purchases property from utter strangers *and* receives it under unusual circumstances, *and* especially where all the facts of the case are passed upon by a jury, *and* the jury has come to the conclusion after hearing the facts and circumstances, *that* the defendant had knowledge *that* it was stolen property, *and* by so rendering their verdict, it cannot be successfully maintained in an appellate court *that* defendant did not believe the property was stolen.[31]

How, then, does one construct well-organized sentences? The first principle is to put the main idea in the main clause. When you have written a long sentence that is sprawling and awkward, find its main idea. Then, identify its subject, verb, and predicate. Put

---

[31]   Camp v. State, 89 P.2d 378 (Okla. Crim. 1939).

them in order, and see how they stack up. When reconstructed into a simple sentence, these parts should state the main idea. Contrast this specimen:

> The factor that was most influential in inducing the legislature to enact the bill was the fact that the governor had strongly endorsed it.

The subject of that sentence is *factor*, the verb is *was*, and the predicate is *fact*. The "main idea" thus is: the factor was the fact.

That says nothing. And you cannot construct a good sentence around a main clause that says nothing. What is the main thing that this sentence tries to say? That depends upon context. Is the main point that the bill finally passed? If so, the main clause might read, "the legislature finally passed the bill." Or, if the main point is the governor's support, then the main clause might be, "the strong support of the governor led to the enactment."

Putting the main point in the main clause also puts subordinate points in subordinate clauses.

> The customers watched in silence as the robbers scooped the money into a paper bag.

Journalists provide useful advice on this matter: "don't bury the lead." The main point in that sentence is surely not the inaction of the customers, but the act of the robbers. That should therefore make up the main clause:

> The robbers scooped the money into a paper bag as the customers watched in silence.

Putting the main idea in the main clause and subordinate ideas in subordinate clauses has a corollary: give the context first, details later.[32] The issue should be put before the facts. A statement that starts by giving us items of information—things that happened, dates, statistics—without "setting the scene," calls on us to hold all this information in our memory until we are finally told what it is about. Similarly, in framing questions presented, putting the question in context means starting with the broadest principle that the point concerns, then moving to the more specific.

The following paragraph dissipates its potential effectiveness because its several clauses, strung together with *ands*, lose their focus and force.

---

[32] James C. Raymond, Legal Writing: An Obstruction to Justice, 30 Ala. L. Rev. 1, 12–4 (1978).

> All of the parties were familiar with all of the terms and conditions of the contract, *and* this being true, Metropolitan cannot now be heard to complain that the contract does not mean just exactly what it says, as hereinbefore indicated. This being true, there is no genuine issue as to any material facts *and* Herkenhoff was and is entitled to judgment as a matter of law *and* the lower court did not err in granting Herkenhoff a summary judgment.

Variation is as important as a solid structure. Vary the types of sentences,[33] their length,[34] and the way they begin.[35]

§ 7.8   Structure Periodic and Cumulative Sentences with Care

Compound and complex sentences have two kinds of structure: periodic or cumulative. A periodic sentence, like this one, is where, by interposing subordinate clauses, phrases, modifiers, lists of items, or other details between the subject and its predicate, completion of the main thought is suspended until the end.

A cumulative sentence completes the main thought early, and then adds details, such as subordinate clauses, phrases, or series of items, instead of injecting them between the subject and its predicate. That last sentence is a cumulative one. Its main thought was stated in the first eight words and was complete after the word *early*. It passed up two other stopping or closing points on its way: *details*, and *items*. The periodic sentence, on the other hand, has no stopping place short of the end.

Both sentence structures are capable of producing clear, effective writing. The periodic sentence is useful for emphasizing the point finally disclosed or for building to a dramatic effect.[36]

> *When* in the Course of human events, *it becomes necessary for one people to dissolve the political bands which have connected them with another*, and to assume among the powers of the earth, the separate and equal station to which the Laws of Nature and of Nature's God entitle them, a decent respect to the opinions of mankind requires that *they should declare the causes which impel them to the separation.*[37]

---

[33] See §§ 7.15, The Passive Voice May Be Just What You Need and 7.8, Structure Periodic and Cumulative Sentences With Care. But see § 5.3, Follow The Expected Sentence Order.

[34] See § 7.9, Vary the Length of Sentences, Keeping Them Predominantly Short.

[35] Richard K. Neumann, Jr., Ellie Margolis & Kathryn M. Stanchi, Legal Reasoning and Legal Writing 214–15 (2017).

[36] See § 6.12, Put Words to be Stressed at the Beginning and the End of Sentences.

[37] The Declaration of Independence (1776).

A long, well-constructed periodic sentence may be easily grasped by children:

> *In the loveliest town of all,* where the houses were white and high and the elms trees were green and higher than the houses, where the front yards were wide and pleasant and the back yards were bushy and worth finding out about, where the streets sloped down to the stream and the stream flowed quietly under the bridge, where the lawns ended in orchards and the orchards ended in fields and the fields ended in pastures and the pastures climbed the hill and disappeared over the top toward the wonderful wide sky, in this loveliest of all towns *Stuart stopped to get a drink of sarsaparilla.*[38]

Periodic sentences are heavy artillery in the legal writer's arsenal; they must be used with discrimination and structured with care. Starting a statement and then holding off its completion calls on the reader to keep the start in mind, while absorbing a number of subordinate details, until she is finally given the complete thought. The reader waits for that completion; until it comes, she is under what has been called grammatical tension.[39] Putting that strain on the reader is justified if deliberate, to emphasize an important idea by putting it at the end or to sustain interest while you build to a climax. But if there is no climax, no reason to keep the reader in suspense, this strain is an imposition. So much legal writing is hard to read because it's riddled with unnecessarily long and involved sentences that have no closure point until the end.

Criminal statutes, for example, typically have a simple main thought:

> A person who commits such an act
> Shall be punished in such a way.

But the prohibited act may be so qualified that it takes many words to describe, and we wind up with a provision that reads like this:

> A person who
> > by means of any
> > or in any manner
> > commits such and such an act
> > in this way or that
> or who
> > does something else

---

[38]   E. B. White, Stuart Little 102 (1945).

[39]   See R.M. Eastman, Style 158 (1970) and James C. Raymond, Legal Writing: An Obstruction to Justice, 30 Ala. L. Rev. 1 (1978).

```
        with intent to do this or that
        and without the consent of such and such a person or persons
        while such and such is something
    or who
        aids, abets, or conspires with any person or persons
        to do any of the acts aforesaid,
    is guilty of something
    and punishable by in such and such way
```

Sentences interposing a thicket of subordinate thoughts between subject and predicate would be more easily understood if broken into several shorter ones.

Sometimes exceptions can be avoided by redefining the category covered, instead of first naming a broader category and then making an exception. Thus, instead of saying, "all registered voters, except those registered before January 1st, 2018," say "all voters registered after December 31, 2017."

The cumulative sentence is easier to construct and to read. But it too must be well organized—it should not consist merely of a string of clauses hooked together like a line of train cars. One trick that may help avoid rambling sentences is to express the thought as in a conversation. We cannot write as we talk,[40] but talking out our thoughts can help produce a good first draft that can then be refined.[41] When we talk it out, we use mostly cumulative sentences, expressing our main idea first and then tacking on subordinate thoughts. We use more periods and other closure points instead of injecting examples, exceptions, and provisos between the subject and the predicate. Qualifications and examples can be left for a later sentence. Trying to get them all into the same sentence with the main proposition contributes to the length and complexity of lawyers' language.[42]

§ 7.9 Vary the Length of Sentences, Keeping Them Predominantly Short

Rudolf Flesch quantified reading ease in terms of number of syllables in words and words per sentence. He ranked sentences from very easy (8 words) to very difficult (29 or more words). For

---

[40] See § 4.10, Should You Write the Way You Talk?

[41] See Robert Zoellner, Talk-Write: A Behavioral Pedagogy for Composition, 30 College English 267 (1969) (explaining the technique of "talking out" difficult propositions).

[42] See § 6.8, Do Not Qualify Unnecessarily.

three out of four American adults, sentences of an average length of 17 words are difficult to process. In addition to average sentence length, other readability yardsticks devised for measuring reading ease and interest take into account the percentage of simple sentences, strong verb forms, active voice, and familiar and concrete words.[43]

The 2003 National Assessment of Adult Literacy (NAAL) showed that 43% of the U.S. population has a literacy level of "basic" or "below basic," a number that has not changed significantly since the 1992 research.[44] Readers of legal prose are presumably of higher than average reading skill. But lawyers don't write only for other legal professionals and college graduates, and their words are likely to be longer, their thoughts more difficult, and their concepts more abstract.

So it is good practice to aim for an average sentence length of approximately 20 words. If the sentence has between 30 and 40, exercise strict scrutiny. Beyond 40, assume you need to cut out useless words or use the forgotten period key. If it runs over three lines, consider breaking it in two.[45] You don't need to use your fingers to count the words: if you highlight a sentence in your word processor, the word count appears at the bottom of the screen. You may not even need to count at all: if you can't read your sentence aloud in one breath, it likely is too long.[46]

Yet most writers have difficulty ending a sentence. William Zinsser was facetious: "there's not much to be said about the period except that most writers don't reach it soon enough."[47] The result is that sentences are generally longer than necessary. Lawyers are particularly guilty of neglecting the period. "There are only two cures for the long sentence: (1) Say less; (2) Put a period in the middle. Neither expedient has taken hold in the law . . . . Lawyers are still reluctant to end a sentence."[48]

---

[43] The Art of Plain Talk 38 (1946); The Art of Readable Writing (1949). See also Robert Gunning, The Technique of Clear Writing 32–35 (1952). Microsoft Word evaluates readability levels according to the Flesch-Kincaid Grade Level Test.

[44] See http://nces.ed.gov/naal/kf_demographics.asp. The NAAL is sponsored by the National Center for Education Statistics (NCES), an arm of the U.S. Department of Education to collect and analyze data related to education.

[45] See § 7.7, Sentence Structure and Organization.

[46] Theresa J. Reid Rambo & Leanne J. Pflaum, Legal Writing by Design 458 (2013).

[47] On Writing Well 71 (2006).

[48] David Mellinkoff, The Language of the Law 366–67 (1963).

Robert Gunning's criticism highlights a troubling stereotype of the legal profession: "Lawyers have an odd idea that it is safer to put all ideas in one sentence. Legal mazes result." After exhibiting a monstrous 300-word sentence, rich with polysyllables, he fired: "with such sentences as these a lawyer can build a secure future. By writing sentences that only he can understand, he succeeds in being retained in order to interpret them later."[49]

Some sentences are so elaborate that the thought becomes inaccessible. You will naturally try to break up the sentence into smaller pieces, but will not know where to pause or which ideas to group together.[50] You will have to read it more than once to understand how the words relate to one another. But judges lack the time, said Justice Ginsburg, "to ferret out bright ideas buried in complex sentences, overlong paragraphs, and too many pages."[51] If your reader needs to write a diagram to understand your sentence, it's probably not a good one.

For Urban A. Lavery,

> The fundamental cause of long and involved sentences is ill-digested thought. The person who uses them habitually is the kind of person who starts to speak or to write before his thought is fully developed in his own mind. The person who writes clear sentences is the person who hammers out his thoughts to a finished product in his own mind before passing it on to the reader.[52]

The suggestion that long sentences should be avoided, however, must not be taken as an absolute rule. Nor does it mean that you should try to make all your sentences of nearly equal length—the advice is to keep the average under 20 words, not to write every sentence under 20 words. Variation is as important as keeping an average sentence short. A style in which every sentence is the same length is monotonous. You want a change of pace: a mixture of long, medium, and short sentences, with an occasional

---

[49]   The Technique of Clear Writing 60–61 (1968).

[50]   Veda R. Charrow, Myra K. Erhardt & Robert P. Charrow, Clear and Effective Legal Writing 170 (2013).

[51]   Ruth Bader Ginsburg, Remarks on Appellate Advocacy, 50 S. C. L. Rev. 567 (1999).

[52]   The Language and the Law, 8 ABA Journal 269, 273 (1922).

extremely short one.[53] You should also vary your rhythm by diversifying sentence structure. Isaac Goldberg put it well:

> Writing is symbolized speaking. In speaking, the relative length of our phrases is determined by their emotional or intellectual content and—more than we realize—by the normal flow of our breathing. We do not, in reading, like an uninterrupted succession of sentences containing two or three words each; we do not like an uninterrupted succession of sentences each containing ninety words. We instinctively ask for variation in sentence-length; we instinctively ask, indeed, for variation in word-length, for variation in accent and pitch—in a word, for equilibrium, for harmonious, dynamic balance.
>
> We dislike the succession of short sentences because they suggest asthmatic utterance; we dislike the succession of long ones because they suggest a different type of breathlessness, caused by talking without pause. Listening to music or singing that is consistently in the high registers induces a feeling of strain, and that feeling may begin in our throats, which unconsciously imitate, or have suggested to them, the vocalism required to produce such high tones. Such refinements of writing as rhythm, cadence, harmony of vowels and consonants, even choice of words, which constitute the aesthetics of rhetoric, of style, have a physical basis.[54]

This lesson was captured by Gary Provost:

> This sentence has five words. Here are five more words. Five-word sentences are fine. But several together become monotonous. Listen to what is happening. The writing is getting boring. The sound of it drones. It's like a stuck record. The ear demands some variety. Now listen. I vary the sentence length, and I create music. Music. The writing sings. It has a pleasant rhythm, a lilt, a harmony. I use short sentences. And I use sentences of medium length. And sometimes when I am certain the reader is rested, I will engage him with a sentence of considerable length, a sentence that burns with energy and builds with

---

[53] Ross Guberman advises, "on every page of your brief, include at least one sentence that starts and stops on the same list of text." See Point Made 177 (2011).

[54] The Wonder of Words 354 (1957).

all the impetus of a crescendo, the roll of the drums, the crash of the cymbals—sounds that say listen to this, it is important.

So write with a combination of short, medium, and long sentences. Create a sound that pleases the reader's ear. Don't just write words. Write music.[55]

The advice to maintain a short sentence average, therefore, does not mean that you cannot venture into an occasional long sentence. After all, "a writer who can't write a clear sentence longer than twenty words or so is like a composer who can write only jingles."[56] A good sentence may be very long. Eighteenth century writers sometimes wrote sentences that ran over a page, yet were logically and clearly organized, so that the reader could follow the thought without undue effort. It is only necessary that a sentence not be so complex that the reader gets confused. Such extremes are not accepted in this century, however, and they are particularly inappropriate in a professional setting. But a well-crafted, focused, concise long sentence still has its place in legal writing.

"If you want to write long sentences," wrote Zinsser, "be a genius. Or at least make sure that the sentence is under control from beginning to end, in syntax and punctuation, so that the reader knows where he is at every step of the winding trail."[57]

An effective long sentence, like a short one, does not just happen; it must be planned, and you must follow a few rules for writing clear, concise, and vigorous long sentences. First, get to the subject and the main verb as soon as possible, in the first eight words of your long sentence. (This advice, therefore, discourages the periodic sentence.) Second, do not interrupt the connections between the subject and the verb and between the verb and the object. Third, avoid long introductory subordinate clauses: if you need to open a long sentence with a subordinate clause, keep the introduction short; if you cannot keep it short, move it to the end or make it a separate sentence.[58]

---

[55]   100 Ways to Improve Your Writing 60–61 (1985).

[56]   Joseph M. Williams & Joseph Bizup, Style: Lessons in Clarity and Grace 137 (2017).

[57]   On Writing Well 71 (2006).

[58]   For these and other suggestions on how to write an effective long sentence, see Joseph M. Williams & Joseph Bizup, Style: Lessons in Clarity and Grace 35–39, 137-59, esp. 140–43 (2017).

In addition, make sure every word counts: a good long sentence is concise when every word is doing a job and cannot be deleted without affecting meaning. Finally, whenever you write a long sentence, follow with a short one.[59]

§ 7.10 Keep Paragraphs Short

There is no ideal size for a paragraph, its size determined by its content. It should be as long as necessary to communicate the message—no more, no less.[60] Modern writing style favors small words, short sentences, and short paragraphs. A short paragraph is a flexible concept, varying between 4 and 10 lines or 2 and 8 sentences.

Short paragraphs are useful for the writer and for the reader. They help writers keep their writing under control and produce ideas that are more precise, concise, simple, clear, and forceful. Short paragraphs also help readers, for they "encourage pause, however brief, to take stock of what has been thus far accomplished, to consider the connection between ideas, to fasten down what needs fastening."[61] Moreover, finding your place after a momentary distraction requires less effort in a text with short paragraphs. Writing, says William Zinsser, "is visual—it catches the eye before it has a chance to catch the brain. Short paragraphs put air around what you write and make it look inviting, whereas a long chunk of type can discourage a reader from even starting to read."[62] Successful lawyers write to the eyes and to the ears.

Experienced writers avoid long paragraphs because they are difficult to write and intimidating to read. If a paragraph gets taller than it is wide, even if it is a well-knit logical unit, consider breaking it up. If you look carefully, you will find a place where a new paragraph can appropriately be started, but you may have to recast the introductory words of the second paragraph to show its dependence on the first, or the relation between the two.

Good writers do not consistently write paragraphs that are too short either—several two-line paragraphs give an impression of

---

[59] See § 7.10, Keep Paragraphs Short.

[60] Anne Enquist, Laurel Oates & Jeremy Francis, Just Writing. Grammar, Punctuation, and Style for the Legal Writer 36 (2017).

[61] David Mellinkoff, The Language of the Law 373 (1963).

[62] On Writing Well 79 (2006). See also H.W. Fowler, A Dictionary of Modern English Usage 434–35 (2d ed. 1965); William Strunk, Jr. & E. B. White, The Elements of Style 15–17 (1979).

superficiality of analysis. But do not be afraid to have a short one-sentence paragraph at intervals—a change of pace is as welcome in paragraphing as it is in sentence size and structure.[63]

§ 7.11 Strive for Continuity

Writing that moves on a logically direct path has a natural coherence; its parts fit together well. It is worth knowing, therefore, some of the devices that help make one's writing flow smoothly from sentence to sentence and from paragraph to paragraph.

"A good transition is like the statue of the [Roman] god Janus: it looks before and after. It refers in some swift way to what has preceded and announces what is to follow."[64] Avoid cumbersome transitional phrases, which impede rather than facilitate the progress of thought: "This leads us to our second point . . ."; "Having proved our first point, we shall now . . ."

Experienced writers weave ideas seamlessly—one thing naturally leads to another. There are at least five ways to do this:

(1) The most common way to indicate the structure of thought are transitional or connective expressions:

(a) Indicating *order in time*:

first, second, third, next, initially, at first, the second, subsequently, previously, eventually, before, after, afterwards, earlier, later, while, formerly, at (by) the time, meanwhile, in the meantime, simultaneously, since, until, when, then, following, recently, at last, finally.

(b) Indicating *order in arrangement*:

next, then, last, final, finally, second, a further reason, most important, former, latter.

(c) Adding *examples* or *specifications*:

especially, specifically, in particular, particularly, at least, for example, for instance, that is, markedly, notably, namely, including, above all, like, such as, chiefly.

---

[63] See § 7.9, Vary the Length of Sentences, Keeping Them Mostly Short.
[64] Chester Noyes Greenough, Frank Hersey & Harold Bruce, Writing Well 108 (1932).

(d) Indicating *additions*:

moreover, in addition, furthermore, besides, further, alternatively, additionally, other, another, as well, again, similarly, like, and, too, also, indeed.

(e) Indicating *contrast, comparison, exceptions,* or *negations*:

but, however, nevertheless, yet, on the other hand, nonetheless, notwithstanding, otherwise, regardless, in spite of, instead of, though, although, even though, except, conversely, in contrast, albeit, comparatively, alternatively, similarly, equally, notwithstanding, instead, like, likewise, unlike, still, whereas, rather, nor, contrary to, on the contrary.

(f) Indicating *cause or effect*:

because, accordingly, therefore, thereby, thus, as a result, consequently, hence, for that reason, in that case, since, so, if so, lest, so that, so as to, for, inasmuch as, due to, in order to, that is why, consequently.

(g) Indicating *condition*:

if, even if, unless, provided that, given that.

(h) Indicating *positioning*:

here, there, above, below, opposite, on the other side, behind, beyond, next to, in front, near, far, close.

(i) *Concluding* or *summarizing*:

in conclusion, in summary, in sum, on balance, in essence, to conclude, to summarize, to sum up, in brief, in short, in a word, all in all, after all, in all, indeed, ultimately, altogether, in any event.

(j) Indicating what is *common*:

generally, in most cases, in general.

(k) Indicating *concession*:

granted, admittedly, while, despite, of course, true, naturally, after all, at any rate, still, that said, even so.

(1)　*Pressing a point* or *helping explain it*:

that is, as a matter of fact, that being so, in fact, still, anyway, in other words, simply put.

These connectors are usually more graceful inside the sentence than in the beginning, except when you shift directions. You make it easier for the reader to follow a new tack if *but* is the first word in the sentence or in the paragraph.

(2)　A word or phrase from the previous sentence or paragraph echoed in the new one links the ideas in the reader's mind. Thus, if the last sentence of the previous paragraph was about a "sense of personal security," the next paragraph may start, "this sense of security . . . ."

(3)　The new sentence or paragraph may start with a brief summarizing phrase referring to the subject just discussed. If you discuss a theory in the previous paragraph, you can start the next one with, "that theoretical approach is unacceptable because . . . ."

These last two devices—sometimes referred to as dovetailing—are usually combined with the use of a demonstrative pronoun, such as *this*, *that*, or *these*.

> From this legislative history,
> Applying these principles to the case,
> Against that background of judicial construction,
> That alone would be considered

(4)　Parallel construction gives emphasis, rhythm, and coherence.[65] Repeating the same sentence structure naturally connects two or more thoughts; there is no need for connective words or phrases such as *and*, *but*, or *moreover*.

The illegality of the scheme is shown by a reading of the court's decision in *Reston*. Moreover, it is absurd, as consideration of the consequences it would have for marital relations makes apparent.	That the scheme is illegal is shown by reading the court's decision in *Reston*. That it is absurd is apparent from the consequences it would have for marital relations.

(5)　You can also use punctuation to make connections between ideas, especially the semi-colon, the colon, and the dash.[66]

---

[65]　See §§ 6.13, Use Parallel Construction and 8.6, Parallel Construction.

[66]　See § 7.13, Continuity Through Punctuation.

These devices can become obvious and monotonous. They can be used generously, but if overdone, the signage may take over the message. The best transitions are those that do not seem artificial or strained, but arise naturally out of the development of ideas— they should be quick and varied, never bringing attention to themselves. Transitions, said Kristin R. Woolever, should resemble careful surgical stitches, not Band-Aids.[67]

If you structure your text carefully, some of your transitions will be implicit: the reader will get it without you having to write them.

Careless writers, however, fail to make clear connections between ideas. Because they know what they want to say, they think the connection is obvious for the reader. Or they omit them in the misguided hope of being concise.[68] But connectors are valuable tools: few words can provide so much organization in so little space.

The choice between explicit or implicit connection is sometimes a matter of feeling and personal taste. Whichever you use, make sure that the bridge between your ideas is clear for the reader, or she may get lost or make the wrong connections. Experienced writers understand that "continuity doesn't magically happen; it's created."[69]

§ 7.12   Lead the Reader by the Hand

A typical reader knows less about the subject than the writer. It's bad writing, therefore, to leave inadvertent gaps in the text and expect readers to connect the dots.

Connectors and transitions not only improve coherence and smooth development, they also provide signals that enable the reader to follow as you move from point to point. They are like a turn signal on a car: they tell those around you what you intend to do next. Just as drivers often fail to indicate their maneuvers, writers often fail to use connectors and transitions appropriately. Unless you continually signal where you are going, you may lose your reader.

But a signal can be misleading.

---

[67]   Untangling the Law: Strategies for Legal Writers 78 (1987).

[68]   Anne Enquist, Laurel Oates & Jeremy Francis, Just Writing: Grammar, Punctuation, and Style for the Legal Writer 50–51 (2017).

[69]   John R. Trimble, Writing With Style 42 (2011).

> Making the decisions of the board final is constitutional. Kentucky has held that the courts may interfere where the property owner alleges that the board's decision deprives him of property without due process of law. Similarly, the Kansas court has held that judicial review cannot be denied. But in most jurisdictions, statutory provisions that the board's decisions shall not be subject to judicial review have been upheld.

Here, the first sentence leads the reader to assume that the subject of the paragraph is that the proposition is constitutional. Instead of expanding on this point, the writer, without any warning signal, switches directions and starts talking about the authorities against it. Reading the words, "Kentucky has held," we expect to be told that Kentucky has supported the proposition just laid down in the topic sentence. But as we get into the sentence, we find it doesn't seem to do so. We start over, thinking we have misread it, cannot find where we went wrong, and end up lost. Only when we get to the end of the paragraph do we see what the writer has done— thrown us off the track by slipping in the minority view when she seemed to be talking about the majority.

There is nothing grammatically wrong with the way the writer developed the point in the paragraph above. Development is stylistic, not grammatical. But she should have made clear to the reader the path she was following. The writer could have done this easily by introducing the second sentence with "it is true that." This would have signaled to the reader that what is to follow is an exception or limitation that the writer wants to get out of the way before going on with the main point.

Good writing is a dialogue in which the reader cannot ask follow-up questions. If the reader does not understand a point, if he thinks of an argument that defeats it, or if he has an unanswered question, the absence of a response is the writer's fault and the writer will suffer the consequences. Therefore, the writer must have the sensitivity to anticipate the reader's reaction, and address those issues at the time he writes—the writer needs to give the information the reader needs at the time he needs it. Writing is, therefore, "a quintessentially empathetic act."[70]

Presenting information effectively is essential to a successful writing style:

> [i]n every sentence there is some . . . order of words more effective than any other; and . . . this order . . . presents

---

[70] Ian Gallacher, Legal Communication and Research: Lawyering Skills for the Twenty-First Century 35–36 (2015).

the elements . . . [so] they may be most readily put together. As in a narrative, the events should be stated in such sequence that the mind may not have to go backwards and forwards in order to rightly connect them; as in a group of sentences, the arrangement should be such that each of them may be understood as it comes, without waiting for subsequent ones; so in every sentence, the sequence of words should be that which suggests the constituents of the thought in the order most convenient for the building up that thought.[71]

§ 7.13 Continuity Through Punctuation

When two sentences have a logical connection, the writer may: (1) write them as two separate sentences, separated by a period; (2) run them together, connecting them with *and* or some other connective; or (3) replace the connective with a semi-colon, a colon, or a dash.

This last possibility is often neglected. Unskilled writers never use punctuation to show continuity; their punctuation is limited to commas and periods, a style that seems simple and vigorous for a short while, but that soon becomes monotonous.

The semi-colon is a connective. Using it instead of a full stop tells the reader that there is a connection between the two statements. As Ernest Gowers has said, the full stop says to the reader, "Have you got that? Very well; now I'll tell you something else." A semi-colon says, "Got that? Now I'll add something else that has something to do with what I just said."[72]

The promisee does not owe a legal debt to the third party, but effectively the third party is receiving a gratuity.	The promisee does not owe a legal debt to the third party; effectively the third party is receiving a gratuity.
The quoted sentence was not the holding in the case, but was mere obiter dictum.	The quoted sentence was not the holding in the case; it was mere obiter dictum.

The colon is another underappreciated mark. It creates anticipation, suggesting a sequel: a list, a specification, an amplification, or a quotation.

> There is only one thing to do: resign.
> This much is certain: we shall never surrender.

---

[71] Herbert Spencer, Philosophy of Style [1852] 16 (1915).
[72] Plain Words 17 (1948).

The parties finally agreed on a compromise: the union would abandon its wage demands in return for certain fringe benefits.

A time comes when people must make up their minds, and on the validity of retribution as a purpose of punishment, the time for equivocation is past: retribution is wrong.

The dash is a deliberate interruption of continuity, similar to a comma but more abrupt and emphatic. Legal writing should be couched in carefully chosen language; it therefore has little use for dashes, which give the impression of breaking off one thought to interject another. Sometimes, however, an abrupt interruption or pause is effective: (1) to indicate a sharp turn of thought or to give a contrasting idea; (2) to interpolate a parenthetical comment or to give a striking detail, and to set it off in a more marked or emphatic way than by using commas or parentheses; or (3) to indicate a pause of suspense.

Made desperate by their depressed plight, the farmers of one district met a lawyer for the mortgagee bank on the courthouse steps and persuaded him—let us hope by fair means—not to proceed with the eviction.

He died in a concentration camp of an incurable blood infection—a Jewish grandmother.[73]

Interjections of any kind, whether set off with dashes, parentheses, or commas, may impair the smooth flow of thought. Inserting a whole sentence within a sentence is particularly disruptive.

Legal writing has been neglected (as have many other techniques and subjects) by many law schools as a vital part of legal education, though some schools have now gone quite far (can one ever go too far?) to correct this situation.

Punctuation marks are like connectors—they are more effective the less you use them.[74]

Losing continuity is not the only penalty for neglecting punctuation. Clarity may also be impaired. And even when the sense is perfectly clear, "a sentence may be deprived of half of its force, its spirit, its point, by improper punctuation."[75]

---

[73] Joseph Gross, Spinoza in Litigation, 11 Shingle 78, 79 (1948).

[74] See § 7.11, Strive for Continuity (excessive use of connectives may become obvious and monotonous).

[75] Edgar Allan Poe, Marginalia, Graham's American Monthly Magazine of Literature and Art 130 (1848).

§ 7.14 Organize Your Paragraphs

The paragraph, not the sentence, is the unit of composition.[76] Yet the paragraph is also a whole: it is not merely a collection of loosely connected sentences, but an orderly series with unity of purpose and logical structure, with a beginning, a middle, and (if necessary) an end. It should have one point to make, and only one.

Paragraphing has many functions. It helps writers keep control of their writing and organize their thoughts, preventing them from wandering or discussing too many issues at the same time. It also helps readers to follow the writer's plan. Paragraphs also have a more mundane function: they break the task of writing and reading into manageable bits, giving writers and readers a psychological and logical break.[77]

For a paragraph to work well, however, you need to (1) clearly establish its topic, and then (2) develop it.

(1) Use Topic Sentences

The first sentence in a paragraph should refer to the previous one, introduce a new point, or both. An effective way to guard against including too many ideas in one paragraph, while maintaining unity and cohesion, is to write paragraphs that can be summarized in single sentences. A summary sentence is usually the best way to start the paragraph. The topic sentence should be short and simple, lest it overwhelm the reader.

In legal writing, the topic sentence can often be the statement of a legal proposition, with the rest of the paragraph devoted to its amplification or to summaries of cases supporting it.

> The contention is unsound for several reasons.
> We have upheld provisions permitting
> . . . has been held to be . . .
> In prior cases, we have upheld warrantless searches involving physical intrusions that were at least as significant as that entailed in the administration of a breath test.[78]

---

[76] William Strunk, Jr. & E. B. White, The Elements of Style 15 (1979); William Zinsser, On Writing Well 80 (2016); Bryan A. Garner, Legal Writing in Plain English 81 (2013).

[77] William Strunk, Jr. & E. B. White, The Elements of Style 15–17 (1979); Anne Enquist, Laurel Oates & Jeremy Francis, Just Writing: Grammar, Punctuation, and Style for the Legal Writer 29 (2017).

[78] Birchfield v. North Dakota, 579 U.S. ___, ___, 136 S.Ct. 2160, 2177 (2016) (Alito, J.).

The most common way of organizing paragraphs in argumentative writing is to state a proposition in the first sentence and follow with its demonstration by evidence, examples, or other data. Many of the paragraphs in appellate court opinions use this structure.

> The conclusion that Section 36B is ambiguous is further supported by several provisions that assume tax credits will be available on both State and Federal Exchanges. For example, ...[79]
>
> The Affordable Care Act contains more than a few examples of inartful drafting. . . . Several features of the Act's passage contributed to that unfortunate reality. . . .[80]
>
> Now, if any fundamental assumption underlies our system, it is that guilt is personal and not inheritable. . . .[81]
>
> The term was applied, then as now, to weapons that were not specifically designed for military use and were not employed in a military capacity. For instance, ...[82]

The topic sentence may be a question:

> The inquiry is, what are the privileges and immunities of citizens in the several states?[83]
>
> The first step in our inquiry must be to answer the question: what is the source of power on which Congress must be assumed to have drawn?[84]
>
> How, then, does the Court weave a clear constitutional prohibition out of pure interpretive equipoise?[85]

A topic sentence may refer to an argument that the paragraph proposes to answer. Such a sentence may start, "the plaintiff contends"; "the Union relies on observations made in"; or "the court below held," and the rest of the paragraph develops the idea:

> Aznavorian urges that the freedom of international travel is basically equivalent to the constitutional right to interstate travel, recognized by this Court for over a hundred years. . . . But this court has often pointed out the crucial difference between the freedom to travel internationally and the right of interstate travel.[86]
>
> Justice Stevens places great weight on James Madison's inclusion of a conscientious-objector clause in his original draft of the Second Amendment. . . . He argues that . . . . It is always perilous to derive the

---

[79] King v. Burwell, 576 U.S. ___, ___, 135 S.Ct. 2480, 2492 (2015) (Roberts, C.J.).
[80] Id.
[81] Korematsu v. United States, 323 U.S. 214, 243 (1944) (Jackson, J., dissenting).
[82] District of Columbia v. Heller, 554 U.S. 570, 581–82 (2008) (Scalia, J.).
[83] Corfield v. Coryell, 4 Wash. C. C. 371 (1823) (Washington, J.).
[84] Perez v. Brownell, 356 U.S. 44, 57 (1958) (Frankfurter, J.).
[85] Boumediene v. Bush, 553 U.S. 723, 833 (2008) (Scalia, J., dissenting).
[86] Califano v. Aznavorian, 439 U.S. 170, 176 (1978) (Stewart, J.).

meaning of an adopted provision from another provision deleted in the drafting process. In any case, what Justice Stevens would conclude from the deleted provision does not follow. . . . Thus, the most natural interpretation of Madison's deleted text is that . . . .[87]

The defendants assert that this court must apply the standards articulated in the Supreme Court's decisions in [*Twombly* and *Iqbal*][88]

The topic sentence need not always be the first sentence of the paragraph and indeed need not actually appear. Some well-written paragraphs have "an implied topic sentence that governs the paragraph as firmly as any written topic sentence."[89]

It is the mark of an unskilled writer to make the structural details of the outline too apparent. To announce the topic at the beginning of every paragraph can be not only monotonous but awkward. The adroit writer does not leave the bones of the skeleton showing so nakedly. For example, the topic of a paragraph may be "the plaintiff's conduct constituted comparative negligence." The paragraph may actually start, "that the plaintiff was also negligent clearly appears not only from the testimony of the impartial witnesses, but also from her own admissions." With such an introductory sentence, the reader knows what should follow—a summary of the evidence showing comparative negligence.

Chief Justice Marshall found that Congress had power to incorporate a bank by starting a paragraph boldly admitting that the power was not expressly given:

Among the enumerated powers, we do not find that of establishing a bank or creating a corporation. But there is no phrase in the instrument which . . . excludes incidental or implied powers. . . .[90]

In the following paragraph, the topic sentence might be worded as follows: "Although the constitutional guarantees of personal liberty are not always absolutes, government may not go so far as to compel public affirmations which violate religious conscience." But no such sentence actually appears. Instead, the idea is developed gradually.

Concededly the constitutional guaranties of personal liberty are not always absolutes. Government has a right to survive and powers conferred upon it are not necessarily set at naught by the express prohibitions of the

---

[87]   District of Columbia v. Heller, 554 U.S. 570, 589–90 (2008) (Scalia, J.).

[88]   Edwea Inc. v. AllState Ins. Co., 2010 WL 5099607, (S.D. Tex. Dec. 8, 2010) (J. Rosenthal).

[89]   Anne Enquist, Laurel Oates & Jeremy Francis, Just Writing: Grammar, Punctuation, and Style for the Legal Writer 36 (2017).

[90]   McCulloch v. Maryland, 17 U.S. 316, 404 (1819).

> Bill of Rights. It may make war and raise armies. To that end it may compel citizens to give military service, and subject them to military training despite their religious objections. It may suppress religious practices dangerous to morals, and presumably those also which are inimical to public safety, health and good order. But it is a long step, and one which I am unable to take, to the position that government may, as a supposed educational measure and as a means of disciplining the young, compel public affirmations which violate their religious conscience. . . .[91]

Starting a new paragraph is the signal to the reader that one point in the development has ended and that the next one is beginning. Where you do not start a new paragraph, you imply that you are still discussing the same point. If your reader finds that you have moved on to a new point without giving him the signal, he is confused. A related error appears in the following paragraphs:

> In 1498, the Venetian Republic granted to Democrito Terracina a monopoly to print all books in Arabic, Moorish, Syrian, Armenian, Indian and Barbary for a period of twenty five years. In 1518, the Holy Roman Emperor Maximilian gave John Shoeffer the exclusive right to print the works of Livy for a period of ten years.
>
> In the Middle Ages another form of copyright protection was developed which we may call "institutional" protection.

The second paragraph's introductory words imply that the writer is about to move on, in the historical development, to the Middle Ages. But we were already there in the preceding paragraph. What the writer meant to say was, "another form of copyright protection developed in the Middle Ages was what we may call 'institutional protection.'"

A topic sentence, therefore, facilitates the transition between paragraphs. A transitional word or phrase will alert the reader whether the new paragraph is a continuation of or a contrast with the idea in the previous one, or whether it introduces a new subject.[92] If you want the reader to follow the path you created, make sure that the needed transitions linking the ideas are expressly or impliedly stated at the outset of each paragraph, not only in your mind.[93]

You might omit topic sentences in early versions. But as you revise your prose, make sure to include them. If you see a paragraph without a topic sentence, ask yourself what you were trying to say.

---

[91] Minersville School District v. Gobitis, 310 U.S. 586, 602 (1940) (Stone, J., dissenting) (internal citations omitted).

[92] Bryan A. Garner, Legal Writing in Plain English 83 (2013).

[93] Bryan A. Garner, The Elements of Legal Style 62–66 (2002).

The answer to that question leads to a topic sentence that will put the paragraph in perspective, giving it meaning and relevance.[94] It could also reveal that you need to rewrite the paragraph or divide it in two.

A topic sentence is such an important part of composition that it should not be wasted with weak statements or citations.[95] But not every paragraph requires its own topic sentence. When you need several paragraphs to develop a complex issue, each new paragraph is merely a continuation of the previous one. These paragraphs need only transitional phrases to show the relationship with an original topic sentence:[96]

> The third element is
>
> Yet another exception may be found

(2) Develop the Paragraph Topic

After a good topic sentence, you should amplify or discuss the point. Do not betray the expectation you have created in the first sentence by chasing some other point. The easiest way to lose unity is to allow yourself to be distracted from your main thought by a side issue, so that a paragraph that started out discussing one thing wanders off into a minor or collateral point.

The following paragraph violates this rule (as well as several others). We are not told the main point at the outset, so we must do some close reasoning to discover it:

> To the extent that any decision relies on the lack of competition between the parties or on the statement that the element of "passing off" was not present, it is submitted that the decision is incorrect. Neither should trivial differences in titles nor in the statement that the adversaries were equally entitled to the use of the title furnish the basis for a decision. The same can be said of the requirement that notice be posted to the effect that the work, blatantly advertised under a title that has elsewhere acquired a secondary meaning, is not that work at all.

This was later rewritten to read:

> Courts have allowed the continued use of competing titles of theatrical performances on several grounds. In *Glazer* the court, in refusing to enjoin, stressed the difference in the titles, although that difference seems insignificant. Other grounds for similar decisions have been the lack of direct

---

[94]   Richard K. Neumann, Jr., Ellie Margolis & Kathryn M. Stanchi, Legal Reasoning and Legal Writing 196 (2017).

[95]   Helene S. Shapo, Marilyn R. Walter & Elizabeth Fajans, Writing and Analysis in the Law 205 (2013).

[96]   Id. at 210.

competition between the parties, the absence of the element of "passing off," and a feeling that both parties were equally entitled to use the title. In one case, the court allowed the continued use of a similar title on condition that the defendant make a public announcement that his was not the plaintiff's well-known production.

None of these are satisfactory reasons for failing to enjoin the continued use of a title. The publicity value of the title is an important part of the originator's property right. The only question with which the court should concern itself is whether the defendant has converted this property right to his own use.

The revised version not only tells us in the first sentence what the paragraph covers, it also complies with another rule, already mentioned: when you have two things to say, say one first, then the other, not both together. Here, the writer wanted to tell us the holdings of several cases and argue that they were unsound. In the first draft, he tried to do both at the same time. In the second, he first did one and then the other, devoting a separate paragraph to each. The second version is longer, but it is concise and clearer than the first.

An experienced writer may not make a conscious choice in paragraph development. The plan she follows, almost without specifically thinking about it, will depend on the point being made. When laying down a legal proposition, especially if it is an intricate one, she may want to develop it by giving illustrations. Or she may want to support it with cases, which may provide illustrations as well as authority. The novice, however, may need to consciously commit to a plan of development, or else the paragraph may become merely a string of loose and unorganized sentences that have no focus and make no point.

You may use several common patterns of paragraph development, including (a) comparison; (b) analogy; (c) example; (d) evidence; (e) definition; and (f) division. The patterns may not always appear in their pure form, but often a dominant pattern may be identified.[97]

Each of these patterns may be illustrated by examples taken from judicial opinions.

---

[97] See Roy Ivan Johnson, Marie Schalekamp & Lloyd A. Garrison, Communication—Handling Ideas Effectively 137 (1956).

(a) *Development by Comparison*

A common method of exposition is to set an object against another, discussing their differences and similarities. That's how Justice Black opens one of his dissenting opinions:

> At the outset I want to emphasize what the crime involved in this case is, and what it is not. These petitioners were not charged with an attempt to overthrow the Government. They were not charged with overt acts of any kind designed to overthrow the Government. They were not even charged with saying anything or writing anything designed to overthrow the Government. The charge was that they agreed to assemble and to talk and publish certain ideas at a later date.[98]

(b) *Development by Analogy*

Development by analogy is a special form of development by comparison. Analogies are helpful to explain an unfamiliar or abstract idea by comparing it to something that is commonly known or widely accepted. Sometimes in an argumentative paragraph the analogy is merely a figure of speech.

> To propose to punish and reform people by the same operation is exactly as if you were to take a man suffering from pneumonia, and attempt to combine punitive and curative treatment. Arguing that a man with pneumonia is a danger to the community, and that he need not catch it if he takes proper care of his health, you resolve that he shall have a severe lesson, both to punish him for his negligence and pulmonary weakness and to deter others from following his example. You therefore strip him naked, and in that condition stand him all night in the snow. But as you admit the duty of restoring him to health if possible, and discharging him with sound lungs, you engage a doctor to superintend the punishment and administer cough lozenges, made as unpleasant to the taste as possible so as not to pamper the culprit.[99]

(c) *Development by Example*

Examples validate an argument. In legal writing, a typical pattern begins with a statement of a rule of law in the first sentence, followed by factual or legal statements from other cases. You need only skim the paragraph below:

> The price paid for property or services is only one of the terms in a bargain; the effect on the parties is similar whether the restriction on the power of the contract affects the price, or the goods or services sold. Apart from the cases involving the historic public-callings, immemorially subject to the closest regulation, this court has sustained regulations of the price in cases where the legislature fixed the charges which grain elevators, Brass

---

[98]   Dennis v. United States, 341 U.S. 494, 579 (1951).

[99]   George Bernard Shaw, Preface to Webb, English Prisons under Local Government XIV (1922).

v. North Dakota, 153 U.S. 391, 38 L.Ed. 757, 4 Inters.Com.Rep. 670, 14 S.Ct. 857; Budd v. New York, 143 U.S. 517, 36. L.Ed. 247, 4 Inters.Com.Rep. 45, 12 S.Ct. 468, and insurance companies might make, German Alliance Ins. Co. v. Lewis, supra; or required miners to be paid per ton of coal unscreened instead of screened, McLean v. Arkansas, supra; Rail & River Coal Co. v. Yaple, 236 U.S. 338, 59 L.Ed. 607, 35 S.Ct. 359; or required employers who paid their men in store orders to redeem them in cash, Knoxville Iron Co. v. Harbison, 183 U.S. 13, 46 L.Ed. 55, 22 S.Ct. 1; Dayton Coal & Iron Co. v. Barton, 183 U.S. 23, 46 L.Ed. 61, 22 S.Ct. 5; Keokee Consol. Coke Co. v. Taylor, 234 U.S. 224, 58 L.Ed. 1288, 34 S.Ct. 856; or fixed the fees chargeable by attorneys appearing for injured employees before workmen's compensation commissions, Yeiser v. Dysart, 267 U.S. 540, 69 L.Ed. 775, 45 S.Ct. 399; or fixed the rate of pay for overtime work, Bunting v. Oregon, 243 U.S. 426, 61 L.Ed. 830, 37 S.Ct. 435, Ann.Cas.1918A, 1043; or fixed the time within which the services of employees must be paid for, Erie R. Co. v. Williams, 233 U.S. 685, 58 L.Ed. 1155, 51 L.R.A.,N. S., 1097, 34 S.Ct. 761; or established maximum rents, Block v. Hirsh, 256 U.S. 135, 65 L.Ed. 865, 16 A.L.R. 165, 41 S.Ct. 458; Marcus Brown Holding Co. v. Feldman, 256 U.S. 170, 65 L.Ed. 877, 41 S.Ct. 465; or fixed the maximum rate of interest chargeable on loans, Griffith v. Connecticut, 218 U.S. 563, 54 L.Ed. 1151, 31 S.Ct. 132. It has sustained restrictions on the other element in the bargain where legislatures have established maximum hours of labor for men. Holden v. Hardy, 169 U.S. 366, 42 L.Ed. 780, 18 S.Ct. 383; or for women, Muller v. Oregon, 208 U.S. 412, 52 L.Ed. 551, 28 S.Ct. 324, 13 Ann.Cas. 957; Hawley v. Walker, 232 U.S. 718, 58 L.Ed. 813, 34 S.Ct. 479; Riley v. Massachusetts, 232 U.S. 671, 58 L. Ed. 788, 34 S.Ct. 469; Miller v. Wilson, 236 U.S. 373, 59 L. Ed. 628, L.R.A.1915F, 829, 35 S.Ct. 342; Bosley v. McLaughlin, 236 U.S. 385, 59 L.Ed. 632, 35 S.Ct. 345; or prohibited the payment of wages in advance, Patterson v. The Eudora, 190 U.S. 169, 47 L.Ed. 1002, 23 S.Ct. 821; Strathearn S. S. Co. v. Dillon, 252 U.S. 348, 64 L.Ed. 607, 40 S.Ct. 350; or required loaves of bread to be a certain size, Schmidinger v. Chicago, 226 U.S. 578, 57 L.Ed. 364, 33 S.Ct. 182, Ann.Cas.1914B, 284. In each of these cases the police power of the state was held broad enough to warrant an interference with free bargaining in cases where, despite the competition that ordinarily attends that freedom, serious evils persisted.[100]

This example illustrates both the pattern and its overuse. Justice Stone piled example on example, citing 24 cases, until we have more than enough.

When you have several items to present, order them coherently: (1) from the lesser to the greater, the order of climax; (2) from the greater to the lesser; (3) from the general to the particular (deduction); (4) from the particular to the general (induction); (5) and from the familiar to the unfamiliar.

---

[100] Ribnik v. McBride, 277 U.S. 350, 374 (1928) (Stone, J., dissenting).

(d) *Development by Evidence*

A general statement or claim can be developed by listing specifics or evidence. This method is often used to explain a process or system.

> Primary elections are conducted by the party under state statutory authority. The county executive committee selects precinct election officials and the county, district or state executive committees, respectively, canvass the returns. These party committees or the state convention certify the party's candidates to the appropriate officers for inclusion on the official ballot for the general election. No name which has not been so certified may appear upon the ballot for the general election as a candidate of a political party. No other name may be printed on the ballot which has not been placed in nomination by qualified voters who must take oath that they did not participate in a primary for the selection of a candidate for the office for which the nomination is made.[101]

(e) *Development by Definition*

Definitions provide meaning to concepts and distinguish them from others.

> Of all the terms used in the Taking Clause, "just compensation" has the strictest meaning. The Fifth Amendment does not allow simply approximate compensation but requires "a full and perfect equivalent for the property taken."[102]

> At the time of the founding, as now, to "bear" meant to "carry." When used with "arms," however, the term has a meaning that refers to carrying for a particular purpose—confrontation . . . .[103]

(f) *Development by Division*

Another form of development by definition is development by division, which explains a subject by dividing it into its essential parts. In legal writing this is typically found where the writer divides a cause of action into elements.

> The district court read plaintiff's complaint to allege three distinct theories.[104]

---

[101] Smith v. Allwright, 321 U.S. 649, 663 (1944) (Reed, J.).

[102] Penn Central Transp. Co. v. New York City, 438 U.S. 104, 150 (1978) (Rehnquist, J., dissenting).

[103] District of Columbia v. Heller, 554 U.S. 570, 584 (2008) (Scalia, J.) (internal citations omitted).

[104] Morse v. Lower Merion School Dist., 132 F.3d 902, 905 (3rd Cir. 1997) (Scirica, J.).

(g) *Development by Classification*

Development by classification breaks down the subject into groups or categories. For example, murder can be classified into first degree murder, second degree murder, and felony murder.

§ 7.15 The Passive Voice May Be Just What You Need

The active voice is more concise, more precise, more vigorous, and more forceful than the passive voice, and leads to more interesting reading.[105] Therefore, you will strengthen your writing style if you consistently prefer the active voice over the passive.

But only the constant and inadvertent use of the passive voice is undesirable—if you know what you are doing, you may and sometimes must use the passive voice. After being relentlessly demonized for decades, the passive voice is now unfairly branded as undesirable. Impressionable writers think it is unacceptable, even ungrammatical. But the passive voice is useful, and a better alternative to the active voice in some situations.

There are several legitimate reasons to use the passive voice. Otherwise, it would not have thrived for millennia in several languages, including Russian, Chinese, Latin, and Ancient Greek. To emphasize the action or the person or thing acted upon (instead of the actor), use the passive voice. If the actor is unknown, or obvious, or irrelevant, using the active voice would be a mistake. Experienced writers also employ the passive voice strategically, when it is undesirable or unnecessary to identify the actor. The passive voice is also useful when, for stylistic reasons, you need to start a sentence with the person or thing acted on. Moreover, moderate use of the passive voice will enliven and diversify your style: you do not want all sentences equally structured or equally forceful.[106]

So, prefer the active voice unless you can articulate a legitimate reason to use the passive.

---

[105] See §§ 3.8, The Passive Voice is Verbose; 5.11, The Passive Voice May Be Ambiguous; 6.5, The Passive Voice is Weak.

[106] See §§ 5.15, Use Ambiguity Strategically (the passive voice is useful to craft strategically ambiguous sentences) and 6.12, Put Words to be Stressed at the Beginning and the End of Sentences ("Although the passive voice is less forceful than the active, the passive may sometimes supply emphasis where you want it.").

§ 7.16 For Emphasis, Build to a Climax

To get the greatest emphasis in a paragraph, put the most important ideas at the beginning and at the end—the topic sentence at the beginning, and at the end the strongest of your examples, or the climax of your argument, or a strong summarizing sentence that echoes the topic sentence without repeating it. It is worth spending extra energy to word this summarizing sentence forcefully to drive home the point.

Skim the paragraph below, focusing on its powerful concluding sentence:

> If we cut through mere details of procedure, the operation and effect of the statute in substance is that public authorities may bring the owner or publisher of a newspaper or periodical before a judge upon a charge of conducting a business of publishing scandalous and defamatory matter—in particular that the matter consists of charges against public officers of official dereliction—and unless the owner or publisher is able and disposed to bring competent evidence to satisfy the judge that the charges are true and are published with good motives and for justifiable ends, his newspaper or periodical is suppressed and further publication is made punishable as a contempt. This is the essence of censorship.[107]

Below is another powerful concluding sentence:

> In the last analysis, jurors will accord mercy if they deem it appropriate, and withhold mercy if they do not, which is what our case law is designed to achieve.[108]

Concluding sentences, however, are not always necessary. Sometimes the idea is so clearly stated in the paragraph that adding a conclusion is ungainly and obvious repetition. A conclusion may be particularly helpful, however, after a long paragraph or one with a complicated issue—use your writer's sense to determine whether your paragraph needs a concluding sentence.[109]

---

[107] Near v. Minnesota, 283 U.S. 697, 713 (1931) (Hughes, C.J.).

[108] Kansas v. Carr, 577 U.S. ___, 136 S.Ct. 633 (2016) (Scalia, J.).

[109] Anne Enquist, Laurel Oates & Jeremy Francis, Just Writing: Grammar, Punctuation, and Style for the Legal Writer 36–37, 40–41 (2017).

Chapter 8

A TOUCH OF ELOQUENCE

The well-written works are the only ones that will go down to posterity: the amount of knowledge in a book, the peculiarity of the facts, the novelty even of the discoveries, are not sure warrants of immortality. If the works . . . are written without taste, without nobility, without inspiration, they will perish; since the knowledge, facts, and discoveries, being easily detached, are passed on to others, and even gain intrinsically when appropriated by more gifted hands.

Buffon (1707–1788)[1]

Nearly always the things a writer says are less striking than the way he puts them; for men in general have much the same ideas. . . . It is the expression, the style, that makes all the difference. . . . True style gives individuality to the commonest things, strength to the feeblest, dignity to the simplest.

Voltaire (1694–1778)[2]

§ 8.1   Introduction

Precision, conciseness, simplicity, clarity, forcefulness, and organization, discussed in previous chapters, are the essential qualities of style—for a lawyer even more than for most writers. Generally, the lawyer must avoid the more literary qualities of eloquence or ornamentation. But occasions will arise when a lawyer will want more than cold clarity or logic, and should be able to express an idea with grace and elegance.

The qualities that make for grace, polish, and effectiveness of expression are not easily identified. No one knows why certain combinations of words move us more strongly than others.

---

[1]   Discours sur le Style [1753], in Lane Cooper (ed.), The Art of the Writer 153 (1952).

[2]   Style [1771–1774], in Lane Cooper (ed.), The Art of the Writer 160 (1952).

She walks in beauty, like the night.—Lord Byron.

Most would agree that this combination of simple words, simply arranged, makes an effective sentence, but we do not know why. Nor can we teach how. There is, as C. E. Montague once said, "a kind of dazzling unreason" about the effect that certain combinations of words has upon us.[3] Indeed, "[t]here is no satisfactory explanation of style, no infallible guide to good writing, no assurance that a person who thinks clearly will be able to write clearly, no key that unlocks the door, no inflexible rule by which the young writer may shape his course."[4]

"Each phrase in literature is built of sounds, as each phrase in music consists of notes. One sound suggests, echoes, demands, and harmonizes with another; and the art of rightly using these concordances is the final art in literature."[5] This lesson was captured by Gary Provost: "Writing is not a visual art. It is a symphony, not an oil painting. . . . The words you write make sounds, and when the sounds satisfy the reader's ear, your writing works."[6]

Do not underestimate the power of eloquence. "Sometimes one memorable line can elevate an otherwise mundane brief. A single sentence in legal discourse can recast or transform the debate."[7] Judge Patricia Wald elaborated: "the well-turned phrase in a brief can capture a judge's attention. . . . [A]n occasional witticism or comparison with some other aspect of life . . . can lighten the somber atmosphere and even create a kind of commonality between judge and counsel. . . . [T]he best ones will reappear in the judges' opinions."[8] Indeed, "[g]ood writing," said Steven Pinker, can flip the way the world is perceived.[9]

---

[3]   A Writer's Notes on His Trade 245 (1930).

[4]   William Strunk, Jr. & E. B. White, The Elements of Style 66 (1979).

[5]   Robert Louis Stevenson, On Style in Literature, 47 Contemporary Review 548, 557 (1885). See also id., Essays Literary & Critical 40 (1923).

[6]   Make Your Words Work 54 (2001).

[7]   Tom Goldstein & Jethro K. Lieberman, The Lawyer's Guide to Writing Well 202 (2016).

[8]   19 Tips from 19 Years on the Appellate Bench, 1 J. App. Prac. & Process 7, 21 (1999). See also Adam Feldman, All Copying is not Created Equal: Borrowed Language in Supreme Court Opinions, 17 J. App. Prac. & Process 21 (2016) ("From 1946 through 2013, Supreme Court opinions shared 9.55 percent of their language, on average, with individual merits briefs.").

[9]   The Sense of Style 14 (2014).

As is true of other arts, good writing is not acquired by mechanical application of rules. "[T]he essence of a sound style," said H. L. Menken, "is that it cannot be reduced to rules."[10] Wide reading and extensive practice are the best recipe to develop the elusive quality of eloquence. Some develop an ear for prose as some develop an ear for music; others seem to remain tone deaf.

But this is of no help and little consolation to lawyers who must write, and who want to write well. They want suggestions that will help them choose the right word or phrase, the right arrangement of words and phrases within the sentence, and the right arrangement of sentences, to get a smooth flow of ideas and to evoke the emotion or impression desired.

Develop the habit of writing deliberately, not by accident. Everything in your text must serve a purpose: "every mark in the document—every punctuation mark, every word regardless where it appears—literally everything in the document should be calculated to have an effect on the reader."[11] This is more easily said than done, for "very few writers really know what they are doing until they've done it."[12]

The good writer, like the good practitioner of any craft, has done enough experimenting to have learned a number of ways to do the job well. She experiments with words, rhythm, and cadence to arrive at "a subtle something that makes of the phrase a whole that is greater than the mere sum of its parts."[13]

Mastery of rhetorical techniques may help you nudge your style from acceptable to memorable.

§ 8.2   Alliteration

Alliteration is the repetition of the same sound or letter at the beginning of two or more adjacent words. The Fowlers were not impressed with it, seeing it as a novice's toy."[14] But a device that Winston Churchill embraced need not be discarded by the rest of us:

---

[10]   Literature and the Schoolma'm, in H.L. Mencken, Prejudices, Fifth Series (1926).

[11]   Ian Gallacher, Legal Communication and Research: Lawyering Skills for the Twenty-First Century 124 (2015).

[12]   Anne Lamott, Bird By Bird 22 (1994).

[13]   Isaac Goldberg, The Wonder of Words 373 (1938).

[14]   H.W. Fowler & F.G. Fowler, The King's English 292 (1906).

> We cannot fail or falter.
>
> We shall not flag or fail.
>
> Let us to the task, to the battle and the toil.
>
> I have nothing to offer but blood, toil, tears and sweat.

Repetition of similar sounds in a sentence gives harmony and swing. It catches attention. That's why it was frequently used in advertising and political slogans:

> Better Buy Buick
>
> Britain's best business bank
>
> Deep clean cream cleanser
>
> Don't dream it. Drive it

Alliteration is everywhere and we don't see it. Some well-known brands are alliterative: Bed, Bath & Beyond, Best Buy, Calvin Klein, Coca-Cola Classic, Dunkin' Donuts, Krispy Kreme, Minute Maid, PayPal, Power Point, Range Rover, Rolls Royce, Sesame Street, TED Talks, Weight Watchers, Word for Windows.

Governor Mark Hatfield nominated Richard Nixon for the presidency in the following words: "a man to match the momentous need" of the times, a man who had "demonstrated courage in crisis from Caracas to the Kremlin . . . a fighter for freedom, a pilgrim for peace."[15] Does this strike you as effective or overwrought?

Alliteration may be used not only as a mnemonic device but also stylistically, for euphony and emphasis. Poets often use it:

> Even the weariest river winds somewhere safe to sea.— Swinburne.
>
> The moan of doves in immemorial elms and the murmur of innumerable bees.—Tennyson.

It has also been used effectively in prose:

> The mind and the mood of the masses is the soil of the policy.—Glenn Frank.
>
> His soul swooned slowly as he heard the snow falling faintly through the universe and faintly falling, like the descent of their last end, upon all the living and the dead.—James Joyce.

The rhythm of a well-placed alliteration may communicate something beyond words. Annoyance, indignation, and frustration ooze from the sentence below:

> As always, there will be a festering low road of speculation about [Hillary] Clinton herself, her health, her hair, her husband.[16]

---

[15]   1960 Republican National Convention.

[16]   Joe Klein, The Myth of Inevitability, Time Magazine, June 16, 2014.

As is true of any artistic device, alliteration can be overdone. If, instead of feeling the words flowing smoothly, the reader notices the alliteration, the emphasis is too heavy. You don't want sentences that sound like "Peter Piper picked a peck of pickled peppers."

Here are the opening words of a book on psychiatry and law:

> There was a time when the medicine man and the lawgiver had much in common. Both were men of mystery and magic, members of a sacerdotal class in close communion with the gods.

Notice that the first sentence has a series of two *m* sounds. The second has a series of four *m* sounds followed by three hard *c* sounds. Is the effect good? Is it overdone?

Alliteration usually refers to the recurrence of consonant sounds in the first letter of words. Recurrence of consonant sounds that are not in the first letter is called consonance, as in Shakespeare's "*All*'s we*ll* that ends we*ll*" or "the ea*r*ly bi*r*d gets the wo*r*m." Recurrence of vowel sounds (not necessarily the first letter) is called assonance: "his escape from the jail, the home chosen by his host."

§ 8.3   Rhythm

Aristotle described prose as neither possessing meter nor destitute of rhythm.[17] Isocrates said, "let not prose be altogether prose, for it would be dry; nor metered, for that would attract too much attention."[18] The ancient Greeks' warning has been repeated by others. Robert Louis Stevenson said, "prose must be rhythmical, and it may be as much so as you will; but it must not be metrical."[19] The Fowlers scorned metrical prose: "the novice who is conscious of a weakness for the high-flown and the inflated should watch narrowly for metrical snatches in his prose; they are a sure sign that the fit is on him."[20]

Experts agree that rhythm is desirable. A sentence's impact depends not only on the words used but also on the effect their arrangement creates. Rhythm is always present in well-written prose. Writing is rhythmical if the words fall naturally into

---

[17]   Rhetoric, III, 8.

[18]   See George Saintsbury, A History of English Prose and Rhythm 2 (1912).

[19]   On Style in Literature, 47 Contemp. Rev. 548, 555 (1885).

[20]   H.W. & F.G. Fowler, The King's English 295 (1908).

groupings whose length and arrangement are such that the sounds roll smoothly off the tongue. Writing without rhythm is lifeless.

The reader may not notice that a sentence has rhythm, but because it rolls smoothly she may get the strong impression that it is good. So the person looking at a painting, or listening to music, or reading good writing, feels that it is pleasing, although she may not know and may not care how the effect was obtained.

There are no rules for rhythm in prose. Unlike the measured rhythm of poetry, prose is irregular. You must develop an ear for timing. Like music, a sentence's rhythm may call for a word of one syllable and be spoiled by a word of three. Or it may call for a word accented on the first syllable rather than on the second. You feel when to speed up or slow down, when to go and when to stop—pauses are as important as sounds.

"Good writers control the pace and emphasis of their sentences by artful use of sentence structure, sentence length, punctuation, and stressed and unstressed syllables. Like good musicians, they 'hear' what they are creating."[21] To be a good writer, then, you must "develop your ear for the sound of written language."[22]

Here's a sentence in which one superfluous word spoils the rhythm:

> The seeds of most mental disorders, of vice and crime, of alcoholism and perversion, of brutality, hatred, miserliness, and innumerable other highly unlovely traits are sown in the first years of childhood.

In the confusion caused by numerous revisions, the manuscript that was sent to the printer contained this one word, which was not intended to be included. It is, as you probably sensed from reading it, the twenty-second word in the sentence (*highly*). "Innumerable other unlovely traits" would have sounded much better.

Would it have been better still to add a word, the word *all*, between *are* and *sown*? To hear what is being written, read the sentence aloud both ways and decide whether *are sown* or *are all sown* sounds more euphonious.[23]

---

[21]   Anne Enquist, Laurel Oates & Jeremy Francis, Just Writing 145 (2017).

[22]   Gary Provost, 100 Ways to Improve Your Writing 158 (1985).

[23]   *Compare* Manfred S. Guttmacher & Henry Weihofen, Psychiatry and the Law 453 (1952) (old version) *with* Henry Weihofen, Crime, Law, and Psychiatry, XXV New Mexico Quarterly (1955) (new version).

Not every writer will notice the difference; not every reader will recognize your effort. But engagement in this level of subtlety and dedication is what produces superior prose.

Consider the pledge of allegiance in its original and current forms. Which version has better rhythm?

I pledge allegiance to the flag, and to the republic for which it stands, one nation, indivisible, with liberty and justice for all.	I pledge allegiance to the flag of the United States of America and to the republic for which it stands, one nation, under God, indivisible, with liberty and justice for all.

One rhythmic device present in every sentence is rise and fall. Consider this famous sentence written by Justice Holmes:

> But when men have realized that time has upset many fighting faiths, they may come to believe even more than they believe the foundations of their own conduct that the ultimate goal desired is better reached by free trade in *ideas*—that the best test of truth is the power of the thought to get itself accepted in the competition of the *market*, and that truth is the only ground *upon* which their wishes safely may be carried out.[24]

The sentence moves in a curve, like the flight of a bird. It rises in a gradual ascent, reaching its highest altitude with the word *ideas*, maintains that height for a time (through *market*), then begins to lose altitude, and glides gracefully down ("upon which their wishes safely may be carried out"). The gentle movement of rise and fall and the variation in tone create rhythm—that's flow, that's cadence.

When seeking eloquence, remember Gary Provost's advice:

> Writing is not a visual art any more than composing music is a visual art. To write is to create music. The words you write make sounds, and when those sounds are in harmony, the writing will work . . . Read aloud what you write and listen to its music. Listen for dissonance. Listen for the beat. Listen for gaps where the music leaps from sound to sound instead of flowing as it should. Listen for sour notes. Is this word a little sharp, is that one a bit flat? Listen for instruments that don't blend well . . . There are no good sounds or bad sounds, just as there are no good notes or bad notes in music. It is the way in which you

---

24   Abrams v. U.S., 250 U.S. 616, 630 (1919).

combine them that can make the writing succeed or fail. It's the music that matters.[25]

§ 8.4   Rhymes—Something to Avoid

While rhythm is desirable, rhyming is not. Keeping the reader's attention requires minimizing friction in the communication between writer and reader. No distraction should interfere with the smooth transmission of thought. When your prose rhymes unexpectedly, it distracts the reader, just like grammatical error, misspelling, or wrong choice of words. So avoid having too many words in the same sentence that rhyme or contain the same sound: they offend the inner ear, even when absorbed only through the eye.

Lawyers use many abstract words that end in *-ation*, *-ing*, *-otion*, *-ly*, *-ty*, or *-ship*. Two or three such words in a sentence may give a jingling effect.

> Your communication to the Administration bears the connotation
> The interest of society in the security of property
> The actual contractual work
> It is presumed that she assumed
> Comparatively recently

Jingling rhymes are especially noticeable when formed by the first and last words of a short sentence.

> Our nation must be saved from foreign domination.

Words that almost rhyme can be just as noticeable as those that actually do.

> Washington set the precedent of a two-term limit for President.

§ 8.5   Reiteration

The chapter on conciseness warned against pointless repetition—the use of two or three words with the same meaning, or two or three phrases or clauses that repeat one thought. But repeating words and phrases is not always pointless—it may be done deliberately, to achieve emphasis, cohesion, or clarity.[26] Reiteration may also convey an emotional effect.

Winston Churchill used reiteration effectively:

---

[25]   100 Ways to Improve your Writing 58–59 (1985).

[26]   See §§ 2.5, Don't be Afraid to Repeat a Word, 3.9, Not All Repetition is Pointless, and 6.11, Use Reiteration Deliberately.

> Do not let us speak of darker days; let us speak rather of sterner days. These are not dark days: these are great days—the greatest days our country has ever lived; and we must all thank God that we have been allowed, each of us according to our stations, to play a part in making these days memorable in the history of our race.
>
> We shall not flag or fail. We shall fight in France, we shall fight on the seas and oceans, we shall fight with growing confidence and growing strength in the air, we shall defend our island, whatever the cost may be, we shall fight on the beaches, we shall fight on the landing grounds, we shall fight in the fields and in the streets, we shall fight in the hills; we shall never surrender.

Others have also used it:

> What do we mean when we say that first of all we seek liberty? I often wonder whether we do not rest our hopes too much upon constitutions, upon laws and upon courts. These are false hopes; believe me, these are false hopes. Liberty lies in the hearts of men and women; when it dies there, no constitution, no law, no court can save it; no constitution, no law, no court can even do much to help it. While it lies there it needs no constitution, no law, no court to save it.—Judge Learned Hand.[27]

> When ideas compete in the market for acceptance, full and free discussion exposes the false and they gain few adherents. Full and free discussion even of ideas we hate encourages the testing of our own prejudices and preconceptions. Full and free discussion keeps a society from becoming stagnant and unprepared for the stresses and strains that work to tear all civilizations apart. Full and free discussion has indeed been the first article of our faith.—Justice Douglas.[28]

Repetition, however, cannot be used in quite the same way in writing as in speaking. When speaking one can repeat essentially the same words and get variety by stressing a different word or phrase the second time, or varying the inflection or the tempo.[29] The printed page does not have these devices: variety in expression must be obtained by rearranging or substituting words.

"To be effective," however, "repetition must be combined with some variety and some progression in the treatment of the subject."[30]

While intentional reiteration may be pleasing and effective, merely accidental repetition of sound is a blemish.

Avoid using the same word in two different senses:

> He wept—something he had never done before before a jury.

---

[27]   The Spirit of Liberty, New York City, May 21st, 1944.
[28]   Dennis v. United States, 341 U.S. 494, 584 (1951) (dissenting).
[29]   See § 4.10, Should You Write the Way You Talk?
[30]   Cleanth Brooks & Robert Penn Warren, Modern Rhetoric 32 (1979).

With all her investments realized, she realized she'd never work again.

Pennoyer was not perfect and the principles it stated were not helpful in some cases, as future cases would demonstrate.

§ 8.6   Parallel Construction

Arranging words, phrases, and sentences in groups of two or three elements of the same grammatical category often aids in building up emotional effect.[31] Lincoln could have said "government of, by, and for the people," or even more concisely, "a people's government," and he would have said just as much as "government of the people, by the people and for the people." But he had goals other than concision. He used three parallel phrases purposefully, deepening emotional reactions with each repetition. He used the same technique in his Second Inaugural Address: "with malice toward none; with charity for all; with firmness in the right . . . ."

Parallel construction gives emphasis, coherence, balance, and rhythm to your prose. The ear likes to hear the pattern of one phrase echoed in another, building cumulative credibility. That's the power of repetition. As with other devices, it is necessary to guard against overuse, but for a climax or a conclusion, it can be very effective. Here again, Churchill is masterly:

> Death and sorrow will be the companions of our journey; hardship our garment; constancy and valor our only shield. We must be united, we must be undaunted, we must be inflexible.
>
> The only guide to a man is his conscience; the only shield to his memory is the rectitude and sincerity of his actions.
>
> "Not in vain" may be the pride of those who survived and the epitaph of those who fell.

Read some balanced sentences from judicial opinions and absorb some of their grace:

> We are not final because we are infallible, but we are infallible only because we are final.—Justice Jackson.[32]
>
> Jurisdiction exists that rights may be maintained. Rights are not maintained that jurisdiction may exist.—Judge Cardozo.[33]
>
> The constitutional protection of religious freedom terminated disabilities, it did not create new privileges. It gave religious equality, not civil immunity. Its essence is freedom from conformity to religious dogma,

---

[31]   See §§ 6.13, Use Parallel Construction and 7.11, Strive for Continuity. See also § 8.7, Antithesis.

[32]   Brown v. Allen, 344 U.S. 443, 540 (1953).

[33]   Berkovitz v. Arbib, 130 N.E. 288, 291 (1921).

> not freedom from conformity to law because of religious dogma.—Justice Frankfurter.[34]

> Freedom to publish means freedom for all and not for some. Freedom to publish is guaranteed by the Constitution, but freedom to combine to keep others from publishing is not.—Justice Black.[35]

> State help to religion injects political and party prejudices into a holy field. It too often substitutes force for prayer, hate for love, and persecution for persuasion.—Justice Black.[36]

> My evangelistic brethren confuse an objection to compulsion with an objection to religion. It is possible to hold a faith with enough confidence to believe that what should be rendered to God does not need to be decided and collected by Caesar.

> The day that this country ceases to be free for irreligion it will cease to be free for religion—except for the sect that can win political power. The same epithetical jurisprudence used by the Court today to beat down those who oppose pressuring children into some religion can devise as good epithets tomorrow against those who object to pressuring them into a favored religion.—Justice Jackson.[37]

> Nothing is to prevent the State from replacing any Motel 6 with a Ritz-Carlton, any home with a shopping mall, or any farm with a factor . . . Any property may now be taken for the benefit of another private party.—Justice Sandra Day O'Connor.[38]

The number three has always had a special attraction for the human race. We make trinities of our most important concepts. We like the sound of words, phrases, and clauses that come in threes. Many of Francis Bacon's memorable aphorisms are in this form.

> Reading maketh a full man, conference a ready man, and writing an exact man.[39]

> Some books are to be tasted, others to be swallowed, and some few to be chewed and digested.[40]

If the first two of the three clauses are short and parallel, and the third longer and more elaborate, we can get not only rhythm but climax. In *Ex parte Milligan*, for example, Justice Davis said:

> The Constitution of the United States is a law for rulers and people, equally in war and in peace, and covers with the shield of its protection all classes of men, at all times, and under all circumstances.[41]

---

[34]   WV State Bd. of Ed. v. Barnette, 319 U.S. 624, 653 (1943) (dissenting).

[35]   Associated Press v. United States, 326 U.S. 1, 20 (1945).

[36]   Zorach v. Clauson, 343 U.S. 306 (1952) (dissenting).

[37]   Id.

[38]   Kelo v. City of New London, Conn., 545 U.S. 469, 503 (2005) (dissenting).

[39]   Essayes: Religious Meditations: Places of Perswasion and Disswasion (1597).

[40]   Id.

[41]   *Ex parte* Milligan, 71 U.S. 2, 120 (1866).

Eleanor Roosevelt ended a foreword with this paragraph:

> Hearing these lectures, he [Franklin Roosevelt] would have understood, as I can understand, the real significance of what Mr. Bowles is telling us: that there is much to do, that the hour is late, and that we must find a President this year who has the will to work, the heart to inspire us, and the wisdom to show us the way.[42]

Justice Davis and Eleanor Roosevelt used three clauses, and the third contained three more.

David Melinkoff's aphorism gracefully mixes some variation into a parallel construction:

> *How* something is said determines *what* is said. *What* and *how* are inseparably joined, and when *how* gets drunk, *what* stumbles.[43]

Parallel construction does much more than create a pleasing writing style; it creates conciseness, clarity, and consistency:

> [It guides] readers smoothly through sentences by signaling the elements that work in pairs and series. . . . [P]utting parallel ideas in parallel form is essentially a matter of thinking straight, of recognizing how the various sentence components fit together. Elements that have the same relation to another element should have a family resemblance, and those that do not function together should not look as if they do.[44]

You will probably not find carefully constructed parallelism in your first drafts. As you revise your prose, however, look for opportunities to connect related ideas in planned symmetrical arrangements.[45] But feel free to disrupt the reader's expectations of parallelism—if done deliberately and with discretion, the effect may be powerful.

§ 8.7   Antithesis

When we express opposing ideas, we create antithesis, the setting of one thing over against another. Bringing opposing ideas together in this way makes them stand out, and has more impact on the reader.

---

[42] Preface, in Chester Bowles, Agenda 1961: New Principles For a New Age (1960).

[43] Sense and Nonsense 116–17 (1982).

[44] Claire Kehrwald Cook, Line by Line: How to Edit Your Own Writing 61–68 (1985).

[45] See Paul Marx, The Modern Rules of Style 9 (2007).

Parallel construction and antithesis enrich one another when artfully combined.[46] A sentence in this form can be pithy and forceful.

> To err is human; to forgive, divine.—Alexander Pope.
>
> It hath been an opinion that the French are wiser than they seem, and the Spaniards seem wiser than they are.—Francis Bacon.
>
> Religion has not civilized man—man has civilized religion. God improves as man advances.—Robert Ingersoll.
>
> A cynic is a [person] who knows the price of everything and the value of nothing.—Oscar Wilde.
>
> It is difficult to make our material condition better by the best of laws, but it is easy enough to ruin it by bad laws.—Theodore Roosevelt.
>
> Let us never negotiate out of fear. But let us never fear to negotiate.—John F. Kennedy.
>
> Ask not what your country can do for you—ask what you can do for your country.—John F. Kennedy.
>
> Proverbs are short sentences drawn from long experience.—Miguel de Cervantes.
>
> That's one small step for man, one giant leap for mankind.—Neil Armstrong.
>
> We must learn to live together as brothers or perish together as fools.—Martin Luther King, Jr.
>
> The world will little note, nor long remember what we say here, but it can never forget what they did here.—Abraham Lincoln (The Gettysburg Address).

In antithetical statements, as in writing generally, the more concise wording is more vigorous; separating the contrasting ideas by punctuation alone (comma, semi-colon or colon) is usually stronger than using words such as *but* or *whereas*. Too many lawyers, if they wrote Pope's line in their usual style, would write, "To err is human, whereas to forgive is divine."

In Lincoln's writing, as one critic has said,

> a delicate balancing of contrasted thought is conveyed in an equally delicate balancing of phrase, that pleases and attracts the mind, no less than the ear, of [whoever] hears it. A tendency toward veiled antithesis, indeed, may be set down as a definite feature of Lincoln's oratory. It enters into nearly all of his most finished utterances; and it is the more effective in that it does not spring from conscious artifice, but is entirely natural; for it arose from the supremely logical workings of an intellect that had been

---

[46] See §§ 6.13, Use Parallel Construction and 8.6, Parallel Construction.

trained to see the other side of every question, to set one fact against another, to weigh and to compare, and then to render judgment with a perfect impartiality. This it was that gave to Lincoln's controversial oratory its great persuasive power; for it struck the note of absolute sincerity and of intense conviction."[47]

§ 8.8 No Time for Style?

You may feel that all this talk of rhythm and cadence and balance is overrefined, that busy lawyers have no time to waste with this level of sensitivity. Lawyers working under pressure struggle to find time for factual investigation and legal research, let alone for crafting their writing. Nor are clients interested in paying attorneys to review their own work endlessly.[48] But this means lawyers are not performing at their highest level of competence, and it hurts their case. If time constraints force a quick and ruthless approach to editing, focus on organization, precision, and clarity. Able lawyers, however, appreciate the importance of expressing their thoughts effectively and find the necessary time to do it.

When Abraham Lincoln took office in 1861, he was under as much pressure as any practicing lawyer is likely to be. Seven states had seceded from the Union and formed a provisional government. Fort Sumter had been under siege for several months. If ever a situation demanded action and did not permit wasting time in word-polishing, this was it. Yet Lincoln, in preparing his inaugural address, took time to seek the best advice he could get. And the men whose advice he sought agreed on the importance of what that address should say. They all made thoughtful suggestions. W. H. Seward suggested a paragraph at the end, and submitted a draft. Lincoln adopted the suggestion, but made revisions.

Seward's original version and Lincoln's revision appear below. Seward had made some revisions of his own; his draft contains words he had first written and then stricken out. Notice the changes he made and the further changes that Lincoln made. Evaluate each one and imagine the reasons for making it. Was it made to give

---

[47] Harry Thurston Pock, Abraham Lincoln, in George Rice Carpenter (ed.), American Prose 257 (1918).

[48] See Charles R. Calleros, Legal Method and Writing 306–07 (2014) (discussing the economic limitations on multiple revisions, including the client's resources and the value of the claim).

precision, conciseness, simplicity, clarity, forcefulness, balance, rhythm, cadence?

Here is Seward's original manuscript (with his changes):[49]

> I close. We are not, we must not be aliens or enemies but fellow-countrymen and brethren. Although passion has strained our bonds of affection too hardly they must not, ~~be broken, they will not,~~ I am sure they will not be broken. The mystic chords which proceeding from ~~every ba~~ so many battle fields and ~~patrio~~ so many patriot graves pass through all the hearts and ~~hearths~~ all the hearths in this broad continent of ours will yet ~~harmo~~ again harmonize in their ancient music when ~~touched as they surely~~ breathed upon ~~again~~ by the ~~better angel~~ guardian angel of the nation.

Here is Lincoln's revision:

> I am loth to close. We are not enemies, but friends. We must not be enemies. Though passion may have strained, it must not break our bonds of affection. The mystic chords of memory, stretching from every battlefield, and patriot grave, to every living heart and hearthstone, all over this broad land, will yet swell the chorus of the Union, when again touched, as surely they will be, by the better angels of our nature.

"Practicing attorneys," said Lucy V. Katz, "can rarely agonize over each sentence to achieve balance and form. Yet awareness of the importance of these factors will gradually make all of us produce better sentences. When there is time to edit, we can then write prose that may be eloquent and truly persuasive."[50]

Literary taste takes time to develop. One learns to appreciate good writing much as one comes to appreciate good music, by hearing much of it. Even without conscious effort, we adopt the style of what we read. With deliberate application, you can do more than emulate good style: you can find your own voice.

---

[49] See 3 John G. Nicolay & John Hay, Abraham Lincoln: A History 317–44 (1890).
[50] Winning Words: A Guide to Persuasive Writing for Lawyers 25 (1986).

Chapter 9

CONCLUSION

What is written without effort is in general read without pleasure.
Samuel Johnson (1709–1784)[1]

Fine writing is generally the effect of spontaneous thoughts and a labored style.
William Shenstone (1714–1763)[2]

But easy writing's vile hard reading.
Richard Brinsley Sheridan (1751–1816)[3]

A hasty, careless, bad style shows an outrageous lack of regard for the reader, who then rightly punishes it by refusing to read the book.
Arthur Schopenhauer (1788–1860)[4]

One arrives at style only with atrocious effort, with fanatical and devoted stubbornness.
Gustave Flaubert (1821–1880)[5]

Easy reading is damn hard writing.
Maya Angelou (1928—2014)[6]

If you believe in the value of your thoughts, you must exert great effort to express them articulately. The journey toward ideal expression starts here, and never ends. But you will find that each step is its own reward.

This book has displayed a compilation of common stylistic blunders. Do not assume, however, that lawyers' writing is worse than that of most people. All writers are tempted at times to indulge in pompous or pretentious words. Others also fail to think through

---

[1]   See William Seward, Biographiana 260 (1799). But see http://quote investigator.com/2014/11/08/without-effort/.

[2]   On Writing and Books, in 1 Essays of British Essayists 315 (1900).

[3]   The Rival Beauties 16 (1772). See http://quoteinvestigator.com/2014/11/04/easy-writing/#note-10041-1.

[4]   On style [1851], in Lane Cooper (ed.), The Art of the Writer 232 (1952).

[5]   Pensées de Gustave Flaubert 15 (1915).

[6]   Maya Angelou: How I Write, The Daily Beast, April 10, 2013.

exactly what they want to say before they say it, neglect to read critically, and fail to revise their writing.

Most lawyers, like most government officials, "write grammatically correct English. . . . Sometimes it is very good, but then no one notices it. Occasionally it reaches a level of rare excellence."[7]

The bad practices denounced in this book are not characteristic of most lawyers' writing. Anyone who habitually commits every error in the book is a poor prospect for the profession. You should concentrate on correcting those you commit. Some can be avoided before they are written. When about to begin a sentence with *it is* or *there is*, remember that this is a weak start and find a stronger opening; when *very* comes to mind, recall that this word is almost never a help.

But no one should expect to attain perfection in the first draft— the key to good writing is rewriting. When you reread your early drafts for style, you will find intensifying adverbs you put there to add force that now sound exaggerated. You will find weak nouns qualified by one or more adjectives; if you think, or consult a thesaurus, you will find a single noun that will do the job by itself, and do it more pungently. You will find loose, unharnessed sentences that you can rearrange and tighten.

When you think you have a passable draft, read it aloud. Or have a friend read it to you. As you listen, you will hear passages that sound flat or awkward. If the reader's voice falters, if he stresses the wrong word, if the rhythm breaks, then the passage needs reworking. Perhaps it needs to be thrown away, in favor of a fresh start.

Finally, with hard work and perhaps a little luck, you succeed in erasing all the evidence of your sweat and toil. You have a paragraph that sounds easy and natural. For that is the aim of all the labor—to make it sound unlabored. "A picture is finished," said James Whistler, "when all trace of the means used to bring about the end has disappeared."[8]

If you succeed, you will have the gratifying feeling that the words you have used and their arrangement hit just the right note to produce the effect you want. As you reread your work, phrases,

---

[7]   Ernest Gowers, Plain Words: Their ABC 291–92 (1957).

[8]   The Gentle Art of Making Enemies 115 (1890).

sentences, whole paragraphs ring pleasingly in your mind and in your ear. "This is good!" you will say, a little surprised and more than a little pleased. That is your reward: the sense of satisfaction with a job well done, the ultimate reward of any creator.

Appendix

FURTHER READINGS

With precious few exceptions, all the books on style in English are by writers quite unable to write.

H. L. Menken (1880–1956)[1]

This book offers an introductory approach to legal writing style. A superb writer, like any artist, is born, not made. Whatever expertise you may acquire will likely come from reading good prose and practicing composition. Extensively.

Although you will not learn to write good prose merely by reading books on style, they can help you reach your finest form. As you gain awareness, you will learn to identify and avoid bad practices and adopt good ones. If you care about your writing—and you should—read several books on style. As you absorb their advice, note which lessons resonate with you, so you can find your own voice. Below are some that even Menken would endorse.

General Writing Style

Joseph M. Williams & Joseph Bizup, Style: Lessons in Clarity and Grace

William Zinsser, On Writing Well

William Strunk, Jr & E. B. White, The Elements of Style

Claire Kehrwald Cook, Line By Line: How to Edit Your Own Writing

Gary Provost, 100 Ways to Improve Your Writing

Legal Writing Style

Bryan Garner, The Elements of Legal Style

Bryan Garner, Legal Writing in Plain English

Anne Enquist, Laurel Oates & Jeremy Francis, Just Writing: Grammar, Punctuation, and Style for the Legal Writer

Ian Gallacher, Legal Communication and Research

---

[1] Literature and the Schoolma'm, in H.L. Mencken, Prejudices, Fifth Series (1926).

Academic Legal Writing
Eugene Volokh, Academic Legal Writing
Elizabeth Fajans & Mary Falk, Scholarly Writing for Law Students

Law Dictionary
Black's Law Dictionary
The Wolters Kluwer Bouvier Law Dictionary: Desk Edition
Garner's Dictionary of Legal Usage
Burton's Legal Thesaurus

Thesaurus
The Oxford American Writer's Thesaurus (Christine A. Lindberg, ed.)
Roget's International Thesaurus (Barbara Ann Kipfer, ed.) [organized by categories]
Merriam-Webster's Collegiate Thesaurus

Dictionary of Usage
Fowler's Modern English Usage [prescriptive or descriptive]
Garner's Modern English Usage [prescriptive]
Merriam-Webster's Dictionary of English Usage [descriptive]

A comment on Fowler's *Modern English Usage*. The first edition (of 1926, still in print) and the second (of 1965, lightly updated by Ernest Gowers and available in the used-book market) adopt a prescriptive approach to usage and grammar, clearly distinguishing right from wrong, good from bad. The third edition, rewritten by Robert Burchfield (1996), and the fourth, by Jeremy Butterfield (2015), have substantially transformed the original work, adopting a descriptive approach, which merely records common usage without prescribing a correct standard.

Fowler's legendary name appears on the cover of the third and fourth editions only for commercial reasons, because his name is synonymous with accurate usage. But neither of these books is a Fowler: the entries are different, the comments are different, the examples are different, the tone is different, the underlying philosophy is different. Fowler is cited, and even quoted, in the third and fourth editions as an author of a different book, usually in disagreement, sometimes in an unfairly dismissive tone.

Despite being dated, containing a few errors, and being indifferent to American usage, the first and second editions are more useful for lawyers, not only because of their intrinsic value but also because the descriptive approach, adopted in the third and fourth editions, is of limited value to formal prose.

Buy the second edition and read it for pleasure; buy Garner's and keep it handy for frequent reference.

Index

References are to Sections
